W9-DER-415

A Divided Poet

Studies in American Literature and Culture

A Divided Poet

Robert Frost, *North of Boston*, and the Drama of Disappearance

David Sanders

CAMDEN HOUSE
Rochester, New York

Camden House is an imprint of Boydell & Brewer, Inc., Rochester, NY 14620, USA, and of Boydell & Brewer Limited, PO Box 9, Woodbridge, Suffolk IP12 3DF, UK

ISBN-13: 978-1-57113-499-8; ISBN-10: 1-57113-499-9

Library of Congress Cataloging-in-Publication Data

Sanders, David, 1942–
A divided poet: Robert Frost, North of Boston, and the drama of disappearance / David Sanders.
p. cm. — (Studies in American literature and culture)
Includes bibliographical references and index.
ISBN-13: 978-1-57113-499-8 (hardcover: acid-free paper)
ISBN-10: 1-57113-499-9 (hardcover: acid-free paper)
1. Frost, Robert, 1874–1963. North of Boston. 2. Frost, Robert, 1874–1963 — Criticism and interpretation. I. Title.

PS3511.R94N637 2011
811' .52—dc22

2011008045

Printed in the United States of America. Printed on acid-free paper.

To
S. Y. S., G. Y. S., and R. Y. S.,
my inspiration and delight.

Only be it understood,
It shall be no trespassing
If I come again some spring
In the grey disguise of years,
Seeking ache of memory here.

— Robert Frost, "On the Sale of My Farm"

I hate to think of the old place when we're gone,
With the brook going by below the yard,
And no one here but the hens blowing about.
If he could sell the place, but then, he can't:
No one will ever live on it again.

— Robert Frost, "The Housekeeper"

The storyteller is doomed to live as two, with one self laughing and weeping and the other seated in a corner, making theater of the event.

— Richard Selzer, *Down from Troy*

Contents

Acknowledgments

Behind any book that has been years in the making, as this one has, lies an exchange with many others through their writing — a virtual conversation from which one's own ideas take shape and definition. In this regard, the work of Lawrence Thompson, Jay Parini, William Pritchard, and Jeffrey Cramer has been invaluable. For me, however, John Evangelist Walsh has a special place among Frost's biographers, for it was *Into My Own*, his study of Frost's "English years," that first fired my interest in the genesis of *North of Boston* and its connection to the lives behind it, including the poet's own.

The citations and notes within this book identify others who have helped me move this work forward, if often rather slowly. But beyond the debts explicitly noted are others that might remain unknown if not mentioned here. Perhaps least aware of her contribution is my former colleague Kate McConnell, whose comment on an essay of mine in 1999 prompted a line of thinking that led ultimately to the "divided poet" I portray here. I thank Carole Thompson, Paola Loreto, and Russell Coward, for their comments on the early sketch that would grow into this study. My thanks to also Tyler Hoffman and Ann Mikkelsen for sharing some of their unpublished work with me, and to Marian Walker and Peter Nelson at the Amherst College Library for checking, and sometimes correcting, quotations in sources unavailable to me here.

I am grateful to exchanges, in person and by email, with George Monteiro, Robert Hass, Donald Sheehy, Mark Richardson, Peter Gilbert, and Robert Faggen, all of whom have been open-handed in sharing their knowledge and insight on questions large and small, and also to Robert Hass and Jay Parini, for encouragement and advice on a completed first draft of this book. The anonymous outside reader of that first draft has my deep appreciation both for his praise of my work and for the criticism that helped me strengthen it. I am immensely grateful to my friend and former colleague Kenneth Mason for his unflagging generosity in reading repeated drafts of the book, as a whole and in parts, and for his sage advice on its emphasis and design. It is hard to describe my appreciation to Richard Wakefield, poet, fellow scholar, and friend, who, over my years of work on this book, has read every part, some more than once, whose conversation has invariably enriched my understanding of Frost, and whose comments, as my readers will discover, have often found a place in the book itself. I thank my wife, Sara, for helping me think through many ideas and, as always, showing me a thing or two I didn't know. I also thank Sara and our children, Gabriel and Rachel, for reading or listening to various parts of this book as they emerged. Their belief in this project has meant more to me than they would ever suspect.

Jim Walker, editorial director of Camden House, has been central to this project since we met in 2009, giving excellent guidance on matters large and small. Expert and professional, always direct yet unfailingly courteous and kind, he has exceeded the high expectations inspired by our first conversation. I am grateful to other members of the Camden House team for their excellent work and collegiality. These include John Blanpied, for his superb copyediting, exacting and smart, managing editor, Ryan Peterson, for his good judgment and various sorts of textual magic, and both for their sympathy and patience with my textual fussing. My thanks to Frank Gutbrod, whose simple and elegant cover design made a superb photograph of Robert Frost even more arresting, and to Jane Best for her deft handling of final production matters. This book is better for all their work.

Many thanks to Tevis Kimball and Kate Boyle at the Jones Library in Amherst, Massachusetts, for providing the Edward Sweetland photograph of Frost that appears on the book's cover. For permission to use it, thanks to them and to Peter Gilbert, trustee for the Frost Estate. Thanks to Peter Gilbert also for permission to quote from Frost's uncollected poems and to Mimi Ross for permission to quote from those published by Henry Holt and Company.

Abbreviations Frequently Used

CPPP Robert Frost. *Collected Poems, Prose, and Plays.* Edited by Richard Poirier and Mark Richardson. New York: Library of America, 1995.

SL Robert Frost. *Selected Letters.* Edited by Lawrance Thompson. New York: Holt, 1964.

Verse Citations

Unless otherwise noted, the Frost poems quoted in this book will be found in the Library of America edition of Frost (*CPPP*) on the pages indicated below. The *North of Boston* poems are listed as they occur in that volume. Other Frost poems are listed alphabetically.

From *North of Boston*

The Pasture	13
Mending Wall	39–40
The Death of the Hired Man	40–45
The Mountain	45–49
A Hundred Collars	49–55
Home Burial	55–58
The Black Cottage	59–62
Blueberries	62–65
A Servant to Servants	65–69
After Apple-Picking	70–71
The Code	71–74
The Generations of Men	74–81
The Housekeeper	82–89
The Fear	89–92
The Self-Seeker	93–100
The Wood-Pile	100–101
Good Hours	102

Other Frost poems

Acquainted with the Night	234
Asking for Roses	525–26

Introduction: The Poet, His People, and the Drama of Disappearance

A Dramatic Arrival

PUBLISHED IN ENGLAND in 1914, *North of Boston* brought Robert Frost to national prominence overnight, astonishing almost everyone but the poet himself, who six months earlier had declared himself ready "to do something to the present state of literature in America" (*SL*, 88). His first book, *A Boy's Will*, had come out the year before to unexceptional reviews and Frost, approaching forty, with a family to support and funds for his stay in England running low, understood that a literary career depended on what he did next. By April 1913, when *A Boy's Will* appeared, Frost had a good idea of what his next book would be.

The seeds for it lay in "the bottom of [the] trunk" that Frost brought with him to England when he arrived with his wife Elinor and their four children in September of 1912.[1] Soon after going to contract for *A Boy's Will* in October, he embarked on an intense period of composition, starting new poems while completing others begun in New England, and by spring had assembled much of his new book. Though unsettled by reviews of *A Boy's Will* as they appeared that summer, too many of which stressed the book's simplicity, Frost was encouraged by the response of English friends to his new poems and, by July 1913, described the new book as "well in hand" (*SL*, 83). He continued to shape it into the fall, adding its three major lyrics — "Mending Wall," "After Apple-Picking," and "The Wood-Pile" — in September or October. He made no mention of his *North of Boston* title before November of that year and, taking pains with the volume's overall design, did not deliver the completed manuscript to his London publisher, David Nutt, until February 1914.

North of Boston was issued in May 1914 and, to Frost's gratification and relief, was well-reviewed in England through that summer. By fall it had gained the attention of Henry Holt in New York, who in February

[1] Frost claimed that the trunk contained *A Boy's Will* and "three other books of verse somewhere near completion" (*SL*, 55). It is clear that Frost had drafts of poems that would appear in his next three books: *North of Boston* (1914), *Mountain Interval* (1916), and *New Hampshire* (1923). To say that these books were anywhere "near completion" would be misleading, but at the time Frost may have had a very different idea of his next volumes.

1915 reissued it just as the poet returned home, making it Frost's first American book. Delighted to be in the hands of such a "fine old firm" (Mertins, 141) Frost was even more pleased to find a review, timed to coincide with the book's release, written for the *New Republic* by Amy Lowell, doyenne of American verse. Ellery Sedgwick, editor of the influential *Atlantic Monthly*, underlined this dramatic reversal in Frost's fortunes. Having formerly turned down every poem Frost had submitted to the *Atlantic*, including three *North of Boston* titles sent from England, Sedgwick now courted Frost and sought his work for the magazine. "No wandering poet," Frost later said, "ever came home to a happier welcome" (Mertins, 141). Within a year, Holt had sold twenty thousand copies, "almost unheard of," according to Jay Parini, "for a book of poetry" (171).

North of Boston's Language and Its People

Both in substance and style, *North of Boston* was a radical departure from Frost's first book, published the year before. Representing a younger Frost, as its title suggests, *A Boy's Will* was composed of lyric poems highly personal and emotional in subject, often weighted with wistful melancholy, and laced with archaisms — a style that Frost later referred to as "the manner of the nineties" (*SL*, 129), the decade in which he turned twenty and began seeking publication for his poems. By contrast, *North of Boston*, published in 1914, announced Frost's poetic maturity. Focusing on the moral and economic struggles of New England's rural poor, it presents characters based largely on the people that Frost came to know as friends or neighbors during the decade, 1900–1910, that he lived in Derry, New Hampshire.

Of the book's fifteen principal poems, twelve are narratives of some few hundred lines and are highly dramatic as well. While in most a narrator formally presides, conveying scene, context, and important details of action, he often disappears in long stretches of unbroken dialogue that give the poems over to the voices of the characters themselves. The other three principal poems, all forty to fifty lines long (and all late additions to the book), are among Frost's greatest meditative lyrics. Framing this carefully wrought collection of fifteen poems, all but two of them in blank verse,[2] are two shorter, rhymed lyrics serving as prologue and epilogue. Both the three major and the two shorter lyrics reinforce the dramatic and

[2] Of the narratives, "Blueberries," in anapestic tetrameter is the exception, which I discuss in chapter 5. Among the major lyrics, "After Apple-Picking" is also rhymed. But since the rhymes occur at irregular intervals, the meter is iambic, and the lines are predominantly pentameter, the effect is highly conversational and very like that of Frost's blank verse.

narrative elements of the longer poems even as they introduce a dimension of intimate address to the book as a whole.[3]

In poetic voice, *North of Boston*, sounds little like *A Boy's Will*,[4] and little like the verse that Isabelle Frost had read to her young son or that Frost had read for himself in Palgrave's *Golden Treasury of Songs and Lyrics*, acquired in 1892, during his single unhappy term at Dartmouth College. Unlike those golden, treasured lyrics, *North of Boston* was written, as Frost boasted to his friend John Bartlett, "in a language absolutely unliterary" (*SL*, 102). Though Frost composed the poems largely in England in late 1912 and 1913, their language came from the decade Frost spent in Derry as a schoolteacher, part-time farmer, and night-time poet. And, while Frost surely found models in the conversational vigor of Browning's dramatic monologues and the lean, contemporary styles of Yeats and Hardy, the language of these poems came largely from rural Derry itself. Even before his years there, Frost had come to the "providential" realization, as he later described it, that he "was after poetry that talked" (Mertins, 197). Because "there are moments . . . in talk," he later explained, "[that] the best writing can only come near, we must go into the vernacular for tones that haven't been brought to book" (*SL*, 159). Led by such convictions, Frost was drawn to the expressive idiom of his rural neighbors, especially as it was used by a fellow poultryman, John Hall, who would later become the primary subject of "The Housekeeper."[5] By bringing this local vernacular into the iambic pentameter of blank verse, the classic yet flexible medium of English stage drama, Frost merged innovation with tradition, playing the dramatic tones of meaning against the regular beat of the meter to create a poetry that spoke in the tongue of the people it portrayed.

These people were the heart of the book's drama. In the dedication to his wife Elinor — "To E. M. F. THIS BOOK OF PEOPLE" (*CPPP*, 970) — Frost calls attention to the human source from which his book drew life, and these people were featured in most of the titles Frost had considered for the book: "New England Hill Folk," "New England Farm Servants," and "Farm Servants and Other People."[6] Dominated by their

---

[3] Beginning in 1930, Frost removed the first of these short lyrics, "The Pasture," from *North of Boston* to serve as a prologue for all editions of his *Collected Poems*. *North of Boston* was then opened by its first principal poem, "Mending Wall," but left otherwise unchanged.

[4] "Mowing" and "Storm Fear" are exceptions. They were the last poems in *A Boy's Will* to be composed and were written in the newer, more plain-spoken voice that Frost worked to develop during his Derry years.

[5] More than anyone else, John Evangelist Walsh has explored the value of Hall's friendship and influence for Frost's development as a poet. See chapter 3 of his *Into My Own,* titled "Never Knew a Man I Liked Better."

[6] A fourth provisional title, *New England Eclogues*, alluded, instead, to the literary model established by Virgil's *Eclogues*, poems in which rustic figures discuss contemporary themes in direct dialogue.

dialogues and monologues, the book's principal poems give ample range for the poet's fascination with their language. Writing in 1915 to the Boston critic William Braithwaite, Frost confessed that "my conscious interest in people was at first no more than an almost technical interest in their speech — in what I used to call their sentence sounds — the sound of sense"; but he also stressed his "discovery in doing The Death of the Hired Man that I was interested in neighbors for more than merely their tones of speech — and always had been" (*SL*, 158–59). Frost had emphasized this point in July 1913 when he described his new "volume of blank verse" to the Maine publisher and bibliophile Thomas Mosher. Boastfully confessing to a "level of diction that even Wordsworth kept above," Frost had called the book's language "appropriate to the virtues I celebrate" (83–84). With "the virtues I celebrate," Frost calls Mosher's attention to the human lives behind the speech that had shaped his verse — hard lives made harder by New England's climate, stony soil and, inevitably, its economics.

The Drama of Disappearance

Considering Frost's emphasis on the "people" named in both the dedication to Elinor and his working titles, it may seem curious that in the end he chose a title that does not mention them directly. Yet here, as in so much of his work, Frost's reticence is eloquent. Like the rest of the book's language, the words "north of Boston" say something about its people not only by pointing to the region and culture that have shaped their lives, but by making clear what they are not. Posed against "Boston," with its history and urbanity, what lies "north" is simply "out there," provincial and exposed, somewhere between the capital and the pole, so that, even before we have read the book, *North of Boston* suggests the fortitude of its people by hinting at the cold and emptiness that they face. And when we have finished its poems about failed and failing farms and the families who have left or will soon leave them, we see a traditional way of life that takes definition and value against the urban wealth and power to which it was literally losing ground each year. With just a mention of these people in his dedication, then, Frost trusted the poems to bring his people to our notice, just as he had trusted their language to shape his poetic voice, and just as most of its poems, with their sparing narration, trust to the speech of the characters themselves.

Considering the cultural and economic conflict that shaped the book, it is both ironic and significant that Frost took the phrase "North of Boston" from a real estate advertisement in the *Boston Globe* that he recalled in England (Thompson, *Early Years*, 434). Drafted for literary use, this commercial heading not only enacts the "renewal of words" that Frost considered essential to poetry (*CPPP*, 757). As the book's title, it initiates a renewal of values by returning us to a world more manual in labor and more personal in scale than the world of urban capital from which the phrase had come and in which the book would be seeking a publisher and audience. So too, the sale of these once-working farms to city-dwellers and investors confirmed the change witnessed by the poems themselves: a culture of independent farmers pushed toward extinction by expanding, urban-centered markets. Underlying each of the poems in different ways, much like the New England bedrock exposed in some places, covered in others, is an encompassing narrative of economic decline that touches all the book's characters, compounding the perennial problems of poor soil, long winters, aging, illness, and death. Reflecting a traditional farming culture in retreat before both natural forces and a growing capital economy, *North of Boston* creates a drama of disappearance sustained from the tumbled-down wall of its first principal poem to the abandoned woodpile of its last.

A Divided Frost

As a poet finding his voice in Derry, New Hampshire, Frost was witness to that vanishing. In his neighbors' resistance to natural and economic forces, he saw something admirable, even heroic. His response surely involved some personal pride, for, though born in San Francisco and living there for his first eleven years, Frost was historically a child of New England. His original American forebear, Nicholas Frost, had sailed from Devonshire to New Hampshire in 1634 and, until Rob's grandfather left his Kingston, New Hampshire, farm for the textile mills of Lawrence, Massachusetts, in 1850 and his Harvard-educated father went west in 1883, six generations of Frosts had spent their lives farming in New England and fighting in the Wars of Independence and 1812.

Equally important, Frost saw in his farming neighbors the individualism and self-reliance that, nurtured in New England soil, had created the American nation[7] but were now threatened by a growing culture of mass-production and mass-marketing. From the time of *North of Boston*, if not before, Frost believed that poetry and rural life collaborated to preserve personal values central to a democratic nation. "Poetry," he said in a 1931 interview for *Rural America*,

> is very, very rural — rustic. It stands as a reminder of rural life — as a resource, as a recourse. It might be taken as a symbol for a man, taking its rise from individuality and seclusion . . . and then going out into its social appeal and use. Just so the race lives best . . .

[7] Frost develops this idea in his essay, "What Became of New England?" first delivered as the commencement address at Oberlin College on June 8, 1937. In it he says, "New England, now . . . What's become of it? . . . The little nation that was and was to be gave itself . . . westward into the great nation that she saw coming, and so gave help to America" (*CPPP*, 757).

> storing strength in the more individual life of the country, of the farm — then going to market and socializing in the industrial city. . . . We are now at a moment when we are getting too far out into the social-industrial and are . . . drawing back — drawing in to renew ourselves. . . . I think a person has to be withdrawn into himself to gather inspiration so that he is somebody when he comes out again . . . when he "comes to market" with himself. (Lathem, *Interviews*, 75–76)

This cultural narrative of individual, rural seclusion leading to wider communal engagement certainly reflects Frost's own story as a poet, as we shall soon see more fully. It also suggests how separate individuals, each engaged in one's own pursuit of happiness, may come together to create democratic rule, and underlying that idea, even the story of yeoman farmers joining to defend a newly declared American nation. Both these ideas suggested by Frost's farm-to-market, individual-to-communal paradigm help to explain the importance he ascribed to the virtues celebrated by *North of Boston*. In fact, in many of his later tributes to the values that he saw basic to American democracy, Frost would make *North of Boston* a point of reference. And though Frost took exception to Amy Lowell's emphasis on "a decaying New England" in her *New Republic* review of the book (Thornton, 48), "What she observed that pleased me especially," he later told Louis Mertins, "was that I had caught a fleeting epoch and stamped it into print, of a people purely American. That was what I had unconsciously tried to do" (Mertins, 141).

In producing *North of Boston*, however, Frost found himself on more than one side of the social and economic struggle it portrays. Seeing the book as his final bid for artistic recognition, perhaps his only chance to bring to market the poetic accomplishments of two decades, Frost understood that his survival as a poet required more than good reviews in the literary journals. It meant reaching a mass audience. He also understood that reaching that audience meant allying himself with the same economic forces that worked against the New England farming culture to which his book pays tribute. Because Frost's attachment to its people was no mere intellectual abstraction, such conflicting commitments are significant as biographical fact. They are still more significant when we recognize that, indirectly but indelibly, Frost etched this personal conflict into the poems of his book. How he did so is the main focus of this study.

1: Frost in Derry

THIS STORY OF A VANISHING New England farming culture Frost knew personally and well, and it affected him deeply. In 1899, at twenty-five, he had taken his family to the farm in Derry, New Hampshire, that his paternal grandfather, William Prescott Frost, had purchased for his use. There Frost, more through his temperament and values than his work raising chickens, soon developed strong ties with various neighbors trying to maintain traditional ways of life in a rapidly changing economy. Many of these New Hampshire people in and beyond Derry appear in *North of Boston*, where even Frost's unsentimental view of character and motive cannot obscure his sympathy and respect. Indeed, by dedicating the volume "to E. M. F.," his wife Elinor, Frost assigns these portraits and the people behind them to a deeply personal place in his life.

Nonetheless, the Frost who loved the people and language of Derry in all of their natural and cultural rhythms had come to it not as a farmer but as an aspiring poet, and the poet had needs that led him back to the same world of commerce that was pushing this culture toward extinction. In the year leading to the book's publication, Frost more than once made clear that this expression of personal values and this assertion of poetic prowess were also a bid for economic success. As a labor of ambition as well as love, *North of Boston* registers indirectly but unmistakably the tension between the poet moved to celebrate a fading culture and the poet determined to find his place in the modern economy that was pushing rural Derry toward the past.

Getting to Derry

For Frost, however, the rural farming life involved complicated feelings, especially at the start, and was chosen partly by default. During his high-school summers, he had done enough farm work[1] to know its drudgery as well as some of its "rituals and mysteries," including the proper handling of a scythe and the old-fashioned, hands-on ways to make and store hay (Thompson, *Early Years*, 86–87). These experiences also affirmed his love

[1] In the summer of his freshman year, 1889, Frost worked on the Loren Bailey farm in Salem, Massachusetts. In 1891, he took a job on the Dinsmore farm in Windham, Massachusetts, but, unhappy with his bunkhouse mates, left after three weeks (Thompson, *Early Years*, 85–87, 103–6).

of the out-of-doors. Upon leaving Harvard in the spring of 1899, worried about his persistent chest ailments as well as Elinor's second pregnancy and his mother's poor health, Frost decided to follow his doctor's advice against sedentary work, and, in June of that year, with the help of a local veterinarian and poultryman, Dr. Charlemagne Bricault, he started a small chicken farm on a rented property in Methuen, Massachusetts. The following summer, however, the Frosts were evicted, not only for unpaid rent but because Frost's hens were overrunning the kitchen they shared with the owners. Aware of their straits, Elinor's mother found an attractive thirty-acre farm at a good price in Derry, New Hampshire, twelve miles north of Lawrence, and when it passed inspection by great-uncle Elihu Concord, Frost's grandfather, who had already loaned him the funds for Harvard and the poultry start in Methuen, agreed to buy it for his use.

The Derry farm, where the Frosts moved in September of 1900, included a comfortable house and accessible barn, an orchard, pasture, spring, and woodlot, and lots of room for additional birds. But Frost and Elinor brought with them the fresh grief of four-year-old Elliot's death from cholera that July and, in November, they felt the loss of Frost's mother Isabelle to cancer. Difficult in another way were the tensions between Frost and his grandfather. Frost's friend, Carl Burrell, had agreed to live at the farm and help with the many chores, from milking to growing vegetables to building hen-coops. Though fond of Burrell and glad for the help, Frost resented that his grandfather had made arrangements with Burrell without consulting him. The following year, when the grandfather died, he left Frost with an annuity of $500 but stipulated that he would gain ownership of the farm only after ten years. All told, by exerting a degree of control along with his generosity, and simply by providing for Frost's future in a way that Frost had been unable to do, the grandfather's help carried with it a painful, if implicit, judgment.

Marit MacArthur aptly suggests that "at first, from 1901 to 1906, Frost gave himself to the land with some ambivalence, at his grandfather's invitation and rather at his insistence" but that "gradually, the Derry farm, and the fading rural life it seemed to exemplify, made Frost into its poet" (42). Guy Rotella proposes that Frost's move to Derry may have "felt like a reversion to the position from which his grandfather had risen, as his failure to graduate from Harvard might have seemed a falling off from his father's attainment" ("Synonymous," 39).[2] Likely as this reaction seems,

[2] It seems equally possible that Frost's Harvard experience did not place him second to his father in his own eyes. No longer the willful teenager his father had been, and making many financial compromises to attend, Frost approached Harvard in a more sober way. And though circumstances influenced his leaving, I believe that, finding his own reading to give him as much or more than his college lectures, Frost also felt that he had gained from Harvard as much as it had to give him — in effect, that he had taken Harvard's measure more than it had taken his.

Frost's first five years on the farm may also have had a more positive personal effect, reconnecting him, whether consciously or not, with a family past discontinued in 1850, when his grandfather left his New Hampshire farm for the textile mills of Lawrence. Whatever Frost's most private feelings, becoming the poet of Derry's rural culture, as MacArthur implies and *North of Boston* makes clear, meant engaging a whole class of people,[3] mostly farmers who, for little more than subsistence, did what they could with what they were dealt by nature and the economy. The overall respect for the skills and challenges of farming that Frost gained in these years would of course have been reinforced by his particular affection for such figures as Carl Burrell, John Hall, and Napoleon Gay.

Derry in 1900

By 1900, when Frost moved to Derry, northern rural New England had lost much of its mid-nineteenth-century prosperity. This decline, felt as a

[3] In my discussion of *North of Boston*, the terms "Derry" or "the Derry world" refer to the larger New England backcountry that Frost came to know during his Derry years and reflect his own poetic liberties as much as my critical shorthand. This place is a rural world, quite different from that of the nearby towns and villages, and in Frost's day poorer. Though Frost encountered it mainly around Derry, this world was spread across New England, especially northern New England, and Frost knew it more broadly. Some *North of Boston* characters — the minister and the old widow in "The Black Cottage" and the neighbor of "Mending Wall" — are based on known Derry figures. John Hall, model for the protagonist of "The Housekeeper," lived in Atkinson, New Hampshire, about eight miles east of Derry. Carl Burrell, model for The Broken One in "The Self-Seeker," was associated with at least three places in Frost's life, Derry only the last of them. The protagonists in "The Fear" were based on a couple from Bethlehem, New Hampshire, and one of three models for the farm wife in "A Servant to Servants" was from Lake Willoughby, Vermont. Other characters and even places derive from more than one source. In Frost's imagination, however, and within his book, they all inhabit the same composite place, sharing the same geography and climate, the same hardships, the same language, and the same cluster of values. The word "composite" is Frost's own, and perhaps the point in best made in his own words, recorded by Louis Mertins in the 1930s, where Frost makes clear that the poetic "terrain" he refers to is a human as well as a natural landscape: "To a large extent the terrain of my poetry is the Derry landscape, the Derry farm. Poems growing out of this, though composite, were built on incidents and are therefore autobiographical. There was something about the experience of Derry which stayed in my mind, and was tapped for poetry in the years that came after. . . . Some of the poems combine many incidents many people and places, but all are real. Take the mountain the man "worked around the foot of all his life" [in "The Mountain" from *North of Boston*]. That wasn't one, but several mountains. But it was just as real for all its being composite. Those mountains surrounded the Derry farm, and stretched farther than the eye could see" (Mertins, 72).

crisis in some places, prompted Governor Frank Rollins of New Hampshire, in 1899, to create Old Home Week, a state-sponsored promotional effort to bring former residents back to their ancestral hometowns as tourists, vacationers, or even buyers of summer properties. As Dona Brown explains in *Inventing New England*, "long-standing economic difficulties, a shifting population, and gloomy social analysis" had collaborated to create "a nebulous sense of looming crisis. . . . During the last quarter of the century, the specter of the 'abandoned farm' arose to haunt the politicians and planners of the northern states . . . and later the reform writers of the national magazine circuit." By the 1890s, she says, "Writers in the agricultural press bemoaned the flight of young people to the cities and the West," and the popular press contained warnings of "decadence" and "decline," even social and moral "'degeneration' caused by isolation and poverty" in the northern New England countryside. "Between 1890 and 1910, titles like . . . 'Is New England Decadent?' were an almost constant presence in the magazines" (135–37).[4]

If such assessments often overstated or oversimplified the facts, actual problems were serious enough. Though immigration kept the overall population of these northern states steady, Brown explains, the native-born left in great numbers between 1960 and 1900 — in Vermont, about 40 percent in every decade. Among those who stayed in New England, many left the more remote hill towns and villages, following their jobs to the growing industrial cities of southern New England, whose production capacity and access to railroads had driven many local factories and workshops out of business. And as small-scale industry went south, northern New England became increasingly dependent on farming (137).

Farming, of course, had its own problems due to a generation of falling prices for wool, its main cash crop, and increasing competition from grain producers in the Midwest. Some experts counseled a shift to dairy farming, but the capital and technical training required was beyond the reach of many farmers, and with farm labor scarce, it was difficult to find the additional workers needed for dairying (137). Even before Old Home Week was instituted, state Boards of Agriculture had promoted tourism in the form of farm vacations as a way to preserve farming itself, but even where a nostalgic vision of rural life appealed to city dwellers, few farm families were prepared to meet their expectations for accommodations, meals, and service (155–67).

Derry, thanks to its location in southern New Hampshire, did not suffer the economic decline of smaller hill towns to the north. It was founded as Londonderry in 1718 by Scottish emigrants who, after a century in northern Ireland, had brought to America the Irish craft of linen

---

[4] For further discussion of this topic in connection to Frost, see Donald Sheehy's "Pastoral Degenerate."

weaving. As a result, until the time of the Civil War, when mechanized production displaced most household manufacture, Derry produced a high-quality linen valued far beyond New England. From 1804 the town enjoyed the economic benefits of a turnpike linking Concord, New Hampshire, to Andover, Massachusetts; and running through eastern Londonderry, the turnpike gave that part of the town sufficient independence to separate as the township of Derry in 1827. Though Derry never achieved the size or industrial development of the nearby cities directly on the Merrimack River — Manchester and Nashua in New Hampshire, Lowell and Lawrence in Massachusetts — it clearly benefited from its rail links to Manchester and Lawrence, established in 1849, which helped the newly mechanized shoe industry become "a major business enterprise" by 1870. Throughout the nineteenth century, Derry was prosperous enough to support two respected private schools — Pinkerton Academy, which remains in operation to this day, and The Adams Female Academy.[5]

When Frost reached the Derry farm in 1900, the local shoe industry was at its height, Derry had enjoyed electric service for eight years, and a trolley line to nearby Chester had been established, followed by another to Manchester and Nashua in late 1907. According to *From Turnpike to Interstate: 1827–1977*, "The first few years of the twentieth century saw a period of prosperity such as the town had never experienced before. The shoe factories were all working at capacity and looking for more help than was available — and a building boom was in progress." In fact, by 1906, demand had outgrown available housing, and the Derry Board of Trade underwrote the building of fifty new homes with a guarantee of five years' rent and a $250,000 bond to reassure potential investors (23, 56–57).

Amidst all this prosperity and the scarcity of labor, farming in Derry, as in most of northern New England, was in decline. For the most part, farms remained small, unconsolidated, and unprofitable — with the notable exception of the Hood farm, to which I shall return in a moment. What little the Derry Historic Committee says about any but the Hood farm is revealing. It states simply that, in 1900, the farms "supplemented the factories" but it acknowledges, without quite saying so, that many of them, as part of a nationwide trend, had already disappeared: "Derry . . . took those *remaining* farmers for granted but their number reflected the fact that *rural* America's overall farm population had declined to only thirty-seven percent of the total population" (44; emphasis added). With larger urban markets nearby, eggs and poultry were the dominant form of produce, and according to *Derry Revisited*, Derry's hen population reached new heights in 1911. Nonetheless, assessing the situation in 1901, when Frost learned the terms of

[5] Enrollment at the Adams Academy declined after 1853, when Pinkerton began to accept female students, and in 1887 it merged with the Derry school system.

his grandfather's will, Lawrance Thompson speaks of "the marginal living" that Frost's farming neighbors "managed to eke out . . . through a meager annual sale of milk, eggs, berries, vegetables, and meat" — most of them gaining cash incomes less than the $500 annuity Frost would start to collect in 1902 (*Early Years*, 276).

By contrast, the success of the Hood Farm makes clear what most traditional New England farmers had been unable to do. Its founder, H. P. Hood, had built up a profitable dairy business in the Boston area before he bought, in 1855, a farm of 320 acres in West Derry, pieced together from sixty-five to seventy smaller properties. Shipping to Boston all the milk and eggs he could raise himself and buy from surrounding farms, Hood had built one of New England's largest dairy corporations by the time his sons inherited the business in 1900. It is revealing that the only really profitable farm in the Derry area began, not as a farm, but as a retail business by a Boston entrepreneur who decided to increase profits by raising and feeding his own cows, becoming his own main supplier, controlling quality and costs at the same time. It may be equally important that Hood was born on a Vermont farm, but it is hard to imagine his success without the established customer base and managerial skill he had already developed when he bought his Derry farm, along with the disciplined expansion that allowed him, by 1893, to ship 20,000 quarts of milk a day by refrigerated railroad car[6] from his large barns to his distribution center in Charlestown, Massachusetts, where he continued to buy up other, failing, milk routes (*From Turnpike to Interstate*, 176–81).

Everyone in the Derry area, whether of the village or the farm, would have been aware of the Hood operation, and Frost's contact with the family, according to Thompson, "developed early, when he had been asked to work there in an emergency candling eggs." He also received his collie, Schneider, as a gift from the farm and bought his "fancy-stepping mare, Eunice," from the Hoods for a mere $150 (*Early Years*, 315–16). Business arrangements with the Hood Farm were less satisfactory, for the near-wholesale price they paid for eggs left little profit for Frost. For the ambivalent poultryman who would become the *North of Boston* poet, all of these experiences, each small in itself, must have been illuminating, revealing the difference between those who could make farming pay and those who could not. The Hood operation underlined the key elements of economic success: access to large urban and suburban markets, technical innovation and efficiencies of scale in production, considerable capital, and of course the entrepreneurial and managerial skills needed to

[6] The capital investment underlying the Hood operation is exemplified by the fact that it included a huge ice operation, including an immense, mechanized conveyor belt that brought blocks of ice from Horne's Pond to the Hood icehouse (Holmes and Dugan, 20).

coordinate all these elements. Clearly, to be profitable, farming had to be a business, probably a large one, perhaps even a corporation, as the Hood partnership had become in 1890. It required personal and material resources beyond the reach of the traditional, solitary New England farmer. Even Frost's early mentor and continuing supporter, Dr. Charlemagne Bricault, veterinarian and expert breeder of White Wyandottes, decided in 1905 to give up his poultry operation. Without the help of Bricault's generous prices for his eggs, Frost had little choice but to sell to Hood or directly to his neighbors nearer the village, which he found personally distasteful. Such changes surely played a part in Frost's decision to end his own six-year experiment as a farmer, but not before he came to know first-hand some of the challenges and hardships it entailed.

Derry Village and Pinkerton Academy

The traditional separation of village life from farm life certainly held true in Derry, as Frost was reminded early in 1906 when, pressed by the needs of his growing family, suffering from poor management of what money he had, and embarrassed by unpaid doctor's and grocer's bills, he decided to look for a job that would pay better and more steadily than the desultory sort of farming he had practiced. Though he had never much enjoyed teaching, he knew how to do it and had taught evening classes as recently as his Harvard days, making it an obvious choice. As Frost later explained it:

> The children were coming along and we needed more and more money for them. So, as I lay thinking, awake in bed . . . I became reconciled to my fate. I decided to do what I hated to do — . . . go back to the drudgery of teaching. I had not made a bad job of it. (Mertins, 89)

Frost's short final sentence hints at some solace in the thought that, like it or not, he had done better work as a teacher than as a farmer or a provider. When, however, the chairman of the Derry school board, a local dentist, rebuffed Frost's approach, Frost suspected his reputation as a hen-man, and rather a poor one, as the cause. He had had a similar suspicion when, on a visit to New York City in 1903, he had tried to place poems and perhaps find salaried work with literary editors. "The literary world didn't want to hear from me when I was a farmer in New Hampshire," Frost said of that disappointment decades later. "I had mud on my shoes . . . and that didn't seem right to them for a poet" (in Parini, 83).[7]

[7] Parini's note (463) reads: "Lecture at Amherst, 1959. Tape at ACL [Amherst College Library]."

Fortunately for Frost in 1906, he had begun his inquiries not in Derry but in Lawrence, where he'd been co-valedictorian of his high school class in 1892, and there William Wolcott, pastor of the First Congregational Church and a friend of William Hayes Ward, had suggested that Frost try Pinkerton Academy back in Derry Village, just two miles up the old turnpike road from Frost's farm. Seemingly an obvious choice, Frost had imagined Pinkerton to be out of reach. In his years on the farm he'd been reclusive. What relationships he'd developed were with other farmers, not village people. And it would be hard to say whether his time at Harvard counted for him any more than his lack of a degree counted against him. But armed with a letter of support from Wolcott, he found a surprisingly warm reception from Wolcott's friend, Charles Merriam, pastor of the Derry's Central Congregational Church and a Pinkerton trustee. Merriam was a man of sufficient intellectual accomplishment and sophistication to appreciate Frost, thought him a good prospect for the part-time position that had unexpectedly opened up at the academy, and ended up speaking for Frost in a quite literal way.[8] Not only did Merriam invite Frost to attend the upcoming banquet of the Church's Men's League, where he would meet a number of Pinkerton trustees and teachers, but he suggested that Frost read a poem as a way of introducing himself, and when Frost declined to read it himself, Merriam offered to recite it for him.

The poem, "The Tuft of Flowers," written at least as early as 1897 and describing an unexpected feeling of fellowship coming to relieve a sense of isolation, was uncannily appropriate to Frost's experience with Wolcott and Merriam. The *Derry Sentinel* published it the next day, March 9, 1906, and it apparently helped with Pinkerton. With the support of another trustee, John Chase, whom Frost met at the banquet, he was hired to teach English to the sophomore class for the rest of the school year. Ironically enough, the poetry that, till then, had kept Frost self-consciously apart from others in Derry, had, through Ward, Wolcott, and Merriam, quickly led to a new level of community involvement and, before long, to practical success at Pinkerton. During the following year, Frost wrote two new poems specifically for Derry audiences: one, "The Later Minstrel" was distributed in broadside for Pinkerton's Longfellow Centennial celebration and another, "The Lost Faith," was read, again by Merriam, at the 1907 Men's Club Banquet and printed next day in the *Derry News*.[9]

---

[8] Merriam, an 1879 Yale graduate, was a founder and editor of the *Yale Daily News,* won an award for writing at Yale, and while studying at the Andover Theological Seminary, taught both music and drawing at Philips Academy (*Bulletin of Yale University*, 811).

[9] Neither "The Later Minstrel" nor "The Lost Faith" exemplify the best work Frost was writing, or the lean, spare style he was developing, in these years, and he published neither beyond the Derry community. As I show in chapter 4, however, "The Lost Faith" played an important role in the genesis of "The Black Cottage."

With the exception of the few who disliked his informality and unconventionality both in and out of the classroom, Frost gained strong support from most Pinkerton colleagues and students, thanks to his ambitious work with dramatic productions, sports teams, the literary magazine, and the debating club — all in addition to his innovative curriculum. One measure of this support — but also of the stigma attached to farm life by many in the village and of Frost's continuing self-consciousness about it — became evident when one of Frost's students wrote "hen-man" on the blackboard in his classroom. Clearly feeling the epithet as an insult, Frost was outraged enough to track down the culprit and insist on his expulsion, and though many, including the principal, urged leniency, the trustees backed Frost and the boy went.

The Movement Forward

The six years Frost spent teaching in New Hampshire involved a series of steps away from the farm he moved to in September of 1899. From the start, his Pinkerton years, 1906–1911, involved him with his college-educated colleagues and with the more prosperous and professional families in Derry and the surrounding towns, many of whom sent their children to the academy. In the fall of 1910, the many demands of teaching prompted a move from farm to village; that winter, somewhat to his surprise, Frost was twice invited to speak about his classroom methods to teachers statewide; and at the end of school year, Ernest Silver, Pinkerton's new principal, recruited Frost to follow him to the State Normal School in Plymouth, New Hampshire — a plan that fitted well with Frost's own plans to sell the farm, once it was his to sell, in the fall of 1911. In all, it seems likely that these successive steps in Frost's teaching career, begun as an economic necessity, strengthened him in ways crucial to the poetic future from which they were an immediate distraction. To be sure, the work itself exhausted Frost and sapped his energies for writing. In sending a Christmas gift of manuscript poems to Susan Hayes Ward in December 1911, he explains that it "represents, needless to tell *you*, not the long deferred forward movement you are living in wait for, but only the grim stand it was necessary for me to make until I should gather myself together. The forward movement is to begin next year" (*SL*, 43). When we see the verse that poured out of Frost the following year, it appears that tremendous creative energies had been held in check, and in speaking of his writing in a December letter to Ernest Silver from England, Frost compares himself to "a pawing horse let go" (60). But when we look at all that Frost did in his first year in England, which included his seeking a publisher and reaching out to other writers, it also seems clear that what he gained in the preceding years of teaching — the affirmation of his unconventional methods by students and colleagues, his ability to work under the pressure of judgment, and his increased comfort in dealing with a wider public — all served him well when he had to make his way among complete strangers without even a letter of introduction.

The greater paradox may be that these years at Pinkerton and Plymouth left an essential part of Frost essentially unchanged. While he became enough of a village man to gain acceptance there, his imagination adhered to the beauty and rigor of nature and to the rural, farming people more exposed to both natural and economic forces. Of the various friends and personal acquaintances from Frost's Derry years who become characters in *North of Boston*, Charles Merriam, model for the minister in "The Black Cottage," was the only one who did not experience that vulnerability and exposure, and Frost's greater sympathies as poet lay with those who did. As an energetic naturalist and an avid reader about geology, archeology, and evolution, he recognized the necessity of change and even its power to prompt renewal. But as one who loved the ancient rhythms of rural life and had come to appreciate, if not to emulate, the virtues of his farming neighbors, Frost felt the demise of this traditional culture both intellectually and personally. It moved him, as a poet, to celebrate and record, preserve and protect.

Not that Frost saw the people of Derry simply as victims. Years later he reflected that he had chosen poems "for *North of Boston*" in order "to show the people and to show that I had forgiven them for being people" (*CPPP*, 784), and as he reveals their complexities of circumstance and character, we see a stubborn strength that can offset as well as intensify their vulnerability. But balancing Frost's refusal to sentimentalize these people is his appreciation of the world he had stumbled into, which stripped life to its essentials and spared little room for pretensions. To his years spent farming, raising children, and overcoming the personal depression that followed the deaths of his mother and his first child in 1900, Frost owed much of his personal and poetic maturity. The natural and cultural rhythms of this rural world had provided material and form for his poetic vision, and the poet who would later say "originality and initiative are what I ask for my country" needed little artistic license to invest its people with all the self-reliance and commitment that Frost thought essential to a healthy democracy ("The Figure a Poem Makes," *CPPP*, 778). With such convictions reinforced by his attachment to particular persons, Frost could not help but view the decline of Derry's farming culture, finally, in partisan terms. And so, while recognizing the necessity of social and economic change, the series of portraits that make up *North of Boston* include strong elements of both tribute and lament for what is being lost. In poem after poem, the overriding fact is attrition, the prevailing mood elegiac.

But with strong ambitions in the world of modern publishing balancing such attachments to a fading rural culture, Frost felt a stake on both sides of this conflict between tradition and change, and *North of Boston* reflects that dual allegiance. That it should do so was almost inevitable. In the winter of 1912–13, when he completed most of the poems for the book, Frost and his family occupied a cottage in the London suburb of Beaconsfield, a publisher for his verse having proved so elusive in America. Their arrival in England that fall was a huge gamble on Frost's artistic and economic future, but with this most decisive of steps away from the Derry life begun twelve years before, the "long deferred forward movement" (*SL*, 43) was finally under way.

The Christmas of 1912 found the Frosts in their Beaconsfield bungalow, with *A Boy's Will* accepted for publication and Frost hard at work on the *North of Boston* poems. Inevitably and profoundly, this process entangled Frost's past and future, his memories and hopes. Even as his writing reimmersed him in the Derry world of the poems, so his success in achieving a "poetry that talked," toward which he had worked for years, would have brought to life the prospect of readers ready to pay money for his books. Not that such success was assured. Few if any readers besides Elinor had seen any of the *North of Boston* poems, and *A Boy's Will*, though accepted for publication, had not yet been issued or reviewed. In fact, when this first book appeared in April 1913, early notices, seeming to read Frost's simplicities of style as a lack of sophistication, gave him cause for concern. By July, however, partly to reassure himself of his conscious artistry and partly to cultivate knowledgeable reviewers for his next book, Frost had begun meetings with English poets Frank Flint and T. E. Hulme to explain the "sound of sense" principles behind the new poems. Buoyed by their response to both his theories and the poems themselves, Frost could crow to John Bartlett: "To be perfectly frank with you I am one of the notable craftsmen of my time. That will transpire presently" (*SL*, 79).

The confidence that *North of Boston* would bring his long-desired recognition would wax and wane through the year of the book's gestation, and during this time, emotionally and intellectually, Frost inhabited both the world from which the poems had come and the one into which they might take him. Or perhaps he was caught between these worlds. Either way, he was both champion of a dying, rural culture and an ambitious man of letters in a growing market economy. Integral to the Frost who loved this Derry world was the poet determined not to vanish with it, and here lay something of a problem. Frost knew that, to be the poet he wished to be, to make his act of poetic creation one of economic advantage, he must turn the people and culture of Derry into a saleable commodity, bringing *North of Boston* into the commerce of capitalism and allying himself with the economic interests that the book portrays as an indifferent and sometimes hostile force.

Frost's uneasiness about this act of appropriation would find expression in comments about his poetic vocation over many years. Still more immediate to the Frost who believed his poetic success to hinge on *North of Boston*, this uneasiness surfaces within the volume itself. Its poems are strewn with examples of disloyalty, insensitivity, and alienation; with suspicions or suggestions of exploitation or betrayal, theft or trespass; and with concern and even jokes about these issues. Each of these instances, whether of actual violation, of implied accusation, or even of denial about such possibilities, can be traced, through a series of displacements, back to the poet himself, creating a cumulative suggestion too pervasive to ignore. How Frost expressed his uneasiness about appropriating the lives of his Derry neighbors for *North of Boston*, displacing these feelings onto his poetic characters is, of course, best seen in the poems themselves. But before looking there, it is helpful to consider some of Frost's statements about his poetic vocation that shed light on the conflicts created by his entry into the literary marketplace.

2: Buttering One's Parsnips

THAT FROST SAW *North of Boston* as the keystone of his poetic and economic success is clear in a letter he wrote John Bartlett from Beaconsfield in November 1913, as he was completing his work on the book. There Frost seems most excited by the growing literary friendships he had formed during his first year in England, which by the summer of 1913 had begun to bear fruit. One June discussion of his poetics with Frank Flint had included Robert Bridges, and Frost felt especially encouraged when he placed his own ideas on prosody alongside those of England's Poet Laureate. But eager as he is "to brag a bit" to Bartlett "about [his] exploits as a poet," Frost finds he must first discount them against his larger ambitions, which in turn make clear how his poetic aims involve the nation's mass-market economy. Beginning in teacherly fashion to his former student, Frost explains that

> there is a kind of success called "of esteem" and it butters no parsnips. It means a success with the critical few who are supposed to know. But really to arrive where I can stand on my own legs as a poet and nothing else I must get outside that circle to the general reader who buys books in their thousands. I may not be able to do that. I believe in doing it — don't you doubt me there. I want to be a poet for all sorts and kinds. I could never make a merit of being caviare [*sic*] to the crowd the way my quasi-friend Pound does. I want to reach out. (*SL*, 98)

These comments reveal the related yet conflicting commitments in Frost's idea of his poetic vocation. Wishing to be "a poet for all sorts and kinds," not for an intellectual elite, Frost slights Pound for slighting the general reader, much as he had slighted Frost himself, and in doing so Frost anticipates the anger he would express decades later about those who condescended to his *North of Boston* characters. In that 1937 talk, called "Poverty and Poetry," Frost made explicit these implied connections between himself, the "general reader," and the human subjects of his poems. "[W]hen I speak of my people," he says there, "I sort of mean a class, the ordinary folks I belong to. I have written about them entirely in one whole book: I called it *A Book of People*" (*CPPP*, 759) — the description Frost had used in his dedication of the book to Elinor. But even as Frost identified himself with these people, it was also, inevitably, in distinction to them, and in that sense against them, that he would have to define himself as poet.

Even as Frost saw economic success as a way of reaching "all sorts and kinds," then, he knew that it would also increase the separation that by 1913 he was already feeling from the rural New England to which his verse owed almost everything. Nor would this conflict be easily resolved, for the farmer-poet determined to make a cash crop of his verse was the same Frost who not only located many of his most admired values in its people, but loved that rural world for itself. From the year of his return to America and throughout his career, he would always own a farm and on road trips would long to return there, finding it hard to write anywhere else. Especially in that most decisive step toward a public career — the sale of the Derry farm and the move to England — Frost felt intense loss over the former life, loss that would soon fill his published poems. In the same "butters no parsnips" letter to Bartlett, he also writes, "I don't want you to grow cold in letter writing. You are about all I saved from the years I spent in Derry, you and Margaret, and the three children born to us on the farm, and the first book that was mostly written on the farm" (*SL*, 97). Frost would later recall that he wrote "Mending Wall," *North of Boston*'s opening poem, completed that same fall, "when I was very homesick for my old wall in New England" (Thompson, *Early Years*, 432–33);[1] and that poem's separation between its sophisticated speaker and his traditionalist neighbor, each on his own side of their shared boundary wall and each representing a part of the poet, aptly reflects Frost's own separation from this rural past.

"Reluctance" and the Poet's Calling

As its title suggests, *A Boy's Will* represents a younger version of the poet who sought a publisher for it in the fall of 1912, and Frost says or implies as much not only in letters of the time, but in glosses he added to the book's original table of contents.[2] Though it was "mostly written on the farm" and displays a close attention to natural things that would remain at the heart of Frost's work, the book contains only a few poems in the direct, idiomatic voice he had labored to develop in his Derry years.[3] In fact when Frost arrived in England in September 1912, "the bottom of [his] trunk" (*SL*, 55) held a good many poems in this more vernacular style, most of which would appear in *North of Boston* (1914) and *Mountain Interval* (1916). Perhaps in the fall of 1912 he was not yet sure of

---

[1] According to his note (594), Thompson quotes Frost "from [a] stenographic transcript of a talk given by RF at Wesleyan University, Middletown, Conn., 19 April 1936."

[2] Beginning with Frost's first edition of *Collected Poems* in 1930, he dropped the glosses from the 1913 table of contents.

[3] Two that exemplify this voice are "Mowing" and "Storm Fear," though one could make that case for a few, or parts of a few, others.

these poems or had too few for a coherent volume. Whatever the reason,[4] the poems he chose for *A Boy's Will* overwhelmingly exemplify the "the manner of the nineties" (*SL*, 129) that he had already left behind. Mannered is just what these poems often are, both in posture and voice, as Frost himself hints in his headnotes to the volume, which seem written by one who looks back on an earlier self. The note appended to "My November Guest," for example, reads, "He is in love with being misunderstood," and to "A Late Walk," "He courts the autumnal mood" (*CPPP*, 969). In actuality, the melancholy of the years that gave rise to these poems was no poetic pose. Between 1900 and 1907, Frost lost his mother and two of the six children born to him and Elinor. Elinor's recurrent bouts of depression, Frost's own depression, and his troubled relations with his sister Jeanie all added to the strains of making ends meet on his limited income, of finding time and energy to write, and of wondering how and when he would sell a poem.

In addition, when we consider the Robert Frost who chose and assembled the poems for this first book — a poet still unproven, newly arrived in England and feeling the loss of a place where he had endured and gained so much — we might also see his break with Derry as contributing to the melancholy that pervades *A Boy's Will.* Thanks to a particular allusion, we can attach these feelings of loss quite firmly to its closing poem, "Reluctance." The poem speaks of the "treason" it is for the heart

> To yield with a grace to reason
> And bow and accept the end
> Of a love or a season.

For a poet such as Frost, who often finds occasions for grief in apparently innocent changes, and for a poem whose final line casts its net so wide, it would be unwise to restrict even so keen a sense of loss to any one season, natural or biographical.

For a biographical connection, however, one would naturally start with the time of the poem's composition, long before Frost's Derry decade. Noting, for example, that Frost wrote "Reluctance" in 1894, soon after the Dismal Swamp adventure that followed a premarital rebuff from

---

[4] Frost may also have felt that these poems, in their more traditional style, might be better received than those in his newer, more experimental style, at this point still untested on an audience beyond Elinor. In November 1912, while still negotiating about *A Boy's Will* with Mrs. Nutt (widow of M. L. Nutt and current head of the David Nutt firm), Frost wrote Mosher about "three other books of verse somewhere near completion" (*SL*, 55). From what we now know of his next books, he may also have felt that the poems he placed in *A Boy's Will* would not go well with his newer work and were best published separately.

Elinor, then still Elinor White,[5] Jeffrey Cramer follows Lawrance Thompson in seeing the poem as young Rob's lament for what he imagined as Elinor's withdrawal of affection (Cramer, 27–28; Thompson, *Early Years*, 188–89, 524). In this vein, the poem might also mourn the youthful, idealizing love that Frost, the disillusioned suitor, feared he would never again be willing to risk. Plausible as such readings are, Gerard Quinn has suggested another that relates the poem not to the time of its composition, but rather to the time, eighteen years later, when Frost decided to seek publication of a first book and to make "Reluctance" its final poem.[6]

Quinn has pointed out that the poem's first stanza ends with "an antiquated phrase, 'lo, it is ended,' that," he says, "does not sound at all like Frost" (4).[7] The whole first stanza of "Reluctance" reads:

> Out through the fields and the woods
> And over the walls I have wended;
> I have climbed the hills of view
> And looked at the world, and descended;
> I have come by the highway home,
> And lo, it is ended.

---

[5] Elinor had insisted on finishing at St. Lawrence University before marrying him, and Frost, feeling uneasy about their separation and Elinor's possible interest in more eligible suitors, made an unannounced visit to her residence in Canton, NY, presenting Elinor with the collection of five poems called *Twilight*, which he had had privately printed in just two copies. Taken by surprise, embarrassed by this visit totally against university rules, and perhaps angry at being pressed in this way, Elinor took the little book but refused to talk with Frost till she came home at the end of term. Crushed and humiliated, Frost returned home to Lawrence, then abruptly set off for a lone trek through The Dismal Swamp of Virginia-North Carolina, a destination dictated, no doubt, by his self-dramatizing mood.

[6] The poem was first published in *The Youth's Companion* on November 7, 1912. Clearly Frost had submitted this poem to the periodical before contracting with David Nutt for the publication of *A Boy's Will.* On November 19, Frost wrote Thomas Mosher that he was negotiating with Nutt but had "signed no contract as yet" (*SL*, 55).

[7] Compelling and significant as I find Quinn's reading, I would qualify this point. Such "antiquated phrase[s]" are, as Quinn suggests, precisely what Frost strove to avoid in *North of Boston* and beyond and would be quite out of place in any of Frost's volumes after *A Boy's Will.* But *A Boy's Will,* despite a few examples of his newly vernacular voice, is full of what Frost himself described as "traditional clichés": such words as "Ah," "O," and here, "lo," contractions such as "'twere" and "'tis," and capitalized nouns and personified abstractions characteristic of nineteenth- and even eighteenth-century verse (Mertins, 197–98) It is characteristic of Frost's allusive practice, however, that he should disguise his reference to Longfellow by placing it among so many outmoded mannerisms, making it seem just another stylized expression of feeling.

This final phrase, as Quinn explains, comes directly from the "Introit" to Longfellow's *Divine Tragedy*, where it marks the moment at which the biblical prophet Habbukuk is made to recognize his own prophetic vocation. There the words "Lo, it is ended" are uttered by the angel who literally lifts the hesitant Habakkuk (by the hair!) into his public ministry, using these words to announce that the prophet's former, private life is now behind him (Quinn, 630–31).

Lifted into "Reluctance," the phrase marks a comparable moment in Frost's life. Once we recognize his allusion to Longfellow's plot, we can see that "Reluctance," in completing Frost's first book manuscript, also completes a developmental journey implied by its title, *A Boy's Will*. This phrase, too, Frost took from Longfellow — significantly, from the refrain of a poem titled "My Lost Youth," which reads: "A boy's will is the wind's will, / And the thoughts of youth are long, long thoughts" (*CPPP*, 968). By incorporating "Lo, it is ended" and all that attaches to it, "Reluctance" marks the symbolic moment at which the boy's will, impulsive and brooding and traced through the preceding thirty poems of this first book, now yields to the designs of a poet's mature ambitions. Biographically, it is the moment where the manuscript poems brought to England are offered for publication, where the years of preparation end, and Frost commits himself to a public career.[8] Behind him is Derry, which — in shaping a newer, more confident and original voice, furnishing subjects for his forthcoming "book of people" (*CPPP*, 970), and providing poetic images for a lifetime — was at the heart of the poet he had become. With Frost in England, far from Derry and the farm where "the first book . . . was mostly written" (*SL*, 97) and moving further from it as he made his bid for public recognition, we can imagine why, at the end of this prefatory volume, he might present the choice to leave it behind as a betrayal — "to the heart," at least, no "less than a treason."

A short poem titled "In Neglect" placed at the middle of *A Boy's Will* helps to explain the complex and even paradoxical feelings of loss that accompanied the long-awaited success of Frost's first book. Almost aphoristic in its brevity and elusive in its implications, the whole poem reads:

> They leave us so to the way we took,
> As two in whom they were proved mistaken,
> That we sit sometimes in the wayside nook,
> With mischievous, vagrant, seraphic look,
> And *try* if we cannot feel forsaken.

[8] In a letter of January 18, 1938, Frost told Robert Newdick that "Reluctance" was a very old poem "except for one very important change (which wouldn't you like to know!)" (Newdick, 164; in Cramer, 26). It is tempting to imagine that the change involved this allusion.

The poem is clearly about Frost and Elinor, co-valedictorians of their Lawrence High School class in 1892, who cultivate a pride in their own unworldly waywardness, trying to believe that by holing up on the Derry farm — the "wayside nook" in which they scrape by on Rob's annuity and a little egg money — they have been dismissed by the world for failing to fulfill their early promise. The last two lines, especially, convey a good deal of self-critical irony, suggesting a condescending pleasure the pair take in seeing themselves as misunderstood and banished by others to the very refuge they needed and enjoyed. Much as Frost kept alive the poetic ambition he first confessed in 1894, there was something safe in the obscurity of his early Derry years (before he began teaching at Pinkerton Academy in 1906), during which, if he did not find public success as a poet, he and Elinor could at least live "a life that [went] rather poetically" (*SL*, 224). With the publication of *A Boy's Will*, the personal blessings of this obscurity, mixed though they were, were coming to an end. They had in fact already done so with the decision to seek publication for a book of his verse. And so, while "Reluctance" recalls the painful disillusionment Frost had suffered at the time of its composition in 1894, it acknowledges at least one cost of the public success he had chosen to pursue.[9]

Whatever the feelings of loss conveyed in "Reluctance" and in Frost's November 1913 letter to Bartlett, they were offset by his growing excitement at new prospects for self-realization and recognition. Keep in mind that the poet who drew so deeply from this rural world had never been wholly of it and would inevitably want a literary community, audience, and marketplace that neither Derry Village or the New England back-country could provide. In a letter written January 21, 1913, to Frank Flint, the first poet to befriend Frost in London, Frost makes clear that the world he'd left behind in coming to England had failed to meet his literary need. Referring to the writers he'd met at the opening of Harold Monro's soon-to-be-famous bookshop, Frost writes,

> I was only too childishly happy to make one . . . in a company in which I hadn't to be ashamed of having written verse. Perhaps it will help you to understand . . . if I tell you that I have lived for the most

[9] In an intriguing way, readings that relate the poem to these two biographical moments — 1894 and 1912 — both involve conflicting emotions around publication. In 1894, Frost composes the poem after returning from his Dismal Swamp venture and seeing "My Butterfly," his first published poem, on the front page of the November 8 *Independent*, but finding that this poetic success did not outweigh his imagined loss of Elinor's love. In the fall of 1912, in England with Elinor and their four children, and with "Reluctance" appearing in *The Youth's Companion* and soon in his first book, the feeling of loss is more closely connected to the act of publication itself.

> part in villages where it were better that a millstone were hanged around your neck than that you should own yourself a minor poet. (in Barry, 84–85)[10]

As Mark Richardson has argued persuasively, the "villages" in which Frost felt himself a likely pariah were not simply Derry or Lawrence but most of American culture, in which writing verse was hardly considered manly work, or manly at all.[11] One might be tempted to imagine Derry, whose newspapers had published two of Frost's poems, as diverging from this paradigm, but it seems unlikely that a community valuing "prayer first, then labor" and believing that "everyone must be productive or suspect" would place Frost among its most respected members. By its own account, it did not. Derry's own history of its first 150 years, *From Turnpike to Interstate: 1827–1977*, dutifully says that "Frost is remembered fondly and the town is grateful for his residency here," but only after describing him as

> a lover of nature but not a farmer, a dreamer whose chores would come second to the dream, a man careless with his credit. Such a way of life was alien to people who could never have built their town under such conditions. . . . In truth, this man of thought, temporarily curtailed in his activities due to hay fever and the weakness in his lungs, remained a stranger in the midst of a town whose residents were traditionally energetic and hardworking. (53, 55)

As Frost would say upon his return from England, he had gone to Derry to escape a world that would "disallow" him, and for five years or so, the farm provided an invaluable refuge for the developing poet who went there. But if, all told, Derry allowed him to gather the materials and develop the confidence he needed to take his verse beyond it, it also retained elements of that "disallowing" world, and finally, when the time came to "test [his] strength against all creation," it could not affirm the poet he had become (*SL*, 158).[12]

---

[10] The original of this letter resides at the University of Texas Library (Austin). Though both Walsh (86–88) and Thompson (*Early Years*, 408–9) have quoted from it at length, the entire letter has been published only by Barry.

[11] This idea permeates Richardson's *Ordeal of Robert Frost*, but see in particular the sections titled "The 'Psychogenesis' of a style: Frost in the 'Villages' of America" and "'Good Hours': Frost's Accommodating Intransigence," 56–95.

[12] When I asked Mark Richardson what he thought of the fact that the "The Tuft of Flowers" had been published in the *Derry Sentinel* in 1906, and "The Lost Faith" in the *Derry News* in 1907, he said, "Most of the readers would have been women" (conversation, October 2, 2010).

Wise Counsel, Bolder Choices

A response to Frost's first published poem illuminates the dismissive attitudes toward poetry held by many of Frost's contemporaries, who considered verse a rarified and effete enterprise properly pursued only by a social elite with time and money to spare. And, while this response is not Frost's own statement but another's reflection on him, it nonetheless illustrates the pressures bearing down on one who, like Frost, wanted his verse to be a working part of a working life, not a diversion from it — one determined "to stand on [his] own legs as a poet and nothing else" (*SL*, 98). The reflection comes from Maurice Thompson, a well-known Indiana novelist,[13] writing to William Hayes Ward, editor of the *New York Independent*, who, in November 1894, had published Frost's "My Butterfly: An Elegy." Ward, impressed by this new, young talent, had solicited Thompson's estimate of Frost's poem, and Thompson, struck by "the extreme beauty of that little ode," identified "an art . . . singular and biting" and a "secret of genius between the lines, an appeal to sympathy lying deep in one's own resources of tenderness" (in *SL*, 23–24). Both the relevance and irony of Thompson's response are underlined by Frost's own excitement at this first taste of literary success. So exhilarated was he by the affirmation and the fifteen-dollar check he had received that Frost then sent Ward and his literary editor, Susan Hayes Ward, more poems and a note confessing to "the astonishing magnitude of my ambition" (*SL*, 20).

Thompson's admiration, however, did not translate into wholehearted encouragement. Combining his words of celebration with a somewhat theatrical lament, Thompson also registers "a pang" in reflecting "that its author is poor," adding "What hope is there" for a poet who must "grind" for his own "bread"? Adding a clearly personal element, Thompson, who had found a living in writing prose, speaks of "the gag in my teeth whenever I wanted to sing . . . a gag that can speak and say to me . . . 'Let the rich men like Tennyson and Swinburne and Lowell and Browning and Holmes do the singing: what right has a poor man to waste his time and breath with song'" (Thornton, 17).

Thompson's reservations about poetry as a livelihood echoed those of Frost's Yankee grandfather, William Prescott Frost. At the same time, Thompson's own choice to give up the practice of law in order to write novels, at least half-ignoring his own counsel here, suggests that his figurative singing "gag" represents some conventional "better judgment" as much as his full-throated conviction. There is, in short, a mixed message in his advice to Frost through Ward, which he concludes by saying:

---

[13] Born in 1844, Thompson began his professional life as a lawyer, but began to publish stories and essays in the 1870s and novels in the 1880s, as well as four volumes of verse. His best-known work was a novel, *Alice of Old Vincennes*, published in 1900, the year before his death from pneumonia.

> If I had a chance . . . I should tell [Frost] to forget that he ever made a poem and to never pen another rhyme. I told my brother that years ago and now he is a great lawyer instead of a disappointed poet . . .! I was a better lawyer than he when I was lured away by the Muses. If Frost has good health tell him to learn a trade or profession and carry a sling-shot in his pocket for [the Muse] Aoede. (18)

Combining his praise with his own choice of a literary career, and noting that slingshot to be carried for art's sake, Thompson almost seems to hope that Frost might ignore the lawyerly advice he feels compelled to send his way.[14]

If Thompson harbored any such wish, he had chosen the right man. For, as Lawrance Thompson and Jay Parini remind us, Frost, upon leaving Dartmouth College the year before, had rejected his grandfather's offer to support him for a year of writing "on the condition that if he did not succeed, he must give up trying to be a poet." In a way as prescient as it was realistic, Frost had responded that such a trial would require not one year, but twenty (Parini, 46; Thompson, *Early Years*, 172). It is mildly ironic that the "poor man" who elicits Thompson's warning would persist as a poet. It is doubly and triply ironic that he would do so, first, thanks largely to inherited wealth; second, that the wealth came from the same grandfather who had first tried to wean him of his poetic hopes; and, third, that this grandfather would later buy the farm and supply the annuity that made possible Frost's Derry years, ultimately seeing

[14] There is no evidence that Ward ever passed on Thompson's pessimistic advice, and Mertins reports that Frost "knew nothing of it" (58). But the praise evidently reached him, and in an inscription to Earl J. Bernheimer, Frost's patron, dated February 1, 1940, Frost says that "pride in what . . . Maurice Thompson had said about . . . 'My Butterfly'" was "probably" what made him get up the small collection of poems that he called *Twilight* and had privately printed for himself and Elinor in the fall of 1894 (Mertins, 293). Frost, of course, was well aware of the accepted wisdom that Thompson expresses. Writing to Ernest Silver in December 1913 — when Frost first mentions "North of Boston" as a title — he says, "At most poetry can pave the way for prose, and prose may or may not make money." Yet he goes on to admit that, even so, he is "less inclined to prose that I thought I was when I looked into the future out of a normal school window in Plymouth. I was always that way: two or three days on end I would write prose . . . [as] the thing for a man with a family to do. But just when I though I bade fair to produce a novel . . . I would bring up another inconsequential poem. Sort of incorrigible I am" (*SL*, 102–3). It's hard to know how seriously Frost ever took the idea of writing prose, for, throughout his life, he avoided writing it for publication. We also know that Silver had argued against Frost's leaving Plymouth, especially to write poetry, and Frost may have hoped to pacify him by agreeing in principle and portraying himself as "incorrigible." As Frost makes clear, however, for him poetry was the only real choice — or hardly a choice at all.

him through the twenty years that Frost had set for his poetic probation. Further compounding these ironies for Frost and *North of Boston* is that this grandfather, long an overseer at the Pacific Mills in Lawrence, had acquired this wealth through industrial commerce.

While this inheritance, beginning in 1901,[15] was perhaps the decisive element in giving Frost these twenty formative years, such resources, at least in Frost's hands, were not enough to support the household of six that had taken shape by 1905, pushing Frost into the five years of teaching, first at Pinkerton Academy and then at the Plymouth Normal School, that increasingly hobbled his writing. Frost's refusal to commit to more than a year at Plymouth, coupled with the sale of the farm that November, suggests a clear recognition that his career as a teacher threatened his future as a poet. No doubt aware that the twenty-year "probation" period to which he'd laid claim was nearing an end, Frost understood that a bold choice was needed. The promise of a "forward movement . . . to begin next year" (*SL*, 43) in the Christmas letter to Ward might be read as an exhortation to himself.

The Frost of two years hence — Frost in England in the fall of 1913 — was thus a man nearing forty with a wife and four children who had abruptly left a promising teaching career to spend the following year almost wholly on his verse. As a poet now with one book in print and another almost ready for the press, he still carried the promise and uncertainty that Maurice Thompson had imagined for the young poet of "My Butterfly" in 1894. Frost also carried a "magnitude of . . . ambition" (*SL*, 43) and resolve that would fully reveal itself only by the choices he would make, and this ambition, combined with his practical needs, determined his course with a powerful logic. As a working man stemming from working people, Frost must earn a living. As a family man, he must do it now. And as a poet, he must do it in verse. To accomplish that — "to stand on [his] legs as a poet and nothing else" — he must reach "the general reader who buys books in their thousands" (*SL*, 98). Not to do so would prove him a "minor poet" in the very American "villages" where Frost saw his audience and would be a badge of dishonor among the working people with whom Frost classed himself. But, as we might expect of one who liked to think of himself as an exception in almost everything, even that affiliation must be understood with qualification, especially with regard to Derry.

In all, Derry had given Frost more than he had hoped to find there. In the daily and seasonal rhythms of rural life and the direct impact of

[15] The annuity payment of $500 did not begin until July 1902, but Wilbur Rowell, the grandfather's executor, told Frost that his grandfather had also forgiven the loans used to start the Methuen poultry farm in 1899. If one counts these, as well as the funds for Harvard and Frost's first year on the Derry farm as advances on his inheritance, then one could say it began in 1898.

natural forces, he found materials for his greatest single volume and beyond. In the language of his farming neighbors, he also found a poetic voice at once exacting and vernacular, subtle but direct. Even his teaching and tangential involvement in village life contributed to the confidence he needed to take his work into the wider world. But much as Derry gave him, it could not provide the literary community needed to affirm and promote the poet Frost meant to be. It left him outside the literary marketplace. Critical as Derry was for the poet Frost would become and much as he would look back to it with longing, he was never quite "of" that place, never rooted there as his poetic subjects were, and when it came time to leave, he had the poetic craft, the courage, and just enough cash to do so.

"The Code" and Frost's Relation to Derry

To describe the poet who remains both inside and outside the *North of Boston* culture he records,[16] Tyler Hoffman has compared Frost to the modern ethnographer. Hoffman proposes that "The Code," a dramatic narrative in which a "town-bred farmer" is schooled in local mores by one of his hired hands, "can be read as a metaphor of the anthropological enterprise on which the whole book pivots" ("Poet as Anthropologist," 11). The ethnographer provides a useful model for the poet who was both observer and participant in the culture he wrote about, but we should be careful not to imagine detachment as either the aim or the result of Frost's efforts to map Derry's human landscape in his poems. In fact, as "The Code" examines the relations between farm laborers and their employers, it reveals what made Frost as much a champion as a recorder of this rural culture.

"The Code" contains two narratives, one growing out of the other, each describing a conflict between a farmer and the hired man he offends. In the first, a "town-bred farmer," unaware of the local code he's violated, is instructed by a more sympathetic farm hand who understands his confusion when the offended man, James, "Suddenly / . . . thrusting pitchfork in the ground, / Marched . . . off the field and home." To illustrate his lesson, the same hand then tells his employer of a similar offense by a local farmer who ought to have known better and got a harsher comeuppance in return.

In the opening, framing story, "The town-bred farmer" reveals his outsider status, first, by asking James to "take pains . . . To cock the hay — because it's going to shower," and then by "fail[ing] to under-

[16] For other discussions of this idea, see Lawrence Buell, "Frost as a New England Poet"; Parini, *Frost: A Life*, especially chapters 4 and 5; and Richardson, *The Ordeal of Robert Frost*, especially pages 56–95.

stand" the offense in his doing so. The other hired man, revealing the "code" of the poem's title, explains that any hand told "to work better or faster" would assume that "you meant to find fault with his work," adding, "That's what the average farmer would have meant." On a still more consoling note, he further adds, "Don't let it bother you. You've found out something."

This more sympathetic hired man affirms both the farm servants' code and the unconventional status of his employer when he says, "I'd have served you just the same. / But I know you don't understand our ways." In doing so he makes clear what's wrong with reducing the theme of "The Code" to the "single-minded inflexibility and stubbornness" of the Yankee farmer (Kemp, 128). As if to emphasize both the seriousness of the code and the special dispensation he has granted this outsider, the farm hand then tells of another employer with no such excuse, a farmer named Sanders whom he "served" more severely for his "bulling" tricks, burying him under a wagon-load of hay — an aggressive act that knocked him down and might have killed him. At the end of the hired man's story, when the town-bred farmer asks whether Sanders had fired him for what he'd done, the man answers, "Discharge me? No! He knew I did just right."

This final exchange completes the poem's demonstration of the way that a system of communal rules distinguishes the insiders who know them from the outsiders who need to have them explained. But the parable about Sanders, whom the farm hand had held to the standards of the code, makes equally clear what the code does for the insiders themselves, protecting and empowering those lowest on the economic scale. For Frost such concerns were central. Born in 1874, he grew up in decades when conflicts between workers and increasingly powerful corporations often became violent, and both Frost's parents were outspoken about the corrupting influence of corporate wealth and power. Aided by two short stints in the Lawrence textile mills during and after his high-school days, Frost understood the systematic exploitation of the mill workers, and two early sonnets, "The Mill City" and "When the Speed Comes," both written in Derry but not published in his lifetime, expressed his sympathy for their plight.[17]

As the moral codes of Derry's farming culture are presented in *North of Boston*, they reveal a crucial part of what he valued in this rapidly passing way of life — something that Frost considered fundamental to democracy and an effort toward something more decent and just than Frost had observed in factory conditions and practices. Unwritten, usually implicit and personally enforced, these codes honored the individuality threatened by the systems of mass production and mass distribution that were replacing them. It should hardly surprise us that the book Frost would later

[17] I say more about both these poems in my next chapter.

describe as his way of forgiving people for their "being people" should emphasize in turn the ways they forgive each other (*CPPP*, 784).

"The Code" shows us allowances of two different kinds, both of which validate the respect due to the ordinary farm laborer and, beyond that, reflect the forgiveness that can operate in a culture that remains as much personal as institutional. First is the allowance that a hired man grants his "town-bred" employer, who is unaware of the code he has violated. Then, in the story the hired man tells, we see the reciprocal allowance that the farmer, recognizing his disrespect for an employee, grants the man who, in redressing the offense, might easily have hurt more than his pride. In a parallel way Warren, in "The Death of the Hired Man," follows Mary's lead in the allowance he comes to grant Silas, putting compassion and personal concern ahead of legitimate grievances. Though Mary has seen Silas's desperate condition for herself and is "sure" that "his working days are done," she urges Warren to accept Silas's assertion that "he's come to ditch the meadow." "Surely you wouldn't grudge the poor old man / Some humble way to save his self-respect," she urges, appealing directly to the kindness that she knows to lie beneath her husband's anger. In fact, what softens Warren toward Silas and his repeated derelictions, allowing him to accept the hired man's "right of return," is not a weighing of rights and wrongs or of gains and losses from his years of service. Rather, it is the memories, called up by Mary, of Silas's quirky ways — their shared recognition of Silas not as a commodity, but as a person, as part in their own personal history, and, in his skills with dousing prong and hay fork, as part of a traditional culture about to disappear.

Respect for the individual, especially one lacking economic power, is again at the center of "Blueberries," where the narrator and a townsman gossip, amused about the artful evasions by which their neighbor Loren, with many mouths to feed, guards the berrying places he considers his by right. In counterpoint to such respectful accommodations are the impersonal and unforgiving forces of a corporate economy portrayed in "The Self-Seeker," in which the protagonist observes that the factory that has literally picked him up and thrown him aside now "runs the same without me there," and where the insurance company lawyer sees the injured man, who may never walk again, as no more than a liability to be limited.

As we might expect of a book drawn so fully from the poet's Derry experience, many *North of Boston* poems contain figures that reflect Frost's marginal position in the culture he observed in those years. In addition to those mentioned above, these poems include, as we shall see, "The Mountain," "A Servant to Servants," and "A Hundred Collars," among still others. But we can also see that, for the poet who made this culture a crucible of endangered values, his role as observer inevitably had to take priority over the involvement that made it possible. Without discounting the solidarity Frost felt with the "people" of his "book," we would be mistaken to let the workingman's assertion of belonging mask the possessive pride of the creator. Tellingly, when Frost announced his "new volume of blank verse" in July 1913 to Thomas Mosher, the American small-press publisher and bibliophile, knowing that the fastidious Mosher might find the "every-day level of diction" in the new poems to be a sticking point, he addresses Mosher as one aesthete to another. Not that Frost abandons his role as the people's champion. Yet the low diction so "appropriate to the virtues I celebrate" is something he has "dropped" into; the individual portraits are "character strokes I had to get in somewhere"; and his vernacular artistry, Frost insists, is "designed" rather than natural, thus separating himself, as poet, from his "untutored" poetic subjects (*SL*, 83–84). How different is Frost's emphasis in writing that same month to Frank Flint, who had read eight of the longer narratives and not only shared Frost's democratic sympathies but already understood his sophistication and admired his craft. "Did I reach you with the poems?" Frost asks Flint. "Did I give you the feeling of and for the . . . kind of people I like to write about?" (in Barry, 82). Here, as Frost has less to prove, his Derry neighbors, rather than the occasion and opportunity for his "character strokes," are human beings whose characters provide a reason for his art.

To ask which of these perspectives and attitudes was the more real for Frost is to ask the wrong question. The people he had left behind in Derry remained at the heart of his voice and vision and embodied the individualism that he valued. Now, though transformed into verse, they were still people he cared for. And while his success as a poet was his own, he was fully aware that they were essential to it. Two months later, in September 1913, Frost would reflect on the Scots poet, Robert Burns, "I wonder whether they [his people] made Burns' poems or Burns' poems made them" (*SL*, 94). With its rhetorical inversion, this question suggests the reciprocity of Frost's relationship with his Derry neighbors. Much as he was both inside and outside the Derry world he preserved in *North of Boston*, the people of Derry are both outside and inside him, helping to make him the poet who could, in turn, make them the dramatic characters of his poems.

Upon his return to America, riding the wave of acclaim for *North of Boston* that broke first in England, Frost's Derry years began to take their place in the longer arc of his developing career. In his 1915 letter to the journalist William Stanley Braithwaite, we see Frost shaping that experience in the light of his recent success, supplying information for articles that Braithwaite is writing about this "new" American poet. When Frost explains that he "kept farm, *so to speak*, for nearly ten years, but less as a farmer than as a fugitive from the world that seemed to . . . 'disallow' me" (*SL*, 158; emphasis added), we might wonder whether his "so to speak" is an apology for the uncommitted farmer he turned out to be or a disclaimer for the vernacular idiom "kept farm" that, on the other hand, belongs to the farmer-bard persona he was trying out on his return to America. Either way, in looking back and presenting himself as a poet by design, Frost presents Derry as a preparatory episode, a way "to save myself and fix myself before I measured myself against all creation." And, though Derry gave Frost the growing room he needed, it could not finally sustain or satisfy the poet that had grown there. As he wrote, "I was never really out of the world for good and all" (158).

Homesick for Derry as Frost may have been in England, something more than nostalgia was at work when, in December 1913, within a month of his plea to Bartlett not to let the Derry connection "grow cold" (*SL*, 97), Frost wrote to Ernest Silver, announcing *North of Boston* as the title of his new book and assuring Silver that "no amount of success can keep us here [in England] more than another year. . . . My dream," Frost continues, "would be to get the thing started in London and then do the rest of it from a farm in New England where I could live cheap and get Yankier and Yankier" (*SL*, 103). But even if Frost was utterly sincere with Silver, his joking tone together with the word "dream" suggests a recognition that the way forward would not lead back — that poetic recognition was at odds with rural seclusion and, in the words of John Milton, could not "be run for . . . without dust and heat."[18]

For the poet who had passed his boyhood in San Francisco and grown to manhood in the industrial city of Lawrence, Massachusetts, the idea of growing "Yankier and Yankier" has elements of self-parody. The phrase suggests the studied unpretentiousness of this New American Poet in Old England, who referred to himself, in another letter back home as a "Yank from Yankville" (Thompson, *Early Years*, 415).[19] This pose of ordinariness looks ahead to Frost's public role as rustic bard rather than back to Derry, where Frost often felt more the aesthete than the farmer and was sometimes teased and even resented as a newcomer with leisurely habits and annuity checks. And if that later public persona paid homage to the rural sources of his poetry, it also underlined Derry not as a place to which Frost could return in fact, but as a symbolic locale that he must recreate by artistic means. In any case, the path that took Frost to Derry also led beyond. Unlike the people of his forthcoming book, he had the talent and the will to leave, and in 1911, when the farm became his to sell, he had the funds as well. Such differences from his farming neighbors in Derry were momentous, and Frost's giving up these attachments for literary success involved something different from and stronger than regret.

---

[18] The quoted words are from *Areopagitica*. The entire sentence reads, "I cannot praise a fugitive and cloistered virtue, unexercised and unbreathed, that never sallies out and sees her adversary, but slinks out of the race where that immortal garland is to be run for, not without dust and heat" (728).

[19] The letter was written to Ernest Silver, July 10, 1913, when Frost was deeply engaged both in composing *North of Boston* and in planting seeds for its reception.

3: Winners, Losers, and the Poet

The Cruelties of Succession

I SUGGEST THAT as Frost left behind the Derry friends who lacked his opportunities, and as he turned their hardship and poverty into his own success, he felt vulnerable to the charge of opportunism. Just as the lyric "Reluctance" calls it a "treason . . . to the heart" to "accept the end / Of a love or a season," no matter how necessary that end may be, so we might imagine Frost's own turning away from his Derry attachments, however right for himself and his family, to carry underlying feelings of betrayal.

"Nature is always more or less cruel," Frost has said, illustrating his idea with the ruthless competition for light among forest trees.[1] In portraying the struggle for survival and the particulars of natural succession, Frost's lyrics often focus on the casualties of this process, making the corollary point that we, with our human awareness of mortality, rarely share nature's indifference. To Frost's perennial lyric persona, who readily identifies with other living things, who values them for their beauty, and who knows the mortal implications of all time and change, nature's routine destructions often feel cruel, giving rise to tones of lament and complaint that border on accusation. In "The Oven Bird,"[2] for example, the poem's protagonist, a woodland warbler who "says" rather than sings his story of "diminished things" and clearly speaks for the poet, is strident and persistent in pointing out the losses brought on by the advancing season. Other poems articulate a more direct resistance. The speaker of "A Leaf Treader" hears the autumn leaves "threatening under their breath" as they fall, feels their "will to carry me with them to death," and pushes back: "But it was no reason I had to go because they had to go. / Now up my knee to keep on top of another year of snow."

---

[1] This spoken comment is included in the 1988 biography *Robert Frost* in the PBS series, *Voices and Visions: The Poet in America.*

[2] None of the four lyrics I discuss in this section come from *North of Boston*, but represent a continuity of perspective over at least thirty years. "The Oven Bird" appeared in *Mountain Interval* (1916), but according to Jeffrey Cramer was written in Derry, probably in 1906–7. "Spring Pools" appeared in *West-Running Brook* (1928), "A Leaf Treader" in *A Further Range* (1936). "In Hardwood Groves," which replaced "Spoils of the Dead" in *A Boy's Will* in Frost's first *Collected Poems* (1930), was completed in 1925 but begun in 1905.

Still other poems offer tones that subtly undercut an ostensible acceptance of nature's way. From the first line of "Spring Pools," for example, the speaker understands that an exquisite moment in early spring — the meeting of sky and flowers in the reflecting surface of forest pools — cannot last, for the trees overhead will need all their water to produce another year's leaves. But, despite this understanding, his response to the coming change spills over into something more than a lament. Referring to "The trees that have it in their pent-up buds / To darken nature and be summer woods," and almost speaking to them, he says:

> Let them think twice before they use their powers
> To blot out and drink up and sweep away
> These flowery waters and these watery flowers
> From snow that melted only yesterday.

Against the beauty and defenselessness of the ephemeral "flowery waters . . . and watery flowers," we have the coming violence of destruction, heavy with consonants, made emphatic by the two spondees, "blot out" and "drink up." The speaker's indirect address to the trees, "Let them think twice," whether heard as a plea, an exhortation, or even a counter-threat by one feeling threatened, asks the impossible. But in urging what nature cannot do, this speaker conveys the difficulty of accepting what it does, underlining nature's quite literal inhumanity.

"In Hardwood Groves" goes further in charging cruelty to the rules of natural succession and reminds us that in nature all winners turn victims in the end. This time it is the leaves' turn to suffer. The poem opens by acknowledging nature's economy in using "The same leaves over and over again!" but quickly shifts to the price to be paid for that efficiency:

> Before the leaves can mount again
> To fill the trees with another shade,
> They must go down past things coming up.
> They must go down into the dark decayed.
>
> They *must* be pierced by flowers and put
> Beneath the feet of dancing flowers.
> However it is in some other world,
> I know that this is the way in ours.

Repeated twice, "They must" becomes increasingly emphatic. The leaves, cast into darkness, are pierced and trampled by nature's spring celebrants, and despite the acceptance of what cannot be changed in the poem's final line, the surmise of how it might be "in some other world" opens a space between necessary knowledge and reconciliation. We notice that the speaker of "In Hardwood Groves," even as he tells of the spring flowers pushing toward the light, keeps his eye on the leaves sent "into the dark decayed." They remain both his grammatical subject and the focus of his concern.

The decline of New England's small-scale family farms in a developing capital economy is another story of natural succession, and as *North of Boston* celebrates this disappearing culture, Frost's sympathy again lies with those left behind in the process of modernization, and sometimes in the dark as well. What, then, does it say that the success Frost envisioned for his book would not only make him another winner in the competition for survival but would link him directly with a modern economy whose mass production and mass marketing were essential to selling his books "to the general reader who buys books in their thousands" (*SL*, 98)? If not answered or even precisely answerable, the question is nonetheless raised in many *North of Boston* poems.

Frost's Anti-Industrial Legacy

The destructive potential of industrial capitalism and its power elite was no new idea to Frost when he came to Derry or when he produced *North of Boston*. The foundation for such an awareness was laid early in his life, for both of Frost's parents were committed to reformist views that saw uncontrolled capitalism as a source of political corruption and social injustice. Rob's father Will had always had an anti-establishment bent and, as a youth in Lawrence, Massachusetts, during the Civil War, had developed strong enough Southern sympathies to run off from home in an unsuccessful attempt to reach Virginia and join the Confederate army.[3] Ten years later, as a journalist with political aspirations in San Francisco, he met and came under the influence of Henry George, a crusading journalist who, in 1871, had become editor and part owner of the *Daily Evening Post*, a newspaper founded to expose public corruption. Will Frost's friendship with Henry George soon extended to their families, who visited each others' homes, and in 1875, George convinced Will to leave his job at the San Francisco *Bulletin* to become city editor at the *Post* (Thompson, *Early Years*, 12–13). George thought highly enough of Will Frost to encourage his protégée's political ambitions even as he himself moved to New York City in the summer of 1880; and in 1885, soon after Belle Frost had herself moved to Massachusetts following Will's death, George visited the widow and her two children in Lawrence.

Jay Parini points out that by this time George's "ideas on Christian socialism had proved attractive to a wide range of intellectuals around the world, including George Bernard Shaw and Leo Tolstoy" (8). It is impossible to calculate exactly how conversations between the Georges and

[3] Born in 1850, he could not have been more than fourteen at the time.

Frosts would have affected young Rob, who was only five in 1879, when George published his famous *Progress and Poverty*, a treatise proposing cures for various economic ills, including private land ownership. But it seems likely that this early intellectual climate encouraged his later interest in Shaw, whom Frost admired enough, John Walsh reports, to see a long-running Shaw production, *Fanny's First Play*, with Elinor on September 2, 1912, their very first night in London (15–16). Just three weeks later, on September 26, though already moved in at Beaconsfield, Frost took the forty-minute train ride back to London to seek out a suffragettes' meeting where Shaw spoke (27). Confirming Frost's interest is an early entry — "Pursuit of G. B. S." — in one of his London notebooks (*Notebooks*, 9.1r).[4] As Tyler Hoffman notes, Frost's reflections on his English years include his resistance to English ways of maintaining imperial and class privilege and, looking back to 1913 years later, Frost described himself as having harbored "a poacher in my blood" who refused to be hedged[5] out by his "alien speech" (*CPPP*, 802). Hoffman also observes that two of Frost's earliest friends among English poets, Wilfrid Gibson and Lascelles Abercrombie, "sought to relieve the conditions of the working poor" and cites examples of social protest in Gibson's poems (*Politics of Poetry*, 19–24).

More telling, however, are Frost's own expressions of sympathy for those whose labor drove the industrial machine. Lawrance Thompson writes that a younger Frost, in his first factory job in the summer of 1891, "found . . . his sympathies allied with the labor organizations which had been stirring up the city with protest-meetings" and that, when they succeeded in having their workweek reduced to fifty-eight hours, Rob's defense of the workers led to a disagreement with his grandfather, the retired Pacific Mills foreman (*Early Years*, 106). "Good Relief," a poem Frost wrote in England in 1913 but never published, conveys the pathos of two young boys at Christmastime, who peer longingly into a toyshop window while their father, an out-of-work collier, looks on. Two unpublished sonnets, "The Mill City" and "When the Speed Comes," both written during Frost's Derry years and drawing on his woolen-mill experience of 1893–94, describe the soul-numbing effects of factory work. The imagery of the latter poem — in which "belts begin to snap and shafts to creak. . . . And breaths of many wheels are on the cheek," and "The music of the iron is a law" — contains both mechanical details and figurative

[4] There is another reference to "GB" [Shaw] on the next page (2r) of this notebook.

[5] This verb refers to the ancient practice, used worldwide and well-developed in Britain since medieval times, of using lines of closely-spaced shrubs, often interspersed with trees, to mark property lines and to keep intruders out. To enhance their effectiveness as barriers, such hedges often included dense and thorny species such as hawthorn.

language that Frost would re-use again in "The Self-Seeker," the last and most directly anti-industrial of *North of Boston*'s dramatic narratives.

Equally important, while both "The Mill City" and "When the Speed Comes" express a strong sympathy for those oppressed by an industrial system, the speaker of "The Mill City," like the young Frost still living and working in Lawrence, Massachusetts, does not place himself in the stream of factory workers, but looks on from apart, as one who reserves another path for himself. Indeed, Thompson reads "The Lone Striker," though not published until 1933, as recording the moment in 1894 when Frost, then employed as a light-trimmer in the Arlington Woolen Mills, declared his independence from a place that left no room for his self-determination and will (Thompson, *Early Years*, 161). Such early experiences surely influenced Frost's choice, five years later, of poultry farming as a way to provide for Elinor and the children they were now bringing into the world. But in Derry, New Hampshire, it soon became clear that even the New England backcounty was touched by the industrial capitalism that Frost first witnessed in the factory town where he had grown from youth to manhood. And as we shall see, a number of Frost's *North of Boston* poems show how a changing economic climate had altered lives in the rural culture portrayed in that volume and beyond.

Within *North of Boston* the conflict between a traditional farming culture and an expanding capital economy is clearest, perhaps, in two poems — "The Death of the Hired Man" and "The Self-Seeker," and these poems occupy prominent and reciprocal positions in the book. As the first and last of its dramatic narratives, they not only call attention to this central, cultural antagonism but also to the book's deliberate design. Frost, who worked on the book throughout 1913 — composing and revising the poems, soliciting responses both to them and his principles of prosody, and considering various titles — would later say, "I took my time getting out *North of Boston*. . . . Nothing random in it. It was the gathering of a larger design" (Mertins, 115).

Though composed mainly of dramatic narratives, the completed volume is punctuated by lyrics of two kinds. While "The Pasture" and "Good Hours," two short, rhymed lyrics, serve as prologue and epilogue, two longer meditative lyrics, "Mending Wall" and "The Wood-Pile," each in 40–45 lines of blank verse, serve as the first and last of its principal poems, creating what Matthew Parfitt has called an "inner frame" for the volume (58). Placed just inside this inner frame, "The Death of the Hired Man" and "The Self-Seeker" initiate and conclude the dramatic narratives that comprise the book's main substance, fulfilling its promise as a "book of people" and giving its drama of disappearance a depth and force that come only from engagement with specific human beings.

Parsing the Options: "The Death of the Hired Man"

In "The Death of the Hired Man," Old Silas — the hired man of the title, who is "worn out" and "has come home to die," as Mary says — is emblematic of the book's vanishing culture, not that Mary and Warren seem far behind as they struggle to manage their farm without the help of children. Harold Wilson, the college student who had worked summers for them and is now "teaching in his college," exemplifies shifts in the economy at large, for the mechanization that had replaced much skilled and physical labor both in factories and on farms was accompanied by a general movement away from oral traditions and toward formal education stressing literacy.

Amidst such changes Silas embodies an outmoded past. His vernacular skills, such as water-dowsing or loading unbaled hay by hand, are no longer needed or trusted, and the exhaustions of old age have left Silas ill suited to a newer work-for-wages arrangement. In his attachment to folkways and practical skills, Silas resembles the neighbor of "Mending Wall," who is devoted to his old boundary wall and his father's proverb, "Good fences make good neighbors." Conversely, Silas sees only a waste of talent in young Harold's study of "Latin like the violin / Because he liked it — that an argument!" As Mary reports Silas's ramblings to Warren:

> "He said he couldn't make the boy believe
> He could find water with a hazel prong —
> Which showed how much good school had ever done him.
> He wanted to go over that. But most of all
> He thinks that if he could have another chance
> To teach him how to build a load of hay —
> . . . .
> He thinks if he could teach him that, he'd be
> Some good perhaps to someone in the world.
> He hates to see a boy the fool of books."

There is of course much of Silas, craftsman of the hay-load, in Frost, who valued both in- and outdoor schooling and hated to see anyone made the fool of books. But Latin-loving Wilson represents an equally important part of Frost, the temporary farmer on his way to somewhere else, who will dare to make a profession of his passion, who furthered his study of Greek and Latin at Harvard, and who later claimed to have forgotten more Latin than Ezra Pound ever knew.

As Richard Wakefield has suggested, "The Death of the Hired Man" is about the death not only of one farm servant, but of hired men as a social institution.[6] Silas is caught between the old and the new. Having lived most of his life as a traditional hired man, mainly exchanging work for food and shelter — an arrangement that naturally generated a larger set of unstated obligations and expectations — Silas is nonetheless tempted by new opportunities for money wages and the new freedoms they might bring. But, too old to thrive in a competitive system, he finds it confusing and unforgiving, and Warren is left to absorb the loss. "Off he goes," Warren complains, "always when I need him most. . . . In haying time, when any help is scarce. / In winter he comes back to us. I'm done."

At the heart of the disruption here and in "The Self-Seeker," and underlying central conflicts in such other poems as "A Hundred Collars," and "The Black Cottage," are the workings of a world ruled by money or social status, neither of which accords much value to need or personal history. It is a world embodied here by Silas's estranged brother, associated with financial interests, unnamed and depersonalized — a "somebody" in the bank, as Warren says, implicitly aware of his own lower standing, as a farmer, in the villages of his world. The insurance company lawyer of "The Self-Seeker" plays a similar role in this cultural drama. So disciplined to his pocket-watch and railroad timetable that he seems a mechanism himself, the lawyer is also bullying and rude, and represents an ethic of corporate profit-seeking that invades a world of caring human relations while remaining unconcerned with what it destroys, much as Silas's brother remains ignorant of the Silas known to Mary and Warren.

Just as the figures in one's dream embody hopes, fears, or other aspects of the dreamer, so the figures in a poem can reveal aspects of the poet. Accordingly, we might read Silas's alienated brother as a warning to one whose future depends on doing business in or with that moneyed world, as Frost's intended future surely did. Considering the "magnitude of [his] ambition" (*SL*, 20) we would not expect Frost to equate such a choice with moral bankruptcy. Even Silas's brother "may be better than appearances," as Mary says, and his separation from Silas may be largely Silas's choice. Both the callous lawyer in "The Self-Seeker" and self-important Dr. Magoon in "A Hundred Collars" call attention to the dangers that come with making worldly position one's main concern. At the same time, Frost makes equally clear that the Silas who is tempted, confused by, and finally left out of the money embodies something that he was determined *not* to be. The protagonist of "The Self-Seeker" — like Frost, a lover of natural things and also something of a writer — presents a counter-example even closer to the poet himself.

---

[6] This observation and a few others related to it come from an email letter of July 29, 1998.

A Broken Will: "The Self-Seeker"

More emphatically than any of the book's other poems, the last of its dramatic narratives, "The Self-Seeker," conveys the violence done to individuals and to codes of personal respect when an industrial, capital-driven economy operates unchecked. The protagonist, referred only to as "The Broken One," is an amateur naturalist whose work on the local flora, especially wild orchids, has possibly been ended by a factory accident that has crushed his feet, and the poem recounts a bedside visit of the insurance company lawyer, who pressures the man to accept a settlement of five hundred dollars before anyone knows how crippled he will be. A second antagonist is The Broken One's friend Willis, called Will, who is furious at the lawyer and what he represents but also exasperated by the injured man's refusal to fight for himself or to let Will fight for him. While The Broken One's injury and its possible outcome are enough to explain his fatigue or depression, Frost suggests that his resignation has deeper roots in factory conditions, making his personal initiative — his will — a subtler casualty of the industrial system and giving his friend's name and ineffectual urging a symbolic status in the poem.[7]

Frost makes the accident itself symbolic. For this man who lives for his botanical exploration, "the feet have nearly been the soul," and the accident that has maimed them has literally snatched him off those feet and pulled him into the factory mechanism. As he recounts it, he saved his life only by going along with the machinery's overwhelming force:

> It's hard to tell you how I managed it.
> When I saw the shaft had me by the coat,
> I didn't try too hard to pull away,
> I just embraced the shaft and rode it out —
> . . . .
> That's how I think I didn't lose my head.
> But my legs got their knocks against the ceiling.

As The Broken One finds that once caught in the machine he can keep his head only by "losing" his feet, so Frost implies that once caught in the industrial system, there are no good choices, only varying degrees of loss. The system's depersonalizing power is underlined by what The Broken One says of the factory from his bed: "Everything goes the same without me there." And just as he "embraced the shaft and rode . . . out" the accident, so he tries to embrace the changes wrought by such mechanization. Describing the sound of the factory saws as "all our music," he says,

---

[7] Robert Hass similarly sees the poem as showing "how a human being . . . becomes an expendable component in the vast machinery of big business." For Hass's detailed reading of the poem, see *Going by Contraries*, 165–71.

> One ought as a good villager to like it.
> No doubt it has a sort of prosperous sound,
> And it's our life —

an accommodation that Willis sourly punctures: "Yes, when it's not our death."

The phrases "One ought" and "No doubt" betray the effort required to accept this form of prosperity, for citizenship in this new sort of village comes hard to one who loved tramping through bogs after wild orchids. In a fine example of grim, comic absurdity, Frost dramatizes the difficulty of that surrender as The Broken One projects his anger onto the leather belt that transfers power from the factory's wheel-pit to the saws — the very thing that, like the human workers, makes the place run. Reflecting his own loss of autonomy in the factory, the injured man portrays the belt, once the skin of a living creature, now part of the machine, as having a suppressed spirit of its own. The "Old streak of leather," says the injured man,

> doesn't love me much
> Because I make him spit fire at my knuckles,
> The way Ben Franklin used to make the kite string.
> That must be it. Some days he won't stay on.
> That day a woman couldn't coax him off.
> He's on his rounds now with his tail in his mouth
> Snatched right and left across the silver pulleys.

This vignette of the belt encapsulates the larger social conflict dramatized by the poem. By associating himself with Ben Franklin and his kite, The Broken One clings to what's left of his freedom and initiative, while giving his own anger to the personified leather, which "doesn't love" him, its seeming taskmaster. He even explains the belt's unreliability as deliberate willfulness. "Some days," like a striking worker, "he won't stay" on the job, bringing the factory's work to a halt. On the day of the accident — perhaps with the lifted man's weight providing some extra tension — the belt couldn't be "coax[ed] off" even by a woman, as if held there by its own self-denying discipline. In the end the system wins. The Broken One is replaced, and the refractory leather belt is back "on his rounds . . . / Snatched right and left across the silver pulleys," a compliant part of the mechanism, as the man had been. By describing the continuous belt as having "his tail in his mouth," The Broken One creates an image not only for the numbing repetitions of factory work, but also for the gag one must assume in submitting to them. In addition, the suggestion of self-consumption hints at the anger he must swallow in refusing to fight the insurance company's lawyer.

The indifference of a profiteering capitalism is put into relief by the young girl Anne, who comes to The Broken One's bedside bearing samples of the orchids he cannot seek for himself, her bare feet standing in for the protagonist's injured ones, each pair reflecting our human vulnerability before the machine. Her exchange with the injured man, which the lawyer will dismiss as "a pretty interlude," exemplifies the culture, local and personal in scale, that *North of Boston* means to record, but what these two preserve goes beyond botanical knowledge. Respect for the natural world and for another's needs are both part of the cultural legacy being passed on to the girl, as we see when The Broken One reflects on what he has taught her:

> I've broken Anne of gathering bouquets.
> It's not fair to the child. It can't be helped though:
> Pressed into service means pressed out of shape.
> Somehow I'll make it right with her — she'll see.

The protagonist's fear of what he's done to Anne reflects his own experience of being "pressed into service" and "out of shape," as if in "[breaking] Anne of gathering bouquets" he has broken something in her. But his worry seems misplaced here, for Anne understands the reasons behind her teacher's directives and feels proud and strong, not broken, in applying them. "I wanted there should be some there next year," she says. Rather than an imposition, The Broken One's pleasure in teaching Anne a botanist's discretion, and hers in learning it, exemplify the caring and willing sacrifice that constitute genuine community. We are reminded of Mary's concern, in "The Death of the Hired Man," that Silas be left a "way to save his self-respect" and of Warren's acceding to her plea. Here, the injured man's wanting to learn what will "make it right" with Anne is precisely what the insurance company refuses to do with him. And when, after The Broken One signs the company's offer and the lawyer adds, "We're very sorry for you," Will punctures the insincerity: "Who's *we*? — some stockholders in Boston?"

Just as the injured man's narrative of the accident reflects his suppressed anger, so Will accepts the task of expressing it for both of them, and the poem's final lines makes clear how his rage has been stoked by exasperation with his friend, who even apologizes for him at the poem's end. "Don't mind Will," The Broken One says to the lawyer; "he's savage. / He thinks you ought to pay me for my flowers." Yet, even as the injured man tries to discount Will's accusation and general hostility toward the lawyer, his apology is undercut by dramatic irony. If by "savage" the Broken One means cruel or inhumane, then the rudeness of Will's angry words pales in comparison to the lawyer's callousness. Despite the injured man's conciliatory tone and forgiving nature, he makes the same point that Will had made in his jibe about the stockholders — that the lawyer, with his utterly material concerns, simply cannot grasp what the accident means to its victim. "You don't know what I mean about the flowers," The Broken One says.

> Don't stop to try to now. You'll miss your train.
> Good-by.' He flung his arms around his face.

It is fitting that the substance of Will's accusation pokes through The Broken One's solicitude, for the injured man's final gesture, despite his brave front, reveals that he is broken in more ways than one.

Frost's provisional title for the poem, "The Wrong," mentioned in an August 1913 letter to Bartlett (*SL*, 89), captures the poem's competing issues, for it suggests not only the injustice that one worker suffers at the hands of an industrial system, but also the wrong he does to himself and the friend who tries to help him. Frost's final title extends and complicates this irony. Most directly, "The Self-Seeker" points to the lawyer focused exclusively on having his way while ironically calling attention to a protagonist who undercuts his own interest, even silencing the "Will" that would defend him. Yet at the same time, and in a way opposite to the lawyer's, The Broken One is also a self-seeker. For, in refusing to negotiate about the settlement, he keeps his distance from a system ruled by money, protecting a position that he can call his own. There is, in short, integrity in his refusal to put a dollar value on what he loves. Of his flowers, he says, "They never earned me one cent: / Money can't pay me for the loss of them." And of the botanical catalogue, his "flora of the valley," that he may now never finish, he adds, "But that — you didn't think / That was worth money to me?"

In his final words to the lawyer — "You don't know what I mean about the flowers" — The Broken One makes clear that his acceptance of the insurance company's unfair offer is also, for him, a proud refusal to expose himself further to a system that cannot comprehend his real loss. But, as Richard Wakefield asks, "Does Frost admire him, or does he see him as quaint, even damaged?"[8] Whether or not we view him, with Robert Hass, as "caught up in" an "archaic idealism," it seems clear enough that he is little better suited than old Silas "to adapt to a society driven by financial competition" (170–71). More important for understanding the poet behind *North of Boston*, the fate of this man maimed and discarded by such a system is not one that Frost would accept for himself.

It is revealing to know that The Broken One of the poem is closely based on Carl Burrell, the high-school friend about ten years older than Frost who served as his mentor in important ways. In the ten years between completing eighth grade and returning to high school, Burrell

[8] This question comes from comments on an earlier draft of this chapter in email correspondence July 25, 2006.

had educated himself in three areas of personal interest — botany, American humor, and evolution — that would become life-long interests for Frost himself. He had also had gained a good many practical skills, most of which would later be of great help to Frost in Derry. Hardworking and loyal, but lacking social refinement or strong ambition, Burrell had many of the virtues that Frost celebrated in *North of Boston* but were unlikely to take him far in a rapidly changing competitive economy.

Burrell remained close to Frost after their high-school years, offering his companionship and encouragement during and after Frost's single, unhappy freshman term at Dartmouth College in the fall of 1892. In July 1896, seven months after Rob married Elinor, the couple took a delayed honeymoon trip to Allenstown, New Hampshire, where Burrell was working in a box factory. Carl found them a cottage to rent near him and took them on evening botanical walks, managing to infuse Rob with his own passion for observing natural things closely. It was during this period that Carl suffered an injury very close to the one described in the poem, and during one of Rob's visits to his recuperating friend that he witnessed Carl's encounter with the lawyer. Burrell did recover reasonably well and three years later helped to get Frost established on the Derry farm, where Burrell and his grandfather "Jont" Eastman shared a room and took meals with the Frosts in exchange for taking on most of the farm chores. During these years, Burrell continued his botanizing with Frost, sometimes with young Lesley Frost along, but within two years, an increase in tensions between the men, present from the start, prompted Burrell to leave when old Eastman died.[9] It seems possible that Frost's relationship with Burrell on the farm contributed something to "The Death of the Hired Man," though the impact of their earlier relationship on "The Self-Seeker" is far clearer and more significant.

It is easy enough to see Frost in the character of Willis, who is angry about an economic system that may have crippled and is ready to discard his friend and who is also exasperated by his friend's acquiescence to mistreatment and injustice. But Frost's relation both to The Broken One in his poem and to his real-life model in Burrell has further dimensions. As one who, like old Silas, has been left behind in a competitive market economy, such a potentially thwarted seeker of his own interest is one whom Frost was determined not to be. The basis for a comparison is especially clear in two of Frost's letters, both written from England during the months of his work on *North of Boston*. In one to Sidney Cox in May 1913, Frost connects himself to Burrell by associating the pursuit of wildflowers with his poetic vocation. Admiring the gardens of his English neighbors in Beaconsfield, Frost says,

[9] In chapters 21 and 22 of *The Early Years* (especially 263–78), Thompson gives a helpful account of these relations.

> I like that about the English — they all have time . . . for the unutilitarian flower. I mean the men. It marks the difference between them and our men. I like flowers you know but I like em wild, and I am rather the exception than the rule in an American village. Far as I have walked in pursuit of the Cypripedium, I have never met another in the woods on the same quest. Americans will dig for peas and beans and such like utilities but not if they know it for posies. I knew a man who was a byword in five townships for the flowers he tended with his own hand. . . . I feel as if my education in useless things had been neglected when I see the way the front yards blossom down this road. But never mind; I have certain useless accomplishments to my credit. No one will charge me with having an eye single to the main chance. So I can afford perhaps to yield a little to others for one spring in the cultivation of one form of the beautiful. Next year I go in for daffodils. (*SL*, 71–72)

Here Frost has deliberately put his poetic pursuits, which had now taken him all the way to England, in a botanist's terms — "Far as I have walked in pursuit of the Cypripedium." This genus is precisely the type of wild orchid that figures in "The Self-Seeker" and the man known in five townships for his flowers is almost surely Carl Burrell. By giving this Burrell-based protagonist feet that "are no common feet" and "have nearly been the soul," Frost has portrayed his Broken One in terms that allude to his own metrical "feet," which have put common language to uncommon use, making poetry, as he liked to think, from words and phrases never before "brought into books" (*SL*, 111). More generally, Frost allies himself with his Broken One by defending his "cultivation . . . of the beautiful" and by disavowing a life focused solely on worldly gain — "an eye single to the main chance." He even makes flowers the main measure of his aestheticism by alluding to his poems — "certain useless accomplishments" of his own — as merely the best he can offer in their place. His preference for the uncultivated kind ("I like em wild") also alludes to the very poems he was preparing for this volume, poems steeped in the uncultivated vernacular — the "language absolutely unliterary" that he boasted of using to John Bartlett on December 8, by which time *North of Boston* was almost ready for the press (*SL*, 102).

For Frost, however, it was one thing to embrace such "unutilitarian" things as flowers or poems against a prevailing materialism. It was quite another, as he would make clear ten years later in the final lines of "New Hampshire," to repudiate financial gain altogether. In fact, as we look again at his November 1913 letter to Bartlett, we see that Frost's parallels between himself and the botanist-Broken One serve mainly to emphasize the radically different goals Frost hoped to reach as a poet, goals toward which *North of Boston* was to be the decisive step. Both Frost and his injured botanist envision success through completion of their books, but the success each envisions takes opposite forms. What The Broken One had hoped for — that his book would bring not money, but "friends" like the eminent botanist John Burroughs[10] — is precisely the success "of esteem," "a success with the critical few who are supposed to know," that Frost would dismiss for himself largely because it "butters no parsnips." For Frost, being "a poet for all sorts and kinds" had financial as well as social implications. It meant reaching "the general reader who buys books in their thousands." And while he "may not be able to do that," he is adamant about the goal: "I believe in doing it," he writes Bartlett, "— don't you doubt me there." Perhaps nothing better captures the difference between the poet and the botanist friend who may not walk again than Frost's image of standing "on my legs as a poet and nothing else" (*SL*, 98). Frost, moreover, means to stand by virtue of the same industrial economy, with its powers of mass-production and distribution, that has felled The Broken One, putting the use of his "uncommon" feet and his future as a botanist equally in doubt.

The mixture of likeness and difference between the poet and the protagonist of "The Self-Seeker" leads us back to the divided Frost we find in *North of Boston* as a whole. For Frost, the division arose from the compromises involved in the economic gains that he hoped his book would bring — gains that required an alliance with the same forces that threatened the culture and people to which the book was devoted. For him, such compromise was painful. In Derry and similar places throughout rural New England, social and economic change, however impartial in its operation, had exacted personal costs in personal lives, and in making his poems from such lives, Frost was building success on their personal loss. What Frost owed to Carl Burrell — a friend and mentor into Frost's early manhood, who opened his eyes to lifelong sources of interest and inspiration and helped him get started on the Derry farm — epitomizes what Frost owed to the whole of his Derry experience, which may be one reason that Frost gave "The Self-Seeker" its climactic placement in *North of Boston*. The character of The Broken One's friend, the Will thwarted in his efforts to help, also reflects Frost's role as poet, able to do no more for his friend than write him into a poem almost twenty years later, an act that had in it as much or more of taking as of giving.

---

[10] John Burroughs (1837–1921), born in the Catskill region of New York State, was a naturalist who wrote extensively on both the flora and fauna of his native habitat and became important in the development of the American conservation movement. Something of a polymath, he wrote philosophic and literary as well as scientific essays while continuing to work as a federal bank examiner. An early champion of Ralph Waldo Emerson and a friend of Walt Whitman, he became friends late in life with both John Muir and Theodore Roosevelt as well as Thomas Edison and Henry Ford (Wikipedia, "John Burroughs").

At least two other *North of Boston* figures — the neighbor of "Mending Wall," and John, the primary subject of "The Housekeeper"[11] — are based on specific persons from whom Frost had received artistic inspiration as well as friendship, while others are derived, in whole or part, from actual persons he knew or could observe at close range. What then does it mean that Frost has made his poems from their suffering, collective and individual? While no simple answer is possible, I believe that Frost's wresting of gains from their losses, his use of their lives to advance his own, only compounds the initial inequities between the aspiring poet and his farming neighbors in Derry, and that the inequality of this exchange accounts for the hints of accusation, the repeated references to violation and trespass, transgression and theft, that surface in the volume, often in surprising places and unexpected ways.

[11] Napoleon Gay, a French-Canadian woodsman, was Frost's neighbor across the rough stone wall that marked the south property line of Frost's farm (Thompson, *Early Years*, 284). Frost celebrates Gay's way of carving ax-handles in "The Ax-Helve," first published in 1916 and later included in *New Hampshire* (1923). In conveying Gay's insistence that a good helve should be carved along "lines . . . / . . . native to the grain," Frost clearly alludes to his own idea that a good written sentence, in prose or verse, should be build upon "sentence sounds," the rhythms and intonations of living speech (*SL*, 111). As mentioned earlier, it was apparently John Hall, Frost's poultryman friend, who inspired Frost's first efforts to capture the local, rural vernacular in writing (Walsh, 44–62).

4: Living One's Democracy

IN EMPHASIZING THE HEARTLESSNESS of corporate interests and the human costs of economic change, "The Death of the Hired Man" and "The Self-Seeker" map a divide straddled by Frost's own sympathies and ambitions. Two more of the book's dramatic poems, — "A Hundred Collars" and "The Black Cottage" — further illuminate Frost's conflicted feelings about the Derry neighbors that, by 1904, were already becoming the subject of his poems. As these two narratives — one mainly dialogue, the other nearly a monologue — portray the social and economic hardship he witnessed in his Derry years, they reflect the discrepancies in wealth and status, education and sensibility that inevitably separated Frost from the very people to whom he felt a deep connection, yet also connected him to those from whom he felt apart.

"A Hundred Collars": The Pursuit of Happiness and Its Costs

"A Hundred Collars" presents a charged and, at moments, comic encounter between two characters — Dr. Magoon, a university professor waiting for a train to his country place and Lafe, a newspaper agent on his weekly rounds — who find it necessary to share a hotel room for a few hours late at night. Though they speak only a few minutes and will probably never meet again, each feels his mettle tested and his self-esteem at stake in the exchange. And rubbing each other the wrong way, each exposes the other's native grain.

Though neither character resembles Frost in an overt way, each feels the experience of being caught between cultures that Frost suffered, enjoyed, and would trade on throughout his poetic career. Magoon, the "great scholar," is one whose intellectual achievements have made him part of the high-culture and cash nexus that Frost may have despised but whose wealth and privilege he longed to break into, if only for the sake of his poetry. Could he gain that success without losing himself to it? Though a country man by birth — not, like Frost, by adoption — Magoon is nonetheless cut off from his origins. The "little town" that "bore him . . . / . . . doesn't see him often." He sends his wife and children back there mainly without him — the children to run just "a little wild." Magoon, concerned with his dignity, is estranged by his self-importance. The letters he receives at the general store mean more to him than the people he sees there. "Rifling a printed letter as he talks" to "old friends he somehow can't get near," he removes himself from the rural world he comes from, and the narrator makes clear that his essential alienation is from himself. "[A] democrat, / If not at heart, at least on principle," he can't feel what he thinks he should.

Frost, though not a country man, was a working man by birth and was troubled by the loss of old attachments. And if the Derry world constituted a moral center for him, what did it cost him to leave it behind? The question of Frost's relation to Magoon is made more intriguing by the fact that Frost's farm in Derry was known locally as "the Magoon place,"[1] and one wonders what concerns about his own future might underlie Frost's portrait of one who allows his achievements to separate him from his humbler past. Is his portrait of the condescending and estranged Dr. Magoon something of a warning to himself? Frost was completing "A Hundred Collars" just as he is forging relationships with fellow poets, stimulated and affirmed by his developing conversation with other educated men, including a discussion of his own poetry and poetics that had not been possible in the Derry life he had left behind. The simple truth that Magoon is a model of something that Frost rejects becomes less simple when the status, security, and recognition that Magoon has gained for his academic achievement is what Frost wants for his literary work. Not that Frost was anything like the prig or snob he shows Magoon to be. Still, his economic differences, work habits, and literary and intellectual interests had all set Frost apart from most of his rural neighbors; the ambition that led him from New England to Old England had further separated him from the people and place that constituted his poetic source; and the path to success on which he was bent had led others to become Magoons.

To understand Magoon's relation to Frost, it is helpful to see how his British friend, J. C. Smith, read the poem when Frost sent him a packet of his new work in September 1913, soon after they first met. Smith's comments are all the more revealing because they include Frost's own comments about the poem. After first judging "The Self-Seeker" to be "quite the best of the bunch," Smith writes, "the one poem I'm not quite clear about is 'The Hundred Collars'":

> I know, because you told me, what the central idea is — the dilemma of the theoretical democrat when he's brought up against the real thing — man and brother . . . and equal, but a little drunk, and wanting to present you — as a token of his brotherhood and

[1] Charles S. Magoon occupied the farm and had recorded land transactions as late as 1896. The *Derry News* of October 5, 1900, carried an announcement that "R. Frost" had moved onto "the Magoon place" (Thompson, *Early Years*, 264).

> equality — with a hundred old collars. The idea's . . . quite important — it *is* a real dilemma for the likes of us. . . . (in Walsh, 144–45)

The first of Smith's two points — that "the dilemma of the theoretical democrat [Magoon] . . . up against the real thing [Lafe]" is the poem's "central idea" — apparently affirms what Frost himself had said. But Smith seems equally confident that Frost shares his second idea — that "it *is* a real dilemma for the likes of us." Is it simply that Smith, after his day of conversation with Frost and the correspondence that followed, and after his reading of Frost's poems, feels that he knows Frost well enough to know that? Or had Frost in fact said as much to him?

We need not answer that question to know that the shared "dilemma" Smith describes — the unease of the educated with the laboring classes, whatever the respect between them — is central to the Robert Frost who had left Derry and made his way to England. Frost had left because his Derry neighbors, for all their virtues, could not provide a community ready to appreciate his verse any more than the American literary establishment, controlled by the Lowells and Sedgwicks, would look at it twice until English reviewers had endorsed it. On the other hand, a man such as Smith, sympathetic, forthright, and Oxford-educated, an inspector of teachers' colleges and a noted Shakespearean scholar, was a good example of what Frost had aspired to. Like Frost, he was both a working man and an aesthete. And aptly enough, the Smith who affirmed Frost as a poet and thinker also provided Frost with a counterpoint to his own condescending Magoon. In discussing modesty in a letter to Ernest Silver back home,[2] Frost uses Smith as his example, citing his unassuming, un-Magoon-like manner, notable in light of his accomplishments. To the Magoon who holds himself safely apart from those he thinks beneath him, Frost contrasts Smith, who "doesn't have to think of holding his own against anyone" (*SL*, 115).

When Smith, then, says that Magoon's situation illustrates "a real dilemma *for the likes of us*" (emphasis added), including Frost in the dilemma, he suggests that what Magoon suffers is not simply the result of his own flawed character but something more widely shared. In phrasing Lafe's offer of his old collars as "wanting to present *you*" (emphasis added) with "a token of his brotherhood," Smith clearly places Frost, as he has earlier placed himself, among those he expects to identify with Magoon's position, the question of character quite aside.

---

[2] Silver was appointed principal of Pinkerton Academy in 1909. When he became principal of the New Hampshire Normal School at Plymouth in 1911, he invited Frost to come with him. Frost went largely because of the light teaching duties he would have, but his apparently offhand approach became a source of contention, and Frost, resigning after a year, left a disgruntled Silver behind him.

In explaining to Frost how his poem had spoken to him, describing an empathic response to a character as unappealing as Magoon, Smith helps us understand Frost's claim that in *North of Boston* he had tried "to show the people . . . that I had forgiven them for being people" (*CPPP*, 784). And if we are interested in ways that *North of Boston*'s characters reflect the poet himself, we might then ask what in himself helped Frost to create Magoon, this celebrated fellow so uncomfortable when put in contact with, to paraphrase Frost, "the ordinary folks" he comes from.[3] It seems likely enough that, for the Frost who had distanced himself from Derry in order to write and publish these poems — who had, in fact, been somewhat apart from that world even when most immersed in it — Magoon exaggerates something in himself that also required some forgiveness.

The character of Lafe, the immediate cause of Magoon's "dilemma" in "A Hundred Collars," provides even clearer and closer parallels to Frost's straddling of cultures and loyalties. Lafe works for the Bow, New Hampshire, *Weekly News*, collecting subscription payments and, more important, local gossip and opinion. Presenting himself as a real democrat and man of the people, Lafe is an ingratiating character — down-to-earth if a bit crude, talkative, and seemingly frank about himself. He is observant and, while not deliberately unkind, feisty enough to tweak Magoon for his stiffness — surely another implication of the collars he wants to give him. And if, as Smith suggests, Lafe's offer is a "token of brotherhood and equality," it includes a challenge, implying that Magoon's neck is no better than his. His resistance to Magoon's condescension even resembles Frost's own response to social slights throughout his life, including his refusal to accept as final his rejection by the American literary establishment and the imperviousness to rejection that he claimed to have developed even in England when he felt like a "poacher . . . hedged off" by upper-class snobbery (*CPPP*, 802).

Like Frost, Lafe is drawn to the rural life that Magoon and, to a lesser degree, Frost have largely left behind, and these affinities include a poet's eye for its seasonal changes, which, as we see, also evoke the drama of disappearance recorded by the book as a whole:

> What I like best's the lay of different farms,
> Coming out on them from a stretch of woods,
> . . . .
> I like to find folks getting out in spring,
> Raking the dooryard, working near the house.
> Later they get out further in the fields.
> . . . .
> There's a hayload a-coming — when it comes.
> And later still they all get driven in:

[3] Frost's exact words, from "Poverty and Poetry," a talk given at Haverford College in 1937, are "the ordinary folks I belong to" (*CPPP*, 759).

The fields are stripped to lawn. . . .
. . . the maple trees
To whips and poles. There's nobody about.

More intriguing and more relevant to Frost himself are Lafe's compromises. His important "business is to find what people want," thereby assuring readership for the paper and profits for its owners. "You seem to shape the paper's policy," Magoon observes, and Lafe does not demur. Whether that's quite true or not, Lafe likes to emphasize his solidarity with the folk: "You see I'm in with everybody, know 'em all." Yet, by his own testimony, all his gathering of local intelligence might equally be seen as spying for the enemies of his class:

A good deal comes on me when all is said.
The only trouble is we disagree
In politics: I'm Vermont Democrat —
You know what that is, sort of double-dyed;
The *News* has always been Republican.

Earlier, when Magoon says he's "Known [the *Weekly News*] since I was young," Lafe replies, "Then you know me." But considering what Lake has told us about his work for the paper, what it tells about Lafe remains uncertain, as much to himself as to us.

His description of the pleasure he takes in his work — "It's business, but I can't say it's not fun" — parallels his political compromise. Though he doesn't exactly accuse or excuse himself, one senses that Lafe would like assurance that he does no harm and doesn't betray his fellow Democrats by collecting their views, sometimes in lieu of their dollars, to advance Republican interests. Robert Faggen has seen something more sinister in Lafe's movements, suggesting that his visits may be tours of inspection on behalf of banks alert to the real-estate opportunities represented by failing farms, and that a farm family's coming out to meet him might be as much a defensive as a sociable response.[4] For Lafe, there is both evasion and revelation in the joke that his mule Jemima, and not he, really decides where and when they stop. He says,

I've spoiled Jemima in more ways than one.
She's got so she turns in at every house
. . . .

[4] Faggen suggested this reading in conversation in October 1997, in Rock Hill, South Carolina. Frost's own Derry farm, purchased for his use by his grandfather in 1899, was an example of the real-estate opportunities created by declining New England agriculture, at least on family farms. As mentioned earlier, Frost's title for the volume alludes to this economic situation, for "North of Boston" was one of the headings under which *The Boston Globe* listed country properties for sale.

No matter if I have no errand there.
She thinks I'm sociable. I maybe am.
It's seldom I get down except for meals, though.
Folks entertain me from the kitchen doorstep,
All in a family row down to the youngest. (emphasis added)

Much as Lafe paints the picture of a social call, his practice of visiting every farm family whether or not they owe a subscription payment does raise the question of other motives. And if such motives are feared or suspected, the family's coming out in force might indicate more than mere interest in a visitor, but a desire to keep Lafe in his wagon-seat, from which he can't see too much, especially with his eyes focused on them.

Lafe himself hedges with regard to his own sociability. Not only does he make it Jemima's idea, but she only "thinks" he's sociable, and Lafe adds uncertainty to "her" assessment: "I maybe am," he admits. Even without sinister intentions, Lafe's role as informant for *The Weekly News* adds ulterior motives to the gregariousness by which he explains these visits, giving him something to disguise and deny. When Magoon suggests,

One would suppose they might not be as glad
To see you as you are to see them,

Lafe does not precisely demur and sounds anxious to persuade himself that he is not taking anything from the people on whom he calls:

Oh,
Because I want their dollar? I don't want
Anything they've not got. I never dun.
I'm there, and they can pay me if they like.
I go nowhere on purpose: I happen by.

By this point in Lafe's narrative, we know that nothing about his stops is happenstance, however casual they might seem or be, and also that writing off a few subscription payments might be laid to policy as well as kindness, for the goodwill it generates and the gossip he collects are worth as much or more than the dollars not paid.

But Lafe's denial — "I don't want / Anything they've not got" — compounds this irony and points toward ethical questions central to the whole drama of disappearance that Frost himself witnessed during his Derry years. Far more than any dollars these farm families may lack, what they have — the farms themselves — are of interest to the bankers and businessmen ready to foreclose or buy them cheap, and they are certainly of value to the families themselves. We know, too, that what "they've not got," the farmers' lack of ready cash, may sooner or later cost them the very farms for which Lafe has shown an appreciative eye. Even if Lafe isn't a conscious party to such schemes, what he learns from the local people only furthers the advantage of the moneyed classes positioned to profit from their poverty. His insistence on what he doesn't take thus calls our attention to what he does and suggests his own uneasiness about the role he plays even as it leaves unclear exactly what that is.

Lafe's harvesting something intangible yet substantial and valuable from the local people, even if it's nothing more than the local gossip, clearly connects him to Frost.[5] But the more significant connection lies in Lafe's confusion of giving and taking, of genuineness and feigning, of admitting and denying motives, all of which parallels the conflicted feelings of the poet about to publish *North of Boston* and bring to market the complex produce of his Derry years. Frost's determination to turn his skills with both words and people into published verse links him, like Lafe, to both the winners and losers in a competitive economic system. Like Lafe, Frost is the genuine democrat, openly affiliated with the losers — "the ordinary folks I belong to" (*CPPP*, 759). And like Lafe, he is genuinely drawn to the traditional farming life that is doomed by larger-scale, more industrialized models. Both Lafe and Frost may be drawn to it all the more by being involved in it only as far as they like, since neither farms for a living. Thus, while cultivating an intimacy with that rural culture as inside outsiders, both Frost and Lafe pursue economic gain by turning that intimacy into saleable print. Frost, the city man with an education, literary talent, ambition, and a bi-annual annuity check, is outside this adopted culture in a different way from Lafe, the landless French-Canadian. But both accept the competitive realities of American democracy. Lafe is a short form of Lafayette, hero of the American Revolution, and Frost, as we have seen, was no less determined than Lafe about his pursuit of happiness in this free-enterprise economy.

Looking Back: Poetry, Poverty, and "New Hampshire"

Like Lafe, then, Frost feels a personal and intellectual connection to the rural poor even as his own economic future required alliances with America's money, and this dual allegiance seems to trouble him like a dream, haunting his thoughts for years to come, making appearances, often fleeting and disguised, in both his poems and public talks. What he does to gain recognition as a poet may be as necessary as anything in nature, where creatures live in constant competition, frequently at another's expense. Yet nothing can make it feel wholly right. Decades later, in his talk "Poverty and Poetry," we hear some uneasiness in Frost's denials about his use of the poor in which accusation seems just about to surface:

---

[5] Frost's connection to Lafe is reinforced by the connection he made between the "actuality and intimacy" of gossip and his own poetic aims. For more on this idea, see my discussion of "Blueberries" in the following chapter.

> "You wrote about the poor," they said. I never measured that; I wouldn't have done it if I knew anything was going to be made of it. I didn't do it to get rid of the poor because I need them in my business. (*CPPP*, 761)

"If I knew anything was going to be *made* of it," says Frost (emphasis added), the maker of poems determined to see that his poems made money. Elusively, he follows this almost-evasive, passive construction with an arch assertion of power and possessiveness. "I didn't do it to get rid of the poor," he says (as if he could), "because I need them in my business": this bit of humor by the man who said "Perhaps you think I am joking. I am never so serious as when I am" (*SL*, 139).

Closer in time to *North of Boston* than "Poverty and Poetry," which Frost delivered at Haverford College in 1937, is "New Hampshire," the title poem of his 1923 Pulitzer-Prize-winning volume. There, within layers of irony that make it difficult to locate the poet himself, Frost's persona praises a long tradition of subsistence farming with the proposition that work is noble so long as it doesn't end in commerce. "I've had to work myself," he says. The disgrace is "having anything to sell." New Hampshire's "touch of gold" is that its lone gold mine produced "Just enough gold to make the engagement rings / And marriage rings for those that owned the farm." Someone else found radium. "But trust New Hampshire not to have enough / Of radium or anything to sell." Nature's withholding becomes a moral blessing, and while Frost here takes no personal credit for his choice of Derry as his personal place of retreat, he presents New Hampshire as a blessed state because of the people he found there, understood to be products of its cultural climate and soil:

> When I left Massachusetts years ago
> Between two days, . . .
>   . . . New Hampshire offered
> The nearest boundary to escape across.
> I hadn't an illusion. . . .
> About the people being better there
> . . . .
> I thought they couldn't be. And yet they were.
> I'd sure had no such friends in Massachusetts
> As Hall of Windham, Gay of Atkinson,[6]
> Bartlett of Raymond (now of Colorado),
> Harris of Derry, and Lynch of Bethlehem.

[6] It was, in fact, John Hall who lived in Atkinson, a few miles east of Derry (Thompson, *Early Years*, 283) and Gay who might be said to live in Windham, a town bordering Derry to the south. Oddly, this is Frost's second slip regarding facts about Hall, whom he, in apparent distraction, calls "Kline" in his letter of July 6, 1913 to Frank Flint (Barry, 83).

All are friends of Frost's Derry period. Hall and Gay are featured in *North of Boston* itself, and implicitly all are exempted from the disgrace of commerce and its dubious returns.

But Frost's conclusion undercuts the proposed New Hampshire virtue of work for love rather than gain. Having accepted a position as consulting editor with Henry Holt for one hundred dollars a month, he can now "choose to be a plain New Hampshire farmer"

> With an income in cash of say a thousand
> (From say a publisher in New York City).
> It's restful to arrive at a decision,
> And restful just to think about New Hampshire.
> At present I am living in Vermont.

This final relocation is deftly symbolic. The poet-speaker is not where he had seemed to be. Frost's move to Vermont was, in fact, one outward sign of his new literary prosperity. Vermont was already a fashionable country retreat for literary New Yorkers such as the Holts when, in 1920, Frost began as consulting editor with Holt and Company, sold his house in Franconia, New Hampshire, remote and inconvenient in many ways,[7] and bought "The Stone House" in South Shaftsbury, Vermont, near the homes of writer-friends Sarah Cleghorn and Dorothy Canfield Fisher. For Frost, now a national celebrity sought by public audiences and college faculties and making money from his books and talks, New Hampshire was clearly more restful to think about than to live in. Perhaps more the point for a poet with a body of work to develop, a reputation to enhance, and both a family and public presence to maintain, "rest" was not the order of the day.

For Frost of the 1920s and '30s, who had learned to manage the contradictions involved in making a business of what was supposedly off the commercial scale, the distance between word and deed and the conflicting loyalties created by royalties and contracts could be expressed in open, if elusive, ironies. In *North of Boston*, completed just when he first stated his hopes of reaching readers "in their thousands" (*SL*, 83) — that is, when the inherent conflict was fresher and less resolved — these discrepancies remain embedded and concealed in the work itself.

Keeping the Faith: "The Black Cottage"

"The Black Cottage" provides one of *North of Boston*'s most revealing examples of such obliqueness and indirection in the character of the wistful, somewhat troubled Protestant minister who tells the poem's main

[7] The practical difficulties of life in the Franconia house are clear in both Robert's and Elinor's letters to Lesley, then at Barnard College, during the early months of 1919 and 1920. See *Family Letters*, 50 and 76–80.

story. Like the poet moved to write all the book's poems, the minister feels an evident need to show his visitor, who provides the poem's framing narrative, the now-derelict cottage named in the poem's title, and to tell about the Civil War widow who had lived there well into old age. In the poem's first twenty-four lines, the narrator describes the cottage, weathered in its overgrown yard, and introduces his minister-guide. The minister's ensuing monologue, thus framed, soon develops into a discourse on "the truths we keep coming back and back to," telling as much about himself as it does about the widow. It also reveals concerns that reflect Frost's own. The minister imagines a sequestered kingdom where these recurring truths might be kept from the changes that force them "in and out of favor," thus sparing us many difficult choices. It is a place that, in significant ways, anticipates the utopian New Hampshire of Frost's 1923 poem.[8] In light of this later, idealized state, we might see the minister's imagined domain to reflect the "life that goes . . . poetically" (*SL*, 224) — life outside a competitive marketplace — which Frost in some measure yearned for, even joked about returning to in his December 1913 letter to Ernest Silver, but of course found incompatible with the life he lived and with the public success he sought and achieved, helping, as he did so, to redefine the poet's cultural role in America.[9]

The key to such a protected world, the minister implies, is its safe distance from the familiar one ruled by acquisition and competition — "so walled / By mountain ranges half in summer snow, / No one would covet it or think it worth / . . . conquering to force change on" — a situation similar to Frost's idyllic New England state that doesn't have "enough / Of anything . . . to sell." The mountain remoteness of the minister's world-apart may even be suggested by the

[8] Robert Newdick — who, according to Lawrance Thompson, handled Frost's anecdotes "with meticulous accuracy" (*Triumph*, 483) — suggests that the minister's imagined refuge has roots in some of Frost's earliest writing: "an endless serial," begun in San Francisco and continued in his first years in New England, "about a tribe of Indians who lived in a far-off mountain canyon secure from the outside world. Sometimes after he was a grown man Frost would put himself to sleep by dreaming of those same strange Indians off . . . in their mountain fastness" (22–23). The idea that this refuge had power for Frost in his adult years only adds to the ways that the minister of the "The Black Cottage" reflects important aspects of the poet himself.

[9] With his teaching appointments that began at Amherst in 1916, then continued at the University of Michigan and again at Amherst, Frost initiated the role of writer-in-residence in American colleges. Between shorter visits to other schools and extensive tours for talks and readings, Frost created a public role for the poet and a widespread interest in poetry that no American poet had done before, prompting Allen Ginsburg to call him "the original entrepreneur of poetry" (in Parini, 319). Parini (475) cites "Interview with Allen Ginsberg, April 5, 1997."

actual New England state from which Frost would craft his poetic New Hampshire,[10] which he happily admired from a more settled Vermont, comforted by monthly checks from Henry Holt and Company. Frost's symbolic and sudden removal from his idealized New Hampshire at the end of the 1923 poem is paralleled by the end of "The Black Cottage," where the minister's rhapsody is cut short by the bees inside the cottage walls, bringing him back to the world of competition and change we all inhabit. Unlike Frost's final sideways step in "New Hampshire," in which his persona wryly confesses an ideal comfortably compromised, "The Black Cottage" outlines a starker conflict. When the minister "struck the clapboards, / Fierce heads looked out," abruptly replacing his changeless kingdom with the reality of a derelict cottage colonized by bees and drenched in sunset light.

Within the tale the minister tells, however, the cottage becomes both model and microcosm of his fantasy refuge. Unlike its weathered exterior and overgrown yard, its inside seems hardly touched by the passing years. It was, in fact, a refuge from time and change for the widow who lived there, for she had made it a shrine both to her dead husband, a Civil War soldier, who presided from "a crayon portrait on the wall, / Done sadly from an old daguerreotype," and to the democratic ideal that, for her, gave meaning to his death in battle. Since her own death, her sons have also kept the cottage undisturbed, "mean[ing] to summer . . . / Where they were boys," though they haven't managed to return for years. Memories keep it alive for the minister too, but what claims him is larger than a family past. More than anything else, the cottage speaks to him of the widow's "serene belief" that

> Whatever else the Civil War was for,
> It wasn't just to keep the States together,
> Nor just to free the slaves, though it did both.
> She wouldn't have believed those ends enough
> To have given outright for them all she gave.
> Her giving somehow touched the principle
> That all men are created equal.

For the minister, the widow's conviction identifies one of those "truths we keep coming back and back to," though, like the sons' promise of a summer return, it remains something he can neither take hold nor let go of fully. What touches him more than the democratic ideal of equality is the widow's devotion to it — a belief he finds at once impressive and exasperating, intriguing and puzzling. We hear his doubts along

---

[10] If so, it is probably the colder, more mountainous and remote northern part of the state, exemplified by Franconia, where, as mentioned earlier, Frost lived briefly before moving to South Shaftsbury, Vermont, in 1920.

with some discomfort when, citing "her quaint phrases — so removed / From the world's view today of all those things," he exclaims:

> That's a hard mystery of Jefferson's.
> What did he mean? Of course the easy way
> Is to decide it simply isn't true.
> It may not be. I heard a fellow say so.

At the same time, he admits, his admiration tinged with complaint, that "the Welshman got it planted / Where it will trouble us a thousand years. / Each age will have to reconsider it."

From his unresolved, agnostic position, the minister looks with longing at the widow's faith. Why, he seems to wonder, must the truths "we keep coming back . . . to" have to go "out of favor" at all? The minister sees the widow as inhabiting her belief as she did her cottage, "hearing and yet not / Hearing the latter wisdom of the world," achieving a distance from its shifting values that he cannot imagine without the help of a mountain remoteness. Yet he sees her faith as affecting others as well as protecting itself. "Strange," he muses, "how such innocence gets its own way. / I shouldn't be surprised if in this world / It were the force that would at last prevail."

The power the minister grants the widow's "innocence" reflects the example he has made of her unswerving belief, which has helped him resist unwelcome pressures to change. Faced with a dwindling church membership, he admits that, were it not for the widow's upright if nodding presence in his church, he might have "changed the Creed a very little" to please "the liberal youth" to whom "the words 'descended into Hades' / . . . seemed too pagan."[11] Yet, even as he recalls drawing strength from her, he casts himself as her protector, imagining that, had he not held firm, she might have missed those familiar words in the Creed "as a child misses the unsaid Good-night."

This reciprocity between the minister and the widow reflects that between Frost and his *North of Boston* subjects. In telling the widow's story, the minister rescues her from obscurity much as Frost does all the people of his book. The cottage that "the world" has "passed . . . by," which the minister feels compelled to show his guest, is that part of the

---

[11] Ironically enough, this "Hades" represents an ancient bit of modernizing — the Hellenizing of first-century Jewish beliefs that created Christian dogma. Whether or not this irony is part of Frost's conscious design is difficult to tell, but the example does fit the minister's and the poet's conservative ethic. Here the "younger members . . . or non-members" of the church eager to expel the "pagan" term "Hades" not only want to set aside almost two thousand years of church tradition; they also fail to grasp that the Christian hell was built on the model of the Greek underworld.

Derry world that would simply vanish without work such as Frost's; but captured in verse, like the cottage brought back to life by the minister's story, it asserts values easily overruled in a world ruled by money and commerce. In describing the cottage as a "mark / To measure how far fifty years have brought us," the minister expresses one of Frost's hopes for his book, reminding us in turn that, whatever he does for the people of Derry, he also relies on them much as the minister relied on the widow. Both relationships, like that of Lafe and his rural informants in "A Hundred Collars," involve a mixture of giving and taking.

Frost, however, has written aspects of his own perspective into the widow as well as the minister. The widow's faith in the central tenet of American democracy aligns itself closely with the social and moral values upheld in *North of Boston* and the "virtues [Frost] celebrate[s]" there (*SL*, 84). At the same time, the minister's reservations about the widow's Jeffersonian faith has its parallels in the realism of Frost's *North of Boston* portraits. His later reflection that the book was a way of showing that he "had forgiven [his people] for being people" (*CPPP*, 784) acknowledges the human imperfections that as poet he takes pains *not* to hide. Just as the minister wonders how the widow could be sure "that all men are created free and equal" when "white was the only race she ever knew," and just as he harbors doubts about the idea itself, so Frost, for his part, reveals the limitations of Silas's pre-industrial attitudes in "The Death of the Hired Man," the reflexive traditionalism of the "Mending Wall" neighbor, the impractical idealism of The Broken One in "The Self-Seeker," the instability of the farm wife in "A Servant to Servants," and the failure of each spouse in "Home Burial" to understand the other's grief. Yet Frost goes further in dramatizing the virtues of this soon-to-be-lost culture in the kindness of Mary and Warren for Silas, in The Broken One's dealings with his young helper Anne, and even in the wall-building neighbor's stubborn wisdom about boundaries. Significantly, too, Frost himself shares the widow's "free and equal" faith in a way that the minister does not.

He shares it more fully because he examines it more closely. In the letter to Frank Flint, written July 6, 1913, just after Flint had read eight of the *North of Boston* narratives, Frost declares himself "no propagandist for equality" but claims to "enjoy above all things the contemplation of equality where it happily exists," then cites the "independent-dependence of the . . . people" he'd written about in the poems (in Barry, 83).[12] In distancing himself from a pure egalitarianism, Frost seems to reject the Jeffersonian ideal of equality for "all men"; yet, when he addresses this issue more than twenty years later in "What Became of New England?" he artfully defends Jefferson's idea.

---

[12] The original of this letter resides at the University of Texas Library (Austin) and so far remains unpublished except by Barry.

In that talk, delivered at Oberlin College in 1937, Frost recalls his first year at Harvard, revealing that he'd thought about the issue for most of his adult life:

> In 1897 I was sitting in a class in college when I heard a man spend quite the part of an hour making fun of the expression that we were all free and equal. So easy to dismiss. Let's have a look at it. All men were created free and equally funny. Before you laugh too much at that, take another look at it. Four hundred years ago the only people who were funny were yokels. . . . Now, today, even kings are funny. We've come a long way. (*CPPP*, 756–58)

In twice urging us to have "another look," Frost issues a challenge to the Harvard professor who dismissed this democratic axiom, and his quirky analysis follows up by dividing the question of equality from social rank, just as the Declaration of Independence had done. In proclaiming "all men" to be "created equal" and "endowed with certain unalienable rights," the document that rejected a king's authority over thirteen American colonies also renounced a class system that dictated who looked up to or down upon whom. In renouncing a fixed scale for determining one's superiors or inferiors, it freed us to recognize "equality where it happily exists" and even to act on that perception. Frost's comical emendation — that we are all "created free and equally *funny*" — hoists the Harvard professor with his own petard, satirically pointing out that, in making fun of Jefferson's words, the professor was enjoying the very freedom and claiming the very equality that they argue for. It follows, of course, that where we are free to find someone laughable or contemptible, we are equally free to find the same person equal or admirable. Gone, in effect, is the idea that social position determines one's "betters" or one's "inferiors." If we see, as does Frost, the Jeffersonian principle not as denying differences in talent or even moral worth, but as freeing us to recognize what is or isn't there in another person, including equality "where it happily exists," then Frost agrees with the widow that "the Civil War . . . / . . . wasn't just to keep the States together, / Nor just to free the slaves, though it did both." For, maintaining the Union meant holding all States to the "free and equal" promise of its founding.

Though "The Black Cottage" minister does not share Frost's own conviction about the "free and equal" issue, he shares a problem that Frost felt when writing the poem: the need to survive in a contemporary marketplace that readily puts aside the "truths we keep coming back . . . to." When the minister describes the pressure to change the Creed as coming from the "younger members of the church, / Or rather say nonmembers in the church, / Whom we all have to think of nowadays," he makes clear that, whatever else it may be, his problem, like Frost's, is economic. We don't know whether his church, or he as its minister, has survived despite his standing firm or because of it, but he clearly feels grateful to the widow for helping to save his soul — which Frost would later equate roughly with his integrity.[13] It may well be that "liberal youth" of the church needed the minister's stubborn example much as he needed the widow's. They may even have profited from his firmness even while failing to recognize its value, much as the insurance-company lawyer sees no more than "a pretty interlude" in The Broken One's conversation with his young helper, Anne.

By contrast, the minister who feels compelled to tell the widow's story is conscious of what he owes her, and that sense of obligation parallels him to the poet who feels indebted to the Derry neighbors behind his poems. We sense the personal importance of this connection when Frost presses Flint early in July 1913 to say more about the manuscript poems he'd just read. "One thing I'd like to ask," Frost writes: "Did I reach you with the poems . . .? Did I give you a feeling for . . . the kind of people I like to write about?" The phrase "the people I like to write about" understates the passion that comes through in the example Frost then provides: "The John [Hall][14] who lost his housekeeper and went down like a felled ox was just the person I have described and I never knew a man I liked better — damn the world anyway" (in Barry, 83). As I have mentioned earlier, Frost's depth of feeling for his "people" is equally clear when, two weeks later, he describes his new eclogues to Thomas Mosher as "character strokes *I had to get in somewhere*" and their low diction as "appropriate to the virtues *I celebrate*" (*SL*, 83, 129; emphasis added).

It is hardly surprising that Frost's feelings for the people of his book should equal or surpass the minister's gratitude, sympathy, and respect for the widow, for these former neighbors and friends have supplied the material for Frost's new blank-verse poems while inspiring both their themes and vernacular music. In a way less material though no less substantial, they have likely had a role, as the widow has for the minister, in saving his vocation, for their stubborn adherence to their convictions may also have helped Frost sustain his ambitions as a poet even as economic pressures and success at Pinkerton Academy pushed him toward a teaching career. The model for the widow of "The Black Cottage" was in fact one of Frost's Derry neighbors, Sarah J. Upton, whose husband George was the town's first volunteer to the Union Army. As his widow

---

[13] In his "Letter to *The Amherst Student*" (1935) Frost says, "Whatever progress may be taken to mean, it can't mean making the world any easier a place in which to save your soul — or if you dislike hearing your soul mentioned in an open meeting, say your decency, your integrity" (*CPPP*, 739).

[14] Frost actually wrote "Kline," though he clearly means John Hall, featured in "The Housekeeper," one of the poems Flint had read. "The 'Kline,'" writes Walsh, "no doubt comes from Klein's Hill, a rise which bordered one end of the Frost farm in Derry" (238).

of more than forty years, she occupied an unpainted, weathered cottage that Frost would pass on his way between farm and village, and Frost first drafted her story in 1905–6, giving it as good a claim as any *North of Boston* poem to being the starting point of the book. In the same talk in which he defended Jefferson's "free and equal" idea thirty years later, Frost would in fact make clear how the widow's story is deeply connected to the book's most fundamental impulse.

In "What Became of New England?" Frost poses a question that he says he was often asked — namely, how New England had lost its earlier position of intellectual, political, and economic predominance. No sooner does Frost state the question than he suggests with familiar indirection that an answer lies in *North of Boston*, though he identifies the book only by his very approximate dating and his allusion to Amy Lowell's review, which had praised it as "the epitome of decaying New England" (Thornton, 48):

> People say to me, "What has become of New England?" Twenty years ago I published a little book that seemed to have something to do with New England. It got praise in a way that cost me some pain. It was described as a book about a decadent and lost society. (*CPPP*, 755)

As the talk unfolds, Frost's answer to the question "What became of New England?" involves revising its premise, asserting that, as early as the break from England, New England had taken "the decision . . . to merge with greater nation that was to be . . . and," rather than fade or decline, "was gradually disolved [*sic*] into the larger nation" (*Notebooks*, 452). He suggests, in effect, that rather than disappearing, the New England of stubbornly independent farmers and passionate Puritan intellectuals, having spread itself across a continent, still exerted its power, as "The Black Cottage" minister put it, in "the truths we keep coming back and back to."

Frost specifically credits New England with "a stubborn clinging to meaning" in which we recognize the old widow's profile. Somewhat surprisingly, he also glosses this "stubborn clinging" as a "a renewal of words and . . . meaning," something he has shown us in his own defense of Jefferson's "free and equal" doctrine. As he implies with that defense, Frost further insists that by "New England" he means not merely that single regional culture but a cluster of original, founding energies that still give character to a nation. "What's become of [New England]," he says,

> is not necessarily . . . restricted to New England. The little nation that was to be gave itself, as Virginia gave itself, westward, into the great nation that she saw coming, and so gave help to America. And so any of us are not New Englanders particularly; any writers we were, any statesmen we were, were to be Americans, United States statesmen, United States writers. (*CPPP*, 757)

For Frost, then, "What has become of New England" might be read as "What has become of our original, collective past?"[15] and, just as *North of Boston* is one way of keeping what that past has given us, so the widow's effort to memorialize and preserve and the minister's tribute to her effort both reflect the poet's own. Of the two, the minister's monologue more directly resembles the poet's work, not only because it takes narrative form, but because his story of cottage and widow, like Frost's poems about former neighbors and friends, conveys his own struggle to balance the demands of the present against the claims of the past.

Like both the poet and the minister, however, the widow also insists on placing her own and her husband's lives in a larger historical frame. When we see that her "stubborn clinging" to that Jeffersonian idea merges the legacies of New England and Virginia just as Frost does in the very talk where he also defends the "free and equal" doctrine, we see that she is as much the poet's hero as she is the minister's. It is too simple to say that the widow represents all the Derry neighbors who have become his *North of Boston* "people." Nonetheless, as Frost articulates the book's formative impulses in the decades following its composition, and as we understand more fully the importance he attached to these "character sketches [he] had to get in somewhere" (*SL*, 83) the widow emerges as an epitome of those people who maintain old beliefs in the face of modern pressures and consider nothing in life more important than the people in it. Frost, in fact, defended the widow in precisely the terms that he did the book itself. Just as he rejected Amy Lowell's description of his book as a portrait of decadence, Frost later said that there was "***nothing decadent*** in a soldiers [*sic*] widow dying poor in a house that hasn't been painted for years; nor in a soldier's widow dying in her belief that her soldier didn't die in vain" (in Robbins, 3;[16] quoted by Cramer, 36; emphasis added).

Frost did not give the widow such power and importance all at once. In his first version of the poem, written in 1905–06, "The Black Cottage" was a melancholy, rhymed lyric owing much to the long tradition of graveyard verse, and the widow was alive but doddering, more forlorn than determined, the "solitary inmate" of a cottage that "day has passed by" who has "but an hour to wait" till she joins her forebears and husband in the family burial plot.[17] Full of sentimental periphrasis, the

---

[15] Frost's sense of Eastern colonial energies moving westward would have been reinforced by his own family history, for the Frosts had been in New England from 1634 until 1872, when the poet's father went first to Pennsylvania, and then, on the new transcontinental railroad, to San Francisco, where Robert was born.

[16] Robbins quotes Frost from an undated holograph letter postmarked Amherst, Massachusetts, April 29, 1937.

[17] A complete text of the poem can be found in Thompson, *Early Years*, 592–93. The original manuscript is in the Huntington Library in Los Angeles, California.

poem's mood and diction follows poetic models that, in most of his writing at that time, Frost was striving to break from, and he later claimed to have lost this early version "on purpose as a failure" (in Newdick, 163; quoted by Cramer, 36).[18] It is, however, more than Frost's use of his expanded eclogue form in his new, blank-verse style that would bring the second "Black Cottage" so fully into *North of Boston.*

Frost's recasting of the poem owes much to Wordsworth's "Ruined Cottage" for its layering of narratives as well as its story of a long-grieving wife. But the moral and philosophical principle that defines the widow's character is one that Frost had explored in a little-known poem, "The Lost Faith," written in 1907, between the two versions of "The Black Cottage." Stylistically, the poem does not display the vernacular voice and "sound of sense" prosody that Frost had been working to develop since 1904, drafting many poems that would appear in *North of Boston* and *Mountain Interval* (1916). Perhaps reflecting the audience and occasion for which Frost composed it,[19] "The Lost Faith," in reaching for elevation, becomes theatrical, even histrionic. The "lost ideal" it speaks of — none other than the "created equal" principle of American democracy — there becomes

> No less a dream than of one law of love,
> One equal people under God above!
> But fallen to a world of easy scorn.
> See if it dies not — if it is not dead!

Although "The Lost Faith" exemplifies a style that Frost grew away from in his Derry years, it makes clear that he did not do so all at once, and

---

[18] Newdick quotes from a Frost letter dated January 18, [1938].

[19] Frost composed "The Lost Faith" during his first year of full-time teaching at Pinkerton Academy, for the annual banquet of The Men's League of the First Congregational Church, where the pastor, Charles Merriam read it for Frost, as he had done with "The Tuft of Flowers" in 1906. Just as "The Tuft of Flowers" had helped Frost get his teaching job, so "The Lost Faith" may have helped him keep it, raising his stature in the Derry community when his position at Pinkerton was still uncertain. Though Frost was known, at this point, as an unexemplary farmer, a college man without a degree, and one wasn't sure what sort of teacher, two poems had at least made him a cultured person before an influential group of citizens. With the appearance of "The Trial by Existence" in *The Independent*, a nationally known periodical, the previous October, he was also a man of recognized literary accomplishment. In addition, Thompson suggests, the religious fervor and patriotic sentiments of "The Lost Faith" were probably reassuring to many church members who were unsure what to make of Frost's skeptical, freethinking attitudes (*Early Years*, 330). Except for its appearance the next day in the *Derry News*, "The Lost Faith" remained unpublished in Frost's lifetime. A complete text of the poem can now be found in *CPPP*, 512–14.

it nonetheless articulates two ideas that would be central to his revised "Black Cottage," introducing a powerful dynamic that would connect the widow and minister of the new poem and making clear, in turn, that the concerns of these characters are those of the poet himself.

One of these issues, as we have seen, is the ultimate reason for the Civil War and its human costs. Just as the widow of "The Black Cottage" insists that the "free and equal" principle of our nation's founding was the reason for the war and thus for her husband's death, so "The Lost Faith," in mentioning Gettysburg and Malvern Hill, makes clear that the heroic sacrifices it refers to are those of the Union dead. It claims that this ideal not only called the Northern states to battle but also sustained them through it:

> It was the dream that woke them in this north,
> And led the young man forth,
> And pitched against the embittered foe their tent;
> And fought their fight for them on many a field;
> Their sword, their shield,
> The still small voice that like a clarion pealed;
> Strong as a dream and deathless as a dream.

This last phrase, "deathless as a dream," reveals the other issue shared by "The Lost Faith" and "The Black Cottage": the ultimate persistence of the ideal. As its title suggests, "The Lost Faith" opens with the complaint that we have forgotten "the cause that was . . . so dear" to "the heroic dead" for whom we "strew flowers . . . year after year." But Frost also insists that, even while overshadowed by "things . . . not beautiful or bright," the dream remains too deeply lodged in our cultural memory to disappear entirely and "must return again." In acknowledging its enduring power, we see how Frost's "Lost Faith" persona anticipates the "Black Cottage" minister, who includes this Jeffersonian principle among the enduring truths we return to and who longs for a world that, like the widow, could hold to such values without letting them drop from view. The unfaltering belief longed for in "The Lost Faith" is precisely what the minister admires in the widow and wishes for himself.

When Frost recasts "The Black Cottage" for *North of Boston*, the formerly forlorn widow grows larger and closer, gaining fortitude, conviction, and determination when seen through the minister's eyes, his admiration and gratitude conveying the poet's own. As the minister guides his visitor past the widow's cottage, she takes hold of his thoughts much as the actual Sarah Upton may have touched Frost on his walks to the village, and she still troubles the minister in a way that helps him imagine how Jefferson's words "will trouble us a thousand years." It is, in fact, the widow's engagement with so central an issue of our culture that connects her most deeply to other *North of Boston* characters. The way that she transmits her commitment to the minister, helping to maintain and even renew a belief by living it, exemplifies the power that Frost hoped that all the book's characters would have — the "reach" that he asks Frank Flint to confirm in his July 1913 letter.

The minister's need to tell the widow's story, then, parallels Frost's desire to find an audience — ultimately an American audience — for his "character strokes" (*SL*, 83). As *North of Boston* took shape by late summer of 1913, when all but one of the dramatic narratives were largely done, these rural subjects had helped Frost confirm his poetic vocation as much as the widow has helped the minister to redeem his clerical one. For both the poet and his minister, however, their humble models have more than personal resonance. Just as the minister sees the widow's faith in Jefferson's idea as helping to sustain one of "the truths we keep coming back and back to," so Frost later defends its meaning for our democracy. Like all of Frost's *North of Boston* heroes, the widow also makes clear that such founding principles, whether of a nation, church, or any other community, exert binding force only when actively believed and debated, lived directly or vicariously, often at some cost. Richard Wakefield has observed that "it costs Silas [in "The Death of the Hired Man"] something to distance himself from his brother and from his brother's world of finance, and it costs the widow something to wall herself off in her timeless kingdom. It may have cost the preacher something to keep the words to the old creed."[20] In "The Self-Seeker" the cost of The Broken One's refusal to fight for mere dollars is certainly clear, and the actions of the hired men against their farmer-employers in "The Code" are not without risk to themselves. Collectively, these renunciations create more than a portrait of stubborn individualism. They point to the principles behind sacrifice — to a legacy of old truths that, for Frost, maintain their power even against a competing need to deal with the world of flux and finance, which entails still other costs. As storyteller and conveyer of the legacy he has received by way of the widow, the minister of "The Black Cottage" is the poet's alter ego, and *North of Boston* extends and enlarges his testimony.

In stressing the "dependent-independence of the people I like to write about" (in Barry, 83) in his July 6, 1913, letter to Flint, Frost conveys a conscious concern with the delicate balance between individual freedom and communal obligations, a theme that *North of Boston* introduces in its first principal poem, "Mending Wall," where one man finds a needless restriction in the same wall that his neighbor values as a cultural and personal legacy. The minister shares Frost's own conviction, explored in many of the book's subsequent poems, that what disrupts this balance of opposed claims are the temptations of a capitalist marketplace and industrial economy, where wealth is too often used to dominate or

---

[20] This observation was made in an email message of July 25, 2008.

oppress, where mass production discourages individual expression, and where corporate imperatives override personal concerns at great social cost. Though the minister names no such problems of modern commerce, they are just what he excludes from his imagined kingdom when, in more biblical terms, he denies it enough wealth to arouse covetousness and limits change to the innocent shifting of sands.

In the world we actually inhabit, such a kingdom is a mere dream from which Frost has the bees rouse the minister at the poem's end. Or perhaps the minister rouses himself and summons the bees in testimony, for as he imagines the details of life in his kingdom, where "The sand dunes held loosely in tamarisk" are "Blown over and over themselves in idleness," its stability sounds more like stagnation and life like a slow burial that begins at birth:

> "Sand grains should sugar in the natal dew
> The babe born in the desert, the sand storm
> Retard mid-waste my cowering caravans —
> There are bees in this wall." He struck the clapboards,
> Fierce heads looked out; small bodies pivoted.
> We rose o go. Sunset blazed on the windows.

As the isolated caravans cower in the blown sand, which gets everywhere, covering even the newborn infant, life approaches a standstill, and the retreat from change and strife sounds like death. Frost's use of the dash to mark the minister's sudden shift of focus leaves unclear exactly what has happened to his reverie. Has the sound of the bees interrupted it? Or has he, seeing where it leads, broken it off on his own? Does he strike the wall in anger at the bee's presence or deliberately, to make them visible to his visitor, or for both reasons? However we read the minister's actions and motives, the presence of the bees makes clear that the cottage, though treated as a shrine, is not ageless, but a part of time and change and now given over to new tenants. Simply wishing away the demands of a competitive world does little, Frost suggests, for the truths pushed aside in that world.

In striking the wall, acknowledging and perhaps even calling attention to the bees, the minister comes to the same realization, however grudgingly or willingly. Having wrestled with his congregation and the problem of "non-members in the church," he seems already to have understood it in practice. With the widow staunch in his memory though no longer in her pew, he may even maintain his integrity in a world that leaves little room for idealism. His longing, however, to be rid of commerce and competition puts him somewhere between The Broken One of "The Self-Seeker," who refuses to engage such forces, and Frost himself, who hoped to harness them to his artistic ends: who, having completed most of the dramatic poems for his new book, was perhaps first believing that he might gain the economic success he was smugly enjoying ten years later, when he published "New Hampshire." There, as we have seen, he jokes that, when faced with the conflict between idealism and commerce, he chooses both: "to be a poor New Hampshire farmer / With an income in cash of say a thousand / (From say a publisher in New York City)."

The minister, owing something to the widow's example, has found a way to maintain his vocation, presumably earning a living while staying connected to both the traditional past and the "liberal youth" of his church. Thanks to the widow and his other Derry neighbors, Frost, too, was able to find his voice and realize his vocation as a poet. To complete this task and earn a living by it, however, he had to leave behind the people celebrated in his verse and gain a congregation of readers who would buy his books in their thousands, honoring a vanishing rural culture through the very economic system that was hastening its end. Such *North of Boston* characters as Silas or The Broken One, both victims of a changing and impersonal economy, exemplify the failure Frost was determined to avoid by leaving the honorable austerity of New Hampshire for the poetic and economic venture of England.

In generating a success more sudden and dramatic than even Frost had quite imagined, *North of Boston* widened the divide between the people of his book and the poet who had lived among them, sharing their obscurity though not their degree of economic hardship. Although the book was a bridge across that cultural and economic divide, neither the respect nor compassion it conveyed could close the distance created by the genius and education that shaped Frost's interests, by the ambition that pointed beyond Derry, or, finally, by the annuity checks that gave him a leisure and security unknown to his rural neighbors — a luxury derived from his grandfather's career in the Lawrence textile mills, thus underwriting Frost's Derry and English years by the proceeds of a world antithetical to the one honored by his verse. Nor could the Frost hard at work on the eclogues about his Derry neighbors during his first winter in England forget the simpler truth that any success created by these poems would be derived from their hardship and suffering: from the loss of an infant child ("Home Burial"), an aged hired man ("The Death of the Hired Man"), or a common-law wife ("The Housekeeper"); from fear of insanity or of confrontation by one's abandoned husband ("A Servant to Servants," "The Fear"); from the difficulty of feeding one's many children ("Blueberries") or of maintaining one's farm without children to help ("The Death of the Hired Man").

And so, as *North of Boston* records the struggles of these former neighbors, it also conveys the poet's awareness of the appropriation underlying his achievement. Not that we hear any direct confession or apology in a voice we can clearly call Frost's. As William Pritchard has said, in most of the volume's poems "we look in vain for the presence of 'Frost himself'" ("*North of Boston*," 39). Rather, as we might expect of so dramatic a poet, and as two of the volume's major poems have shown, that awareness finds its way into the voices of such characters as Lafe or the minister, whose appreciation of others hints at uses made, debts owed, trusts violated or compromised, and whose expressions of gratitude thus include elements of apology. In further poems we will see further accusations or suspicions and further references to inequity, trespass, or theft, often elusively ironic. These expressions fully fit the characters who utter them and require no knowledge of Frost himself to be convincing within the poems. Yet, when read with awareness of the poet's struggles and doubts, they not only open new dimensions of the poems themselves but reflect the personal drama underlying this pivotal moment in Frost's career.

With that drama in mind, it is illuminating to consider Frost's own use of the term "trespass" in a short poem — "On the Sale of My Farm" — written late in 1911 in something close to the poet's own voice.[21] There Frost claims "cheerfully [to] yield / Pasture, orchard, mowing field" as well as "house, / Barn, and shed" to their new owner, but his farewell summary — "These I can unlearn to love" — suggests that such a renunciation will be hard. The difficulty is emphasized by the condition Frost attaches to the agreement of sale. "Only be it understood," he adds,

> It shall be no trespassing
> If I come again some spring
> In the grey disguise of years,
> Seeking ache of memory here.

Besides underlining the depth of Frost's feeling about his Derry years and the pain involved in the choice he has made, this passage raises a crucial question. Does the denial of trespass here contradict the qualms about trespass woven through *North of Boston*? On the contrary, this addendum affirms them. For, in laying lifelong claim to his memories of the farm, even implying that they confer his right to revisit what someone else now owns, these lines raise the question of what it would mean to convey one's most intimate materials to another's hands — precisely the question that so many *North of Boston* poems raised for Frost himself. His refusal to yield such personal things of his own correlates closely with his uneasiness about appropriating them from others' lives. Frost's artistic ambitions and need to secure his financial future may have made this intrusion necessary, but, as we shall continue to see, the qualms resulting from that choice found their own way into the poems themselves.

---

[21] This was one of seventeen handwritten poems that Frost stitched into a packet and sent Susan Hayes Ward as a Christmas present in December 1911 (*SL*, 42–43). The original manuscript resides in the Henry E. Huntington Library, San Marino, CA. The poem remained unpublished during Frost's lifetime.

5: The Poet and the Burden of Reproach

BOTH "THE DEATH OF THE HIRED MAN" and "The Self-Seeker" portray the antagonism between the rural New England culture championed by Frost and the industrial capitalism with which his literary ambitions required an alliance. "A Hundred Collars" offers two characters, Lafe and Magoon, who in their different ways reflect Frost's position between these opposed forces. Of all Frost's *North of Boston* protagonists, the one most like the poet himself is the minister of "The Black Cottage," whose relation to the widow reflects Frost's own relations to his Derry neighbors, and who must, like Frost, steer a course between his own idealism and economic necessity. In further and often more oblique ways, many other *North of Boston* poems reflect Frost's uneasy position between his former Derry neighbors and the social-economic position he was striving to reach by means of his second book. At the same time, most of these poems remind us of the demographic changes, felt keenly in northern New England, that intensified problems endemic to small-scale farming and contributed to the drama of disappearance traced by *North of Boston* as a whole.

"A Servant to Servants"

"A Servant to Servants," for example, provides a revealing moment in a conversation between the farm wife and the amateur botanist who is camping on her land at the edge of Vermont's Lake Willoughby. The poem is a monologue, its form reflecting the distressed, obsessive outpouring of the woman, who carries burdens of more than one kind. If she and her husband Len have ever farmed seriously, they have had to look beyond farming to eke out a living and now maintain a crew of hired men for road work and other town projects, boarding the men in their home, so that it falls to the wife to feed and clean up after them. She and Len live with the hope that someone will rent the tourist cabins Len has built or that their lakeshore land will yet prove to "be worth something," though the wife is quick to add, "I don't count on it as much as Len." Exhausted and demoralized by her daily tasks, she says with Calvinist fatalism at the end of her monologue, "I sha'n't catch up in this world, anyway."

As taxing as she finds her daily labors, they are less onerous than the ghosts from her family past awakened by the crude and careless talk of the hired men she is forced to hear each day. Depressed, she lives in fear that she will succumb to the insanity that afflicted her father's brother, who "went mad quite young" over a lost love and was confined — for everyone's safety, including his own — behind home-made bars in the attic. Though he died before the narrator was born, he has deeply affected her family life by blighting the early years of marriage for her mother, who, as a new wife, "had to help take care of such a creature / And accommodate her young life to his." Perhaps worst for that young wife, and most haunting for the daughter who now tells her story, was the inability to contain the uncle's thwarted sexual and emotional energies, which spilled out in his crowing and the "twang[ing]" of his wooden bars[1] at night, and in his making "love things . . . dreadful /By his shouts" as she lay in bed beside her husband. He may even have left behind a deeper legacy of guilt, for the narrator had heard her parents "say . . . / They found a way to put a stop to" the situation, suggesting not only some dire act, but layers of secrecy and repression throughout her family culture. It is hardly surprising that now, though surrounded by men, she feels lonely as well as overwhelmed and depressed, probably like her mother. At the end of her monologue, though behind in her work, she says to the visitor willing the listen to her story, "I'd *rather* you not go unless you must."

Early in her monologue, the woman asks the visitor[2] how he had heard of the lake that she sees every day through the bars of her emotional and economic prison. His answer is reflected in her response:

> In a book about ferns? Listen to that!
> You let things more like feathers regulate
> Your going and coming.

It would be peremptory to equate "things more like feathers" — the ferns — with aesthetic concerns, and one need not do exactly that to appreciate the parallel between the poet and the botanizing tourist who prompts this response from a depressed and overworked farm wife. In the summer

[1] Apparently the floor-to-ceiling bars, made from "hickory poles," were flexible enough to vibrate audibly when "pull[ed] . . . apart like bow and bowstring."

[2] Some readers see the auditor as a woman, arguing that the poem's speaker would surely not divulge such intimacies to a man. I find this a defensible though not persuasive reading. More important, the gender of the poem's speaker doesn't alter the implications of the situation for Frost himself. Seeing the auditor as a woman would not change the speaker's surprise at her freedom to travel and explore and would only reinforce the prevailing view of a farming culture that pursuing wild flora, like writing poems, is not quite real or manly work.

of 1909, Frost had, in fact, taken his family on a camping and botanizing trip to Lake Willoughby in Vermont, pitching the family tents on land belonging to a farmer named Connolley and making regular visits to the farmhouse to buy fresh milk and eggs from Mrs. Connolley, who became one of three models for his "Servant to Servants" protagonist (Cramer, 38). Frost had chosen this place partly because he hoped it would be high enough in elevation and far enough north to escape ragweed pollen in hay fever season, partly because the lake provided appealing recreation for the children, and also because he had learned from Carl Burrell that the combination of mountains and bog land was a "paradise for botanists" (Thompson, *Early Years*, 350). As we have seen in "The Self-Seeker" and in his May 1913 letter to Sidney Cox, Frost used his interest in wild flora — his pursuit of the "unutilitarian flower" — as an emblem for the poetic vocation that, as he told Frank Flint in January 1913, he had often borne as a stigma in the American "village." As Mark Richardson suggests, the judgment Frost registered there almost surely combines a general American suspicion about aesthetic pursuits by men (58) with the related disapproval that many Derry villagers felt for Frost's dependence on inherited wealth, which is precisely what allowed him to be more of the poet and less of the farmer than many of them thought he ought to be.

"The Mountain"

Earlier in the volume, "The Mountain" offers a more extended and comic parallel to this encounter, in which the narrator — whose main business, like the poet's, seems to be wandering and wondering over the local landscape — barrages a passing farmer with questions about the mountain that dominates the view. The local mountain is called Hor, named for a peak near Lake Willoughby,[3] suggesting that Frost's 1909 summer in Vermont made a contribution to *North of Boston* beyond "A Servant to Servants." As Frost later made clear to Louis Mertins, however, the mountain "wasn't one, but several mountains" yet was "just as real" and no less true to his Derry experience "for all its being composite," adding, "Those mountains surrounded the Derry farm, and stretched farther than the eye could see" (Mertins, 72).

The more significant connection between "A Servant to Servants" and "The Mountain" resides in the subtle tensions between the local farm people, held captive to their daily labors, and their visitors, who are free to travel and do as they wish. In response, the old farmer, more mischievous than the Lake Willoughby wife, enjoys tweaking the outsider's seemingly

---

[3] Hor is also the mountain on which Moses's brother Aaron is said to have died (Num. 20:22–29), and Frost refers to this tradition in his high-school essay, "Petra and Its Surroundings" (*CPPP*, 633).

idle interest in the local mountain, which the farmer measures in pragmatic terms as a place to hunt deer or catch trout, and as an impediment to the town's prosperity:

> "There is no village — only scattered farms.
> . . . .
> We can't in nature grow to many more:
> That thing takes all the room!" . . . .
> The mountain stood there to be pointed at.

When the farmer teases the visitor's curiosity with intriguing but vague reports about what's up there, including a spring situated — impossibly, it seems — at the summit, the narrator asks him directly, "You never saw it?" to which the farmer answers:

> I've always meant to go
> And look myself, but you know how it is;
> It doesn't seem so much to climb a mountain
> You've worked around the foot of all your life.
> What would I do? Go in my overalls,
> With a big stick, the same when the cows
> Haven't come down to the bars at milking time?
> Or with a shotgun for a stray black bear?
> 'Twouldn't seem real to climb for climbing it.

The farmer begins by trying to explain his lack of firsthand knowledge, but his reply to this curious visitor turns out to be more teasing than apologetic. It has something even of a judgmental edge, for his rhetorical questions and final tautology, "to climb for climbing," imply the folly and waste of expending such effort without a practical purpose, especially when, as he demonstrates, one can have so much fun just with words on level ground.

The narrator's reply — "I shouldn't climb it if I didn't want to — / Not for the sake of climbing" — gently takes issue with the farmer's tautology by implying a value to the climb, though not a tangible one. It also connects such an ascent to other pursuits in *North of Boston* that are valued for the seeing and knowing they yield: botanizing in the woods, raising beautiful fowl, playing the violin, picking wild berries, walking into a frozen swamp, or even, for the narrator of "Mending Wall," repairing a stone fence mainly to engage with one's neighbor. And such intangible aims lead us back, in turn, to Frost's own pursuit of the "unutilitarian flower" and his poetic vocation. In correcting the farmer's tautology — he would climb, he says, "*Not* for the sake of climbing" (emphasis added) — the narrator implies that for him there would be a reason *for* the act, but that a good reason needn't be a practical one: that such nonutilitarian efforts, including the poet's work, have a value beyond themselves, whether aesthetic, intellectual, or even spiritual.[4] And perhaps more radically, his saying "I shouldn't climb it if I didn't *want* to" (emphasis added) implies that desire, pleasure, and a free expression of the will are worthy reasons for such an effort.

The Farmer-Poet

Significantly, this distinction between different kinds of work and different kinds of value points to aspects of Frost's life in Derry that set him apart from the local economy and people. While Frost enjoyed life on the farm, selling eggs and chickens through local channels, his five-hundred-dollar annuity allowed him, for a few years at least, to immerse himself in the daily and seasonal rhythms of farm life without being submerged by them. This degree of financial freedom gave Frost what Robert Penn Warren has called the "cultivate[d] leisure" necessary to a writing life (in Parini, 84–85),[5] and even permitted certain extravagances that, for Frost, were corollary to his imaginative freedom and productivity. If writing meant sitting up long after Elinor and the children were asleep at night, he could sleep late. If it meant a month-long family trip to New York City, where Frost could try to make literary contacts, he could manage the expense, even if it raised local eyebrows — or something more. Both Thompson and Parini report resentment among the local Derry people over the money and habits that set Frost apart yet left him owing money while he waited for his next annuity check. Thompson tells of a butcher's caustic remark about the fancy trap and pacer that Frost had driven to the store where he expected to add to his unpaid bill. Both Thompson and Parini report the bank teller's comment when Frost deposited one of his semi-annual checks — "More of your hard-earned money,

[4] The idea of intellectual and spiritual ascent was central to Frost's conception of poetry. In "Education by Poetry," a talk given at Amherst in 1930, he claims that metaphor — "just saying one thing in terms of another" — is the basis of nearly all thinking, and that to tell students so "is to set their feet on the first rung of a ladder the top of which sticks through the sky" (*CPPP*, 723). In *North of Boston* Frost anticipates this comment with the opening lines of "After Apple-Picking": "My long two-pointed ladder's sticking through a tree / Toward heaven still. . . ." In "Birches," which Frost considered for inclusion in this volume, he speaks of wishing "to climb black branches up a snow-white trunk / *Toward* heaven" (*CPPP*, 70, 118).

[5] Parini cites an "Interview with Robert Penn Warren" (463) as his source for this statement, but gives no date.

Mr. Frost?" (*Early Years*, 315; Parini, 92).[6] Louis Mertins reports that Frost, when older, often "laughed at a reputation he got among his farm neighbors" and quotes him directly:

> They would see me starting out to work at all hours of the morning — approaching noon, to be more explicit. I always like to sit up all hours of the night planning some inarticulate crime, going out to work when the spirit moved me, something they shook their heads ominously at, with proper prejudice. They would talk among themselves about my lack of energy. I was a failure in their eyes from the very start — very start. Certainly I couldn't be a farmer and act like this. Getting into the field at noon! What a farmer! (78)

Despite the degree to which Frost felt connected to the farming people of Derry — as an admirer of particular neighbors, a hereditary if heretical member of their laboring class, and a defender of their culture — he could never quite be one of them, for reasons of his money and education, his poetic sensibility and values, and most of all, for the poetic career, always pointing beyond Derry, that his genius and ambition made both necessary and possible. When we add that this poetic future hinged on the poetic produce of the Derry soil, we have the ingredients of a conflict that we should be surprised *not* to find imbedded in *North of Boston*, the book designed both to celebrate that world and to move beyond it, paying tribute to a collective past while opening the way to a personal future. Like Ishmael in *Moby Dick*, sole survivor of the wrecked Pequod, who makes a life preserver of Queequeg's intended coffin, Frost's escape from that Derry world depends on what he can make from the remains of his former community. And if his survival is necessary for bearing witness to the life that is lost, he must nonetheless, like Coleridge's Ancient Mariner, bear a burden for that survival. In Frost's case, that burden includes an awareness of life's inequities, which include his personal fame and fortune gained in apparent exchange for a way of life that he could save only in imagination.

This burden has not been Frost's alone. In a literary age that demands and rewards realism, writers have often aroused resentment by their artistic use of individuals and communities they knew personally. Among Frost's contemporaries, there is Thomas Wolfe's Asheville, North Carolina, William Faulkner's Oxford, Mississippi, and Willa Cather's New York City and Paris, all full of friends and acquaintances

[6] Parini describes the teller's attitude as "undisguised contempt" (92). Thompson says, "The teller may have intended the remark pleasantly, but Frost resented the insinuation" (*Early Years*, 313). Judging from the Derry community's prevailing view of Frost (see *From Turnpike to Interstate*, 53–55), I incline toward Parini's view.

turned into literary subjects. While objections to this common artistic practice may vary, they often return to the question of self-interest: to what degree these writers have pursued their own ends without regard for the persons made to serve their literary aims — for the privacies they have compromised. A writer's typical defense is that artistic truth may require such intrusions and that its value outweighs the costs involved. Using as a model Thomas Gray's "Elegy Written in a Country Churchyard," which reflects on the circumscribed lives of rural eighteenth-century villagers, one might add that such art pays the respect of notice, if not always of praise, to lives otherwise unrecognized, giving them a kind of voice. In the dramatic narratives of *North of Boston*, Frost gives a voice to more than one Derry neighbor, just as these neighbors have helped Frost find his own.

What distinguishes Frost from so many contemporary writers accused of self-serving appropriation is that he himself calls attention to the transaction between writer and subject, including the question of boundaries that he as artist may have transgressed. In a poem originally published in *A Boy's Will* but omitted in later, collected editions, Frost focuses even more directly on the uneasiness that would show itself repeatedly in the *North of Boston* poems, as if drawn to the surface by the dying New England culture of which he was briefly and marginally a part. The poem's title, "Spoils of the Dead," with its associations of looting, violence, and theft, minces no words about the trespass and transgression that arises when we take possession of what has belonged to others. Unfolding in eight stanzas of parabolic narrative followed by two of homiletic reflection, the poem tells of fairies who find a man's corpse in the woods and carry off his glittering ring and watch-chain in the same careless way that they had earlier plucked and strewn wildflowers. The rhetorical question-and-reply of the final two stanzas captures the poet's conflicted feelings about the issue of survival and appropriation, expressing even a sense of horror at something that may be an unavoidable part of life, especially for a writer:

> When *you* came on death,
>   Did you not come flower-guided
> Like the elves in the wood?
>   I remember that I did.
>
> But I recognized death
>   With sorrow and dread,
> And I hated and hate
>   The spoils of the dead.

In the first of these two final stanzas, the italicized "you" implicates all readers in a charge implicit in the earlier description of the wood-sprites, who move from plucking flowers to taking the dead man's precious things without fear, sorrow, or any other emotional response to the human corpse they find. But as these lines move our attention from elfin to human action and we again recall Frost's own equation between his pursuit of wild orchids and his writing of poems, this poem raises the question of what license we grant our aesthetic aims — how far we shall go in pursuit of the beautiful.

At the end of the penultimate stanza, the speaker admits to being "flower-guided" — instinctively drawn, like the butterflies, bees, and fairies, to gather what one wants from the living and dead alike. By making this admission in a line and sentence all its own — "I remember that I did" — he anticipates the opening "But" of the final stanza, where the emotions of his empathic mortal heart, refusing to stay unheard, set him apart from the uncaring elves and in fact from all nonhuman creatures. Frost's use of the fairies here provides an opportunity to explore an issue of particular relevance to a poet, for without concern for material survival, the fairies are freed to value things for reasons we might call aesthetic. Nearly all earthly creatures live at another's expense, if only by competing for the same resources. Yet the immaterial fairies, if able to reflect, have no need to do so. Freed from the pressures of survival and fear of death, they are as unable to understand the stakes in this competition as are the equally "flower-guided" bees or butterflies, who, though directed by these pressures, are unable to reflect. To "recognize death / With sorrow and dread," as the speaker does here, is to feel and acknowledge death's meaning for one's self, as the immortal fairies and other mortal beings cannot. In addition to direct competition, all creatures — and poets in a conscious and deliberate way — live by appropriating what others leave behind, if only the places they have vacated. That is what inheritance means, and accepting such inheritance may require our putting aside various griefs and qualms. In fact, our pursuits of life and beauty may allow us such qualms only upon reflection, like the speaker who "remember[s]" here. But to feel them not at all is to become entirely elfin — to undo our humanity, which asks a tribute of both "sorrow and dread": of sorrow for the life lost and dread of the death that will one day be our own.

It is perhaps the utter rejection of such "spoils," the unqualified "hate" heaped upon them in the poem's closing lines that might explain Frost's withdrawal of the poem from his published works after 1913 (Cramer, 230). Not that *North of Boston*, full as it is with the "spoils" of Frost's Derry years, would dictate such a retraction. More likely for a poet whose best work points up the unavoidable cruelties of a mortal world, in which living creatures, animal or plant, always compete for finite resources, such a condemnation is too absolute. While "Spoils of the Dead" identifies something that might have especially troubled Frost in the poems of his second book, so substantially crafted from others' lives, it fails to acknowledge the complex give-and-take between poet and poetic subject — the subtler modulation of competing claims as they apply to *North of Boston* itself.

I have suggested that both the overworked wife in "A Servant to Servants" and the local farmer in "The Mountain" pronounce what we might well hear as a judgment on the poet's seeming exemption from the curse of labor as he follows the freedom of his fancy, which in their view might seem almost elfin. The leisure to travel and observe others in their daily tasks, a license enjoyed by both the botanist-auditor in "A Servant to Servants" and the observer-narrator of "The Mountain," clearly parallels Frost's own relation to his *North of Boston* subjects. Compared with them, Frost enjoyed a greater freedom from the work he disliked and took a greater pleasure in the work he choose — a pleasure derived from his ability to find profit in such "trivial" pursuits as walking, seeking wild flora, climbing mountains, or talking with neighbors. If this merging of vocation and avocation, as Frost described it in his 1934 poem "Two Tramps in Mud-Time,"[7] remained as much an "aim" as an accomplished fact, he was, as poet, closer to achieving it than were any of the laboring poor portrayed in *North of Boston*.

How acutely Frost felt this inequity, and how it distanced him from the people he wrote about, is clear in Frost's note to Frank Flint written January 21, 1913, two weeks after they met at the opening of Harold Monro's Poetry Bookshop in London. There, Frost explains how good it felt to have escaped the discomfort he felt in the American "village," describing himself as "only too childishly happy to be . . . in a company in which I hadn't to be ashamed of having written verse" (in Barry, 84). Just as Frost is somewhat hyperbolic ("only too childishly happy") in describing what he was beginning to find in England, we might recognize some exaggeration about what he had left behind. Derry Village was not a cultural desert. Even the Pinkerton colleagues and trustees who distrusted Frost's unconventional ways and didn't much care for poetry were pleased to count among them a poet whose work had appeared in a nationally circulated periodical.[8] In 1906 and 1907, as mentioned earlier, the Men's League of Derry's Congregational Church had invited Frost to read a

[7] 1934 is the year of its first appearance in the *Saturday Review of Literature*. In *A Further Range* (1936) it was subtitled "A Full-time Interest" (Cramer, 103).

[8] "The Trial by Existence," later included in *A Boy's Will*, appeared in the October 11, 1906, issue of *The Independent*, a periodical available in the Pinkerton Academy library (Thompson, *Early Years*, 328). It was one of only three poems published beyond the Derry or Pinkerton communities during Frost's Derry years.

poem at its annual banquet, presentations that helped Frost to gain and then affirm his appointment to the Pinkerton faculty, and on both occasions a Derry newspaper had printed Frost's poem on the following day. Still, for all that, Derry could offer no community of writers like those Frost was now finding in London, two of whom, Frank Flint and T. E. Hulme, would soon be responding to Frost's new poems and poetic theories. Almost the only person to whom he confessed the "magnitude of [his] ambition" (*SL*, 20) before his move to England was Susan Hayes Ward, literary editor of *The Independent*, one of only three widely circulated periodicals that, until the summer of 1912, had accepted Frost's work.[9] So, while we may detect some self-aggrandizing hyperbole when Frost says that he had "lived for the most part in villages where it were better that a millstone were hanged around your neck than that you should own yourself a minor poet" (in Barry, 84–85), we might also trust that the sense of his difference must often have been painful and deep.

Mrs. Connolley and the Poem

By the time Frost wrote this first note to Flint late in January 1913, he was living just outside London, he had a contract with David Nutt for *A Boy's Will* and further books, and he was actively writing and revising the poems for *North of Boston*. That Frost's removal from Derry did not remove the burden of the old apartness is made clear first by the frequency with which the poems of the new book place figures, especially narrators, in positions much like his own position in Derry. His later reflections on the poems both before and after the book's publication confirm that he carried this burden with him to England and beyond. As Frost felt closer to turning his Derry experience into public success, however, any shame attached to being known as a writer of poems shifted toward the guiltier burden of rewards reaped at another's cost.

In the case, for example, of Mrs. Connolley, the overworked farm wife who helped to inspire "A Servant to Servants," Frost clearly came to feel that he had committed a wrong in using her as a poetic subject. Lawrance Thompson observes, approvingly enough, that of all the persons Frost met in his summer at Lake Willoughby, Mrs. Connelley was the only one who "touched him deeply enough to inspire a poem" (*Early Years*, 352). Yet, in a 1937 letter to Albert J. Robbins, Frost accounts it a "reproach" to himself that the woman later "went insane," adding, "I never should have written her into a poem if I had really

[9] The other two periodicals were *The Youth's Companion*, which published "Ghost House" in 1906, and the *New England Magazine*, which published "Into My Own" in 1909. Frost included both poems in *A Boy's Will*.

realized her destiny" (Robbins, 4; in Cramer, 38).[10] Since it does not appear that Frost did anything to worsen Mrs. Connolley's condition or could have done anything to improve it, his self-reproach implicitly comes from having taken more of value from her situation, made more of her life, than she herself could — in effect, gaining from her loss by making an artistic success of her failure. For artists this transformation is an old story. "Out of my great pains / I make little songs" joked the nineteenth-century poet Heinrich Heine (20),[11] reminding us how slight (something "more like feathers"?) the artistic product might seem when compared to the weight of suffering behind it. Different questions naturally arise, and such "feathers" take on greater weight, when the suffering made into song belongs to another.

John Hall and "The Housekeeper"

In the case of John Hall, the fellow poultryman portrayed in "The Housekeeper," the feathers are more literal, and Frost's burden of inequity all the greater for the parallels between himself and the friend who became his poetic subject. Hall's role in Frost's life was much like that of Carl Burrell. Both were older men who gave crucial support to the fatherless Frost at critical junctures in his life, including the period of depression that followed the deaths of his son Elliot and his mother, Belle Frost, in 1900. Beginning in Frost's high-school years, Burrell, ten years his senior, had mentored Frost in subjects of lifelong interest,[12] offered emotional support during Frost's unhappy freshman semester at Dartmouth College, and later helped him get established on the Derry farm. Hall was fifty-seven when Frost, then twenty-five, met him at the Amesbury Fair in 1899, shortly before moving to Derry. An expert poultryman and bird fancier whose fowl were perennial prizewinners at local shows, Hall was surely helpful to Frost as a "hen man," but

[10] The letter is undated but postmarked April 29, 1937. The full passage reads: "I made a Servant to Servants out of three overworked women I have met, one in San Francisco, one in New Hampshire, and one in Vermont. One I never knew the end of: I lost track of her. One to my reproach went insane. I never should have written her into a poem if I had really realized her destiny" (Robbins, 4). As we see, Frost doesn't name Mrs. Connolley as the one who "went insane," and Cramer relies on Thompson for that identification, probably with good reason. However, even if Frost meant another of the women, the self-reproach he reports would likely remain unchanged.

[11] In the original German, "Aus meinem grossen Schmerzen / Mach' ich kleinen Lieder." The translation above is my own.

[12] As mentioned earlier, these were American humor and natural science, with special emphasis on evolution and botany. The latter included intensive field work focused particularly on ferns and orchids.

his intelligence, colorful speech, and love of beauty made him far more important as a friend and conversationalist. Frost's artistic debt to Hall is probably as great as his intellectual debt to Burrell, for it was Hall's inventive language that inspired Frost's first attempts, in prose pieces for two trade journals, *Farm Poultry* and the *Eastern Poultryman*, to catch the tones and rhythms of the local vernacular in writing.[13]

By the time Frost was assembling *North of Boston* a decade later, he had already placed himself, in imagination if not yet fully in fact, on the other side of the drama of disappearance recorded by his book. As Frost develops Hall's character in "The Housekeeper," where he is identified simply as "John," he becomes, like Silas in "Death of the Hired Man," an emblem of quirky individualism doomed in an increasingly competitive and unforgiving economic climate. As Frost describes him through the eyes of the housekeeper's mother, who is about to leave the farm with her daughter Estelle after fifteen years of living with John, her prediction of his personal demise becomes an image of a more general cultural decline. "I just don't see him living many years, / Left here with nothing but the furniture," the mother says of John, continuing with a description that could fit many another small New England farm:

> I hate to think of the old place when we're gone,
> With the brook going by below the yard,
> And no one here but the hens blowing about.
> If he could sell the place, but then, he can't:
> No one will ever live on it again.
> It's too run down. This is the last of it.

The ensuing dialogue between Estelle's mother and the friend who has come to see John, a figure clearly parallel to Frost, reveals the reason for Estelle's departure. After her years as his common-law wife — years in which she shared John's farmwork as well as his bed and supplied most of their household cash by selling her decorative bead-work — Estelle has grown tired of asking John to marry her, and when a willing man "was found," she accepts. Good dramatist that he is, Frost creates sympathy for both characters. Estelle understandably wants the respectability as well as the personal affirmation and security of a recognized marriage, may want children, and may, some readers surmise, even be pregnant. John, who "knows he's kinder than the run of men," as Estelle's mother affirms, thinks that "Better than married ought to be as good / As married." In his July 1913 letter to Frank Flint, Frost classified the poem as "a tragedy" (in Barry, 83), and like many

---

[13] The complete texts of these articles are reprinted in *Robert Frost: The Collected Prose*, and in Lathem, ed., *Robert Frost: Farm Poultryman*.

tragic protagonists, this one finds defeat more through blindness than ill intent. Kind as he is, he fails to understand both the pain his refusal causes Estelle and the possible consequences of that failure, including the devastation he feels when she leaves him.

Hall, like Burrell, possessed all the qualities, including a love of beautiful things, necessary to gain Frost's admiration, friendship, and gratitude, but he lacked those needed to thrive economically. In fact, when Estelle's mother says, "I never saw a man let family troubles / Make so much difference in his man's affairs," we can count Hall's emotional sensitivity as yet another connection to Frost and another quality that both share with Carl Burrell, who could not bear to fight for a fair insurance settlement when he was injured in the box factory. In "The Housekeeper," Estelle's mother stresses John's impractical, extravagant ways. Like Frost and Burrell, who could ignore a farm chore in order to transplant a choice wildflower, the actual Hall also neglected his business for his birds. With his passion for raising fancy fowl and winning ribbons for them, he was, like Frost, less a farmer than an artist. What little his poultry business made he would spend on new birds to groom and show and, while he'd boast of the offers he had for them, he would rarely make the sale. "He never takes the money," Estelle's mother says of John. "If they're worth / That much to sell," she continues, paraphrasing him, "they're worth that much to keep." Even "Our cows and pigs," she adds, "are always better / Than folks like us have any business with."

Clearly enough, Hall's conflicts between extravagance and necessity, between the fowl fancier and poultryman, reflect those between the artist and farmer, and later the artist and teacher, in Frost himself throughout his Derry years.[14] But compounding Frost's relation to Hall is a larger and subtler conflict that arises when Frost writes him "into a poem," underlining the radical difference in their fates, reflecting and even symbolizing their changed relations. Looking again at Frost's July 1913 note to Frank Flint, we should note Hall's prominence in the whole moral-aesthetic enterprise represented by *North of Boston*. "Did I reach you with the poems?" Frost begins, and continues:

> Did I give you a feeling of and for the independence-dependence of the kind of people I like to write about[?] I am no propagandist of equality. But I enjoy above all things the contemplation of equality where it happily exists. I am no snob. I may be several other kinds

[14] Here I conflate the John Hall Frost knew personally with John in the poem. While this would normally be doubtful critical practice, Frost effectively equates them in his July 1913 letter to Flint.

> of fool and rascal but I am not that. The John [Hall][15] who lost his housekeeper and went down like a felled ox was just the person I have described and I never knew a man I liked better — damn the world anyway. (in Barry, 83)

Here Frost's desire to "give [Flint] a feeling . . . for . . . the people I like to write about" is, first, a concern with the success — the expressive power — of the poems on which his future depends. From this concern he moves directly to the John Hall he so admired, and he seems genuinely concerned that the poems pay due respect to the people of his book, of which he makes Hall the prime example. But this sequence is revealing, and regarding the questions Frost raises, I would add: What did it mean to Frost that the questions about John Hall have become those about the success of his poems and book?

The shifts in Frost's paragraph suggest that the answer is not simple. Frost's concern about his poems moves, in effect, from what they convey about his people to ways that they reflect his own convictions and feelings. Realist that he is, he denies any pure egalitarianism, instead claiming to recognize equality "where it exists." But by insisting on a personal equality with the people of his book that transcends class difference, Frost tacitly acknowledges the inequities between their lives and his that it leaves untouched — the social and economic difference that enabled him to become their elegist, standing on the verge of public success. As son, suitor, husband, father, brother, and friend, Frost has suffered alongside them, but in ways they often could not, he has surmounted his losses. He has done so largely through his own will and genius, but he has had the advantage of educated parents and his grandfather's money, and he has had the help and inspiration that friends such as Burrell and Hall could provide, contributions that reached their most enduring value as they passed from his life into his poems. Frost's uneasiness about the inequities between Hall's fate and his own is evident when he protests a bit more than necessary: "I am no snob. I may be several other kinds of fool and rascal but I am not that." It is reflected more obliquely in his parting comment, "damn the world anyway," especially when we consider Frost's very deliberate efforts to make his way in that world.

The grief and anger that surface in this outburst even ten years after Frost's last contact with Hall suggest how fully Frost's work on *North of Boston* re-immersed him in the experience and emotions of his Derry years. But what besides these raw emotions do we find in this exclamation? For what is the world to be judged and damned? For its heartlessness,

[15] As earlier noted, Frost clearly means John Hall, though he says "John Kline," a mistake likely prompted by Klein's Hill, a knoll bordering Frost's farm where the Frost children often played (Walsh, 238). The pain of recalling Hall's demise may also have contributed to Frost's slip.

its saying that passion and caring and talent are not enough and that, for success and security, one must have foresight and calculation and at times even a ruthlessness like its own? Is the world to be damned for exacting its penalties — for its refusal to forgive the "people" in *North of Boston*, as Frost said he'd tried to do, "for being people" (*CPPP*, 784)? Much as Frost suffers over the world's indifference both for Hall's sake and his own, might he also feel a share in that indifference simply by having left Hall behind as he went forward in his life? And whatever the world is to be damned for, is it not same world in which Frost now strives to take a place? Considering the self-reproach he felt simply by learning that the Mrs. Connolley he had "written . . . into a poem" later "went insane" (Cramer, 38), we must wonder what reproach he feels not only for making his way in the world that "felled" John Hall, but for making Hall's loss a rung on the ladder of his own success.

Such questions resonate with a small incident at the very end of "The Housekeeper." When the narrator learns that Estelle has married another man and will not return, he says to her mother, "Then it's all up," and quickly adds, "I think I'll get away. / . . . . You ought to have the kitchen to yourself / To break it to him. You may have the job."[16] The narrator's wish to escape does not put him in a flattering light. However much he might, as he claims, be thinking of Estelle's mother or of John's need for privacy at such a moment, he would also spare himself the "job" of breaking the news and responding to his friend's pain and humiliation.

Since John returns just as the narrator declares his intention, making moot his escape plan, we might wonder why Frost included this brief episode in the poem. His mixing the narrator's self-concern with his concern for John underlines Frost's realism, illustrating the weaknesses he suggested by describing *North of Boston* as an attempt "to show that I had forgiven [the people in it] for being people" (*CPPP*, 784). Within this particular drama, however, and in light of the ironic timing here, the incident also embodies something inescapable about the tragedy that overtakes John. Like most tragedy, this one touches those around him. Tragedy reminds us that in human communities, pain is not readily contained. In this case, the devastation that Estelle's mother has predicted for John has already begun when, in the poem's final lines, he returns to the farm angry and distraught. We also understand that, for the mother, who feels "built in" at the farm "like a big church organ," leaving with Estelle will involve pain and loss beyond mere disruption, and there is little to suggest that Estelle will be happier with the man who "was found" to wed her than she was with John. Here at the end of the poem, we also

[16] My thanks to Robert McDowell and Mark Jarman (56) for calling my attention to this passage in the poem.

see how the pain touches John's friend, transparently modeled on Frost himself, and this, in turn, takes us back to his June 1913 letter to Flint.

There, in his own voice, Frost speaks more fully of what he suffers on Hall's behalf more than ten years after the events themselves. And if, as I have suggested, Frost's work on the poem had revivified that suffering, then the poem and the letter become alternate but eloquent expressions of the same pain, the poem as artfully reticent as the letter is agonized and raw. Both expressions, as we have seen, entangle self-concern with concern for another, so that in "The Housekeeper," the narrator's divided motives mirror Frost's dual concern with the success of his poem and the fate of his friend. The poet's empathy for his characters was at the heart of "this book of people," and it is not surprising that this phrase in the book's dedication "to E. M. F." entwines his feelings for them with the love and gratitude he felt toward his wife Elinor. Yet equally necessary to this book was the ambition and discipline underlying his artistry. In this year of 1913, when Frost's crucial trial by market rested with these dramatic narratives, many of them based on suffering seen close at hand, there was bound to be dissonance between the empathy he felt for his "people" and the calculating work of writing them into poems. The narrator's mixture of motives at the close of "The Housekeeper" is one more way that the poet's complex feelings find their way into the poems themselves.

Both more directly and less, Frost's statements about using John Hall and Mrs. Connolly in his poems anticipate the statement we have seen in "Poverty and Poetry," where Frost says, "I wouldn't have [written about the poor] if I knew anything was going to be *made* of it" (emphasis added). Considering that Frost delivered this talk in 1937, this comment might well be an effort to counter any efforts to construe his concern with economic hardship as support for Franklin Roosevelt's New Deal, which Frost clearly disliked. But even if read in the light of national politics, Frost's statement also captures the discomforts and paradox of his position more simply as artist. By using the passive voice, leaving vague just who might have cast what aspersions, he distances himself from the possible accusations of misuse even as his words suggest all that he has "made" from the rural poor — the poems, money, and fame that divide him further from them. And he supplies further fuel for such aspersions when he goes on to joke, "I need them in my business" (*CPPP*, 761), calling further attention to the material gains of his work, which he had never tried to deny.

By 1937, when Frost delivered "Poverty and Poetry" as a talk at Haverford College, more than twenty years had passed since he had brought his Derry years to market, and in that time he had become a public icon. Did the acclaim of an adoring public help to offset the qualms he felt at turning others' suffering into his own success? Did his personal losses in the intervening years tend to balance or atone for the moral debts he felt as a poet? Whatever the many ironies in his 1937 statement, and whatever of accusation it contains, Frost's claim that he needs "the poor" in his "business" also defends his choices as poet. The mixture of self-accusation and self-defense have settled into a mutual embrace, like the "restful . . . decision" at the close of "New Hampshire," which allows the speaker to admire that mythically noncommercial world across the state line from his comfort and prosperity in Vermont.

Similarly, Frost offsets his acknowledged distance and difference from "the poor" by claiming, nonetheless, that they are "my people" — "the people I belong to" (*CPPP*, 759). So too, whatever Frost may have made from the poor as an artist, setting him apart from them, his work has also brought their humanity home to his readers, helping to bridge a social divide it could not close — a divide that Frost knew from both sides, thanks on the one hand to his experience as a working man born of working people and, on the other, to his education and inheritance, and later to his success both as a poet and a public figure.

Frost, Robert Burns, and Their People

Tellingly, the very question of what a poet gives and takes from his poetic subjects surfaces in a letter that Frost wrote during the last stage of his work on *North of Boston*, and it does so in a way that acknowledges the reciprocity of this complex exchange. The particular remark comes toward the end of a letter to Sidney Cox, a high-school teacher who befriended Frost during his year in Plymouth, New Hampshire, his final year before sailing for England in September 1912. Here, rather than regretting or defending what a poet may owe his human subjects, Frost raises the issue as a wondering speculation abruptly thrust into his summary of recent events. Considering that Frost wrote the letter in September 1913, after a summer in which he cultivated friendships with English writers, solicited their responses to his poems and poetic theories, and was hard at work on *North of Boston*'s final contents and design, it may seem odd that the relevant passage does not mention the book directly and is itself somewhat disjointed. Yet, when the unstated connections are understood, its coherence emerges, and there is no mistaking Frost's preoccupations or their relation to his work-in-progress.

"We are just back from a two week's journey in Scotland," Frost writes Cox from Beaconsfield:

> The best of the adventure was the time in Kingsbarns where tourists and summer boarders never come. The common people in the south of England I don't like to have around me. They don't know how to meet you man to man. The people in the north are more like

> Americans. I wonder whether they made Burns' poems or Burns' poems made them. And there are stone walls (dry stone dykes)[17] in the north: I liked those. My mother was from Edinburgh. I used to hear her speak of the Castle and Arthur's seat, more when I was young than in later years. I had some interest in seeing those places. (*SL*, 94–95)

It was toward the end of this trip north that Frost had met J. C. Smith, the British Shakespearean scholar with whom he had immediately arranged a day of conversation and walking in the local hills and among the stone walls that had taken him back to Derry and the years of spring wall-repair with his neighbor Napoleon Gay. On arriving back in Beaconsfield, Frost sent Smith a copy of *A Boy's Will*, and within days of Smith's September 15 letter reporting his family's pleasure in the book, Frost sent the promised poems planned for *North of Boston*, which now included a new one, "Mending Wall," previously unmentioned in any list of the book's possible contents. In his letter of November 24, Smith not only confirms the late composition of "Mending Wall,"[18] but, as we have seen, recognizes other poems that Frost had described to him, making clear that the new book had been a major topic of their conversation in August.

When we learn how fully Frost had discussed *North of Boston* with Smith, we can recognize it as an unspoken part of his reflections to Cox upon his return from Scotland. It seems clear, for example, that the Americans by which Frost measures these north-Britons are those in his forthcoming book — another "common people" who "know how to meet you man to man" and have left their own mark in stone across a northern landscape. But when we see that the book is connected to everything else Frost mentions about that day in Kingsbarns, we can also see that his question about Burns — "whether they [the local people] made Burns' poems or Burns' poems made them" — raises other questions both immediate and far-reaching at this moment in Frost's career. As another poet of democratic and vernacular impulse whom Belle Frost had read to her son from his earliest childhood, the Scottish Burns was part of Frost's primal poetic consciousness, enriching the legacy of his own Scots blood. Even more germane to the Frost about to publish *North of Boston* is the Robert Burns whose 1786 *Poems, Chiefly in the Scottish Dialect* had

[17] Douglas Wilson, reasoning that Frost, having "taken note of the Scottish form 'dykes,' . . . would likely have used 'stane' as well" (72), examined Frost's holograph letter at Dartmouth College Library and concluded that Frost's parenthetical insertion was, in fact, "dry stane dykes," not "dry stone dykes." I too have examined the original letter, and while Frost's handwriting is not wholly clear at that point, I confirm Wilson's reading.

[18] Smith writes, "Of course I recognized 'Mending Wall' at once as the poem . . . suggested by our walk at Kingsbarns." (Wilson, 73).

not only asserted the worth of a rural people and their language to his nation's literary elite, but had established the reputation of their poet-champion — precisely what Frost was counting on *North of Boston* to do for him.

As Frost recalls that day with Smith in his letter to Cox, with the Scottish hills and people stirring thoughts of New England, of his Scottish mother, and of her literary legacy,[19] and with all these elements touching his forthcoming "book of people," Frost merges Burns's people with his own and himself with Burns, asking of Burns the question at the heart of his own ambitions. With Frost's hopes for the forthcoming book so entwined with feelings of gratitude and obligation toward his former Derry neighbors, his question about the mutual act of "making" between Burns's poems and his culture is one that Frost ponders for himself. Would those farming neighbors whose stories and speech, whose endurance and self-reliance, had helped to "make" his poems now "make" him as a poet, announcing him to the literary elite of Boston and New York, just as Burns's book of rural people had taken him to literary Edinburgh? And if they did, what would Frost's poems do for those to whom they owed so much? Could Frost's book, like Burns's book, make "his people" live for readers who would not otherwise know them, gaining them a respect and recognition they could never win for themselves, preserving a part of their vanishing culture, perhaps even giving them a glimpse of their own human substance?

Jewels and Thieves: "Blueberries," Gossip, and the Poet

Frost's sense of entangled rights and wrongs in his poetic use of former friends and neighbors and the persistence of such unsettling questions for the *North of Boston* poet emerge again in "Blueberries," where the narrator subtly defends his right to gather the same wild berries with which his poorer neighbor Loren feeds his hungry children, much as Frost had chosen to live, and then to write about, a rural life that most of his poetic subjects lived by necessity. The narrator understands and accepts a certain coolness from Loren, who sees him "as having no right / To pick where they're picking." As he tells his story and answers questions posed by an unnamed townsman, the narrator seems to enjoy, even to admire, the polite evasions by which Loren protects his berrying places, and he ends by describing the berries he finds, glistening with raindrops, as "a vision for thieves" — presumably thieves like him.

[19] We should keep in mind that Frost also owed New England to his mother, who insisted on returning there from California upon the early death of her husband, when Rob was eleven years old.

Like the narrator's verbal sparring with the old farmer in "The Mountain," this encounter offers an indirect defense of the poet's work in the narrator's treasuring of an experience that raises life above mere survival. About Loren's viewing him and his children as intruders, the narrator says:

> But we won't complain.
> You ought to have seen how it looked in the rain,
> The fruit mixed with water in layers of leaves,
> Like two kinds of jewels, a vision for thieves.

Some conflicts, Frost implies, just can't be helped. And even as he defends Loren's assertion of his native rights, the narrator's montage of raindrops and berries among the blueberry leaves argues for his more poetic intrusion. Appropriately, the poet's argument is implicit, resting on the narrator's descriptive extravagance. Though nominally a thief, rather than taking, he has added to what he has found by valuing the water and leaves as well as the berries. His aesthetic view, layered with the practical — his composite "vision" of fruit, water, and leaves — creates "two kinds of jewels," two kinds of value, while Loren, his vision narrowed by a different need, is credited with only one. As part of the same poetic extravagance, the narrator's final image, which assigns him the role of thief, overstates Loren's claim in a way that undercuts it. Does picking of berries for pleasure rather than survival really make one a thief? His leveling so bald a charge invites us to temper it and leaves us feeling that, just as there is a beauty as well as food to be found among the leaves, and just as there are reasons to climb a mountain besides finding a stray cow, so there is another way of seeing the issue of rights and trespass. So, while this passage recognizes the Lorens of the world, who look to the berries as sustenance and income, this "thieving" narrator conveys the poet's conviction that there is something beyond basic survival worth reaching for — an extravagance that must sometimes be stolen from necessity.

The design of Frost's argument for poetry reaches even to the verse form of "Blueberries." Its couplets are composed in anapestic tetrameter, which produces a rolling emphatic gait that has made it a frequent choice for comic use, most notably in Clement Moore's "Visit from Saint Nicholas," which, published in 1823, may have become the most often recited American poem through the nineteenth and twentieth centuries.[20] The established use of anapests for light verse naturally raises the question of why Frost chose the form for "Blueberries," especially when *North of*

---

[20] Other well-known examples are Lewis Carroll's "Hunting of the Snark" and Dr. Seuss's "Cat in the Hat." Lord Byron's "Destruction of Sennacherib" is not comic, but its anapestic couplets gallop with the horses in the poem.

Boston is almost wholly in blank verse.[21] The answer is not far to seek — or quite simple. In addition to varying the music of his book, the jauntiness of the lines fits the poem's dramatic situation, in which the narrator shares with a fellow gossip his amusement at Loren's evasions. In light of his elective berry-picking, however, we see that, while setting "Blueberries" apart from the rest of the book, the verse form also connects it by supporting the poetic license that has been questioned and defended in other poems. Just as, in "The Mountain" and "A Servant to Servants," stand-ins for the poet explore the terrain or study ferns (light as "feathers") simply because it pleases them to do so, so this narrator asserts his right to nature's jewels on the ground not of need, but desire. And long before the end of the poem, where he ironically owns his "thievery," he has done so through his playful anapests. In making light of his conflict with Loren by formal means, the narrator defends his right to enjoy himself where others struggle to survive, and even to make one's work a kind of play. In the poem's final line, by claiming yet undercutting the label of thief, the narrator brings his defense to a sharper point, but through the subtler effects of poetic convention and tone, his anapests have urged it from the start. We also see here, as throughout *North of Boston*, that what he defends against, however resisted, insists on being heard.

In fact, while the framing narrative of "Blueberries" creates a reason for the lightness of its verse, it also raises the ethical questions that troubled Frost about making a negotiable commodity of his Derry experience. Richard Wakefield has observed that, in Frost's poem, the narrator who talks about Loren with another neighbor "feeds the village gossip mill" and, in doing so, creates yet "another kind of value for the berries," one "very close to the value of making a poem out of them."[22] In fact, Frost's own comment on the genesis of these poems points to the parallel. In recounting his Derry experience for the Boston critic William Braithwaite in 1915, Frost cites his enjoyment of local gossip as the key to recognizing that he was interested "in neighbors for more than merely their tones of speech. . . . I like the actuality of gossip, the intimacy of it," he explains. "Say what you will[,] effects of actuality and intimacy are the greatest aim an artist can have" (*SL*, 159). As Frost found the local gossip a source for both the vernacular tones and the "character strokes" (83) at the heart of his book, it becomes, almost like the blueberries, something the poet "picks up by chance and *steals* . . . to new uses" (emphasis

---

[21] The book's prologue and epilogue, "The Pasture" and "Good Hours," are in tetrameter quatrains, but of its sixteen principal poems, all but "Blueberries" and "After Apple-Picking" are in blank verse, and the latter, with its loose iambics and rhymes at irregular intervals, produces an effect like that of blank verse.

[22] Wakefield offered this observation in comments on an earlier draft of this chapter (July 23, 2006).

added), as Frost said of another piece of local currency transported into *North of Boston* (Burnshaw, 164).[23]

Like poetry itself, gossip not only puts experience into language, but connects the participants in an exchange of concerns and judgments, becoming a mirror or even a crucible of community values. Since trading in gossip uses another's experience to promote one's own social standing, often at the other's expense, gossip invites and often deserves the charge of self-interest. If we connect such aspersions to the actualities and intimacies we find throughout the *North of Boston* poems, we see precisely what troubled Frost about using the lives of his Derry neighbors to establish himself as a poet. And trouble him it did. Frost's remarks about his appetite for gossip in his March 1915 letter to Braithwaite contain elements of boast, confession, and apology, including this elaborate, elusive disclaimer: "I justified myself by the example of Napoleon as recently I have had to justify myself in seasickness by the example of Nelson" (*SL*, 159). Like any justification, Frost's implies a charge that asks to be answered. Yet by comparing his poetic intrusion into others' lives to seasickness — first his own, then Nelson's, further dwarfing this foible by the admiral's heroic achievements — and also by claiming some unexplained parallel to Napoleon, Frost jokingly yet doubly defends himself to Braithwaite. Hailed the month before by a laudatory review in the *New Republic* upon his February landfall in New York (after a dangerous Atlantic crossing)[24] and finding himself courted by publishing notables soon after, Frost, in fact, writes to Braithwaite much as a conquering literary hero whose right to these intimate materials is now beyond question — or whose artistic triumph at least overrides such concerns. Nonetheless, as his elaborate joking might lead us to expect and his later comments on his use of the poor make clear, questions about such appropriation would haunt Frost for decades. Nowhere, however, are they more alive than in *North of Boston* itself.

---

[23] The specific "new use" to which Frost was referring here is the "slow smokeless burning" in the final line of "The Wood-Pile." As Frost told Stanley Burnshaw, the phrase was inspired by a firearms advertisement in the *Literary Digest* boasting of an "Infallible Smokeless" gunpowder. Notably, the book is almost framed by such "thefts," for, as I point out in the introduction, the phrase "North of Boston" was originally a heading in the real estate section of *The Boston Globe*. Years later, in "The Figure a Poem Makes," written as a preface to *Collected Poems*, 1939, Frost poet says, "The artist must value himself as he snatches a thing from some previous order in time and space into a new order with not so much as a ligature clinging to it of the old place where it was organic" (*CPPP*, 778).

[24] When Frost sailed from Liverpool on February 13, 1915, his ship was escorted, with others, to the open sea by British destroyers. German submarines had already sunk a British merchant ship and, within three months, the "*Lusitania*, following the same route, was struck by German torpedoes and went down with the loss of more than a thousand lives" (Walsh, 216).

Voices from the Ground: "The Generations of Men"

Another of *North of Boston*'s less celebrated poems, "The Generations of Men," has the added distinction of a doubtful assessment by Frost himself when he first mentioned it in an August 1913 letter to John Bartlett. There listing the poems he was then considering for the new book, he also makes clear that having determined the book's general plan, he is now turning his attention to more particular questions of design, coherence, and audience appeal. Frost writes:

> You will gather from the Bookman article (which I sent yesterday) what my next book is to be like. . . . I may decide to call it New England Eclogues. Which do you think of the following list of titles you would prefer to read? The Death of the Hired Man, The Housekeeper (or Slack Ties), The Wrong, A Servant to Servants, The Code (of Farm Service), Swinging Birches, Blueberries, The Mountain, A Hundred Collars, The Cellar Hole, The Black Cottage. All are stories between one hundred and two hundred lines long. I have written one today that I may call The Lantern if Mrs. Frost doesn't dissuade me: she doesn't think it a fit. None of the lot is a love affair except the Cellar Hole and I am not sure that that isn't the least successful of all. (*SL*, 89)

While at this point in 1913, the book was taking shape, major decisions about content and design still lay ahead. Of the twelve poems Frost lists here, eleven would make his final selection. Still there is no hint of "Home Burial," possibly the greatest of Frost's dramatic narratives. Nor does he mention any of the book's three major lyrics — "Mending Wall," "After Apple-Picking," and "The Wood-Pile" — though his inclusion of "Swinging Birches" reveals that Frost had begun to write longer lyrics of a kind not found in *A Boy's Will.*

Frost's question to Bartlett — "Which do you think from the following list of titles you would prefer to read?" — also makes clear the care he took with titles themselves. Eight of the twelve already read as they would when published, but two of these are not quite settled. For "The Housekeeper" Frost poses an alternative title — ("or Slack Ties)"; to "The Code," he considers an addition — "(of Farm Service)." In the end, as he did with the book's title, Frost chose reticence over explicitness, leaving "The Code" and "The Housekeeper" richly unadorned. Of the remaining four titles, "The Wrong" became "The Self-Seeker," "Swinging Birches" would become "Birches" when published elsewhere,[25] and "The Lantern," newly drafted as Frost wrote to Bartlett, would be titled "The Fear."

---

25 "Birches" appeared in the *Atlantic Monthly* in 1915 and in "Mountain Interval" in 1916. While Frost dropped it from *North of Boston*, its inclusion among the dramatic narratives on the list of prospective contents suggests the new dimensions in Frost's lyric practice and in his view of the book's design. I discuss these changes in the following chapter, "*North of Boston's* Major Lyrics."

Among all these revisions, Frost's change of "The Cellar Hole" to "The Generations of Men" is atypical, as it moves away from a concrete factuality toward a breadth of reference verging even on vagueness. Frost does not explain his concern that the poem may be "the least successful of all," but it probably stems from an absence of the overt suffering or sharp conflicts, interpersonal and internal, that are central to the other *North of Boston* narratives. Yet, while "The Generations of Men" lacks such overt drama, it engages a cluster of issues critically important to Frost during his year of intense work on the book that he hoped would establish his name among contemporary poets, as in fact it did. Among these issues is the poet's freedom to play where others struggle to survive, reflected here by characters who, like him, have a merely provisional involvement in the world they explore, leaving them free to make what they will of what they find.

In "The Generations of Men" the characters are two distant cousins, a young man and woman, who have never before met and have returned to the site of their ancestral New England home as part of a family reunion. The reunion itself is part of Old Home Week, an institution introduced in New Hampshire around 1900 in order to encourage tourism and vacationing in areas where New England's rural population had declined, resulting in many abandoned farms. Frost opens the poem with these background facts, underlining, in effect, the drama of disappearance that exerts its force throughout the book:

> A governor it was proclaimed this time,
> When, all who would come seeking in New Hampshire
> Ancestral memories might come together.
> And those of the name Stark gathered in Bow,
> A rock-strewn town where farming has fallen off,
> And sprout lands flourish where the ax has gone.

Within this landscape of mowing fields returning to woods, the old Stark home is now an overgrown cellar hole, placing it among the abandoned dwellings, modern and ancient, that punctuate Frost's published volumes from *A Boy's Will* (1913) to *Steeple Bush* (1947).[26] Because of rain on the day the Stark clan had planned to visit the ancestral site, this young man and woman are the only two members to turn up. As they seat themselves on the old cellar wall, Frost evokes a strong sense of human absence. "The road," his narrator says,

> Bowed outward on the mountain halfway up,
> And disappeared and ended not far off.

---

[26] For an excellent discussion of abandoned houses in Frost, see MacArthur, *The American Landscape*. For a broader discussion of Frost and human remains, especially archeological ones, see Sanders, "Earth, Time, and England."

No one went home that way. The only house
Beyond where they were was a shattered seedpod.
And below roared a brook hidden in trees,
The sound of which was silence for the place.

As in many other poems in *North of Boston* and beyond, Frost makes a particular question into an archetypal one. When the young woman says, "What will we come to / With all this pride of ancestry, we Yankees?"[27] we focus, with her, on New England, and perhaps on its declining share of national prosperity and influence. But as she goes on — "Tell me why we're here / . . . . / What do we see in such a hole, I wonder" — Frost invites us to contemplate the literal ground to which all things return and the vastness of time that swallows all human generations along with their social distinctions, so that the woman questions not only our interest in family roots, but the very meaning of our lives on earth.

This evocation of mortality suggests why Frost might have changed the poem's title from "The Cellar Hole" to "The Generations of Men," reminding us not only of successive lives through the ages, but of the various forms that human beings generate in order to hold our ground against time and change. Such shades of mortality add to the drama slowly building around this young couple, giving their already flirtatious conversation a turn toward courtship and making the rain, which has already made their meeting private, into a catalyst for fertility. In a playful passage that seems headed toward a marriage proposal, the young man, obeying the oracle he claims to hear in the brook that runs through the old cellar, renames his cousin "Nausicaa," because he hopes that she too will prove "unafraid / of an acquaintance made adventurously." The oracle further tells him, he says, to "take a timber" from the old house,

And hew and shape it
For a door sill or other corner piece
In a new cottage on the ancient spot.
. . . .
And come and make your summer dwelling here,
And perhaps she will come, still unafraid,
And sit before you in the open door
With flowers in her lap until they fade.

[27] Frost's choice of the name Stark has particular relevance for Derry, the birthplace of of General John Stark, a Revolutionary War hero who commanded brigades at Bunker Hill, Ticonderoga, and Bennington, and whose often-quoted exhortation, "Live free or die!" later became the New Hampshire state motto. In 1897, the Daughters of the American Revolution erected a tablet marking the birthplace of John Stark on Stark Road in Derry. When Stark was eight, the family moved near to Amoskeag Falls, a few miles away on the Merrimack River. Bow, where this poem is set, is fifteen miles further north on the Merrimack (*From Turnpike to Interstate*, 119–20).

While admitting the uncertainty of all things natural, the oracle's "perhaps" reflects the young man's diffidence and tact. The woman's response is not to be forced; the two have barely met. But she does seem somewhat charmed by this flirtation and, as she agrees to meet again next day, the poem remains hopeful. "The only love affair" among the *North of Boston* poems (*SL*, 89), "The Generations of Men" may well be the only openly hopeful poem in the volume. Frost had a soft spot for young love. Yet even as it proposes new life from a ruin, that Keatsian vision of the woman, the fading flowers in her lap symbolizing her own fleeting powers of generation, inject a note of *carpe diem* urgency.

Like the poet himself, the two young cousins dwell upon but do not dwell in the rural world they contemplate here. Just as Frost in his Derry years did not depend on his farming for survival but could indulge his appetite for exploration, be guided by his imaginative and aesthetic impulses, so the cousins play at imagining the characters from whom they have sprung — forebears who knew little of the leisure and security their modern descendents now enjoy:

> "I can make out old Grandsir Stark distinctly, —
> With his pipe in his mouth and his brown jug —
> Bless you, it isn't Grandsir Stark, it's Granny,
> But the pipe's there and smoking and the jug.
> She's after cider, the old girl, she's thirsty;
> . . . .
>
> "Tell me about her. Does she look like me?"
>
> "She should, shouldn't she, you're so many times
> Over descended from her. I believe
> She does look like you. Stay the way you are.
> The nose is just the same, and so's the chin —
> Making allowance, making due allowance."
>
> "You poor, dear, great, great, great, great Granny!"

The young man's teasing narrative provides a way to let his cousin know that he likes looking at her, and he invites her involvement in the story as he hopes to do in his life. In accord with romantic conventions, he also takes the opportunity to display his worth as a suitor by showing his intellectual and verbal mettle. And so, in answer to his cousin's question, "What do we see in such a hole?" he shares a bit of arcane lore by bringing up the

> myth of Chicamoztoc,
> Which means The Seven Caves that We Came out of.
> This is the pit from which the Starks were digged.

In her reply — "You must be learned. That's what you see in it?" — she seems as puzzled as she is impressed by the association, but, by taking us back to Frost's own interest in Aztec history,[28] this dramatically contrived moment invites us to notice other ways that the poem's young protagonist alludes to Frost's concerns as the *North of Boston* poet.

To appreciate these connections, we should be aware that, for Frost as poet, the importance of play goes far beyond the relative leisure that set him or these two young protagonists apart from the harder-working characters he portrayed in *North of Boston*. In poems written throughout his career, play becomes a figure for poetry itself. In "Swinging Birches," for example, written largely in England around the same time as "The Cellar Hole," the boy's climbing "toward heaven," then being lowered to earth — a metaphoric swinging between elevation and gravity, escape and return — dramatizes poetry's dual commitment to invention and fact. So too, in "Directive," the "make-believe" of the children's playhouse becomes the symbolic source of mutually redemptive play between poet and reader.[29] In "Two Tramps in Mud Time," Frost, refusing to separate vocation from avocation, calls his poetic work "play for mortal stakes."

As wooer and suitor, Frost's male protagonist here is also playing for mortal stakes, but besides this parallel to the poet, "The Generations of Men" uses the young man's play to allude specifically to the principles of poetic prosody that Frost strove to realize in *North of Boston* and repeatedly to articulate in 1913 and 1914, both in conversation with English writers Frank Flint and T. E. Hulme and in letters to John Bartlett and Sidney Cox back home. In all of these efforts, Frost tried to identify poetry's root sources. Insisting that the strength of all good writing, including verse, lay in the vocal patterns of ordinary speech, he strove not only, like Wordsworth, to expunge all false refinements, all "bookish language" (*CPPP*, 694) from his poetic diction but also to capture the cadences he heard in the speech of his farming neighbors. When, for *North of Boston*, Frost explicitly avoided the singing harmonies of Tennyson and Swinburne that had remained part of *A Boy's Will*, he was rejecting an aestheticism largely English and upper-class in favor of one American, rural, and vernacular, placing a cultivation of the soil at least on a par with the cultivation of the drawing room.

---

[28] Frost's very first published poem, "La Noche Triste," described the perilous retreat of the Spaniards from the Aztec capital of Tenochtitlan after the death of Montezuma. Inspired by Frost's reading of William Hickling Prescott's *History of the Conquest of Mexico* in the summer of 1889, the poem appeared in the Lawrence High School *Bulletin* the following April.

[29] For discussion of this idea, see Sanders, "Revelation as Child's Play in Frost's 'Directive.'"

For Frost the key to bringing poetic language so literally down to earth lay in capturing the tones that convey the feelings behind our words, the inflections that often shape the meaning of the words themselves. Writing to Bartlett in February 1914, shortly after *North of Boston* went to press, he announced his "new definition of a sentence" as "a sound in itself on which other sounds called words may be strung." Frost saw these "sentence sounds" as "very definite entities" and believed that "no writer invents them" but "only catches them fresh from talk" (*SL*, 110–11). Writing to Walter Prichard Eaton the following year, Frost extends the idea, insisting that these "sentence sounds" underlie and determine our communicative natures. "No one makes them or adds to them," Frost says. "They are always there — living in the cave of the mouth. They are real cave things: they were before words were" (*SL*, 191).[30]

As the conspicuous image of the cave suggests, "Generations of Men," composed in 1913, anticipates and reflects many of the ideas about poetry that surface in Frost's correspondence of the same period. Just as, in Frost's later masterpiece, "Directive," the spring of the "house no more a house," providing a draft of impermanence, becomes the poet's elixir of inspiration, so, in "The Generations of Men," the young man finds inspiration for his love song (rendered in Frost's blank verse) in the "voice" of the brook running through the old cellar hole, the very ground of his ancestry. So, too, did Frost find the true ground for his poetic voice in the speech of his ancestral New England, from which he'd been temporarily cut off by his father's migration west and his own early years in San Francisco. Just as Frost's young protagonist is guided in his profession of love by forces and sounds more primitive — by the inarticulate "voices" of this "pit from which we Starks were digged," which he then connects to the caves of Aztec myth — so Frost himself means to secure a poetic future by bringing "to book" (*SL*, 159) these traditional New England voices with their "cave things" intact. The poet and his protagonist woo different audiences, but both find inspiration for their songs in the persistent voices of their New England past.

The brook that speaks from this figurative New England cave yields still another, perhaps more surprising, allusion that reflects the poet during his intense year of work on *North of Boston*. In a way that accords with Frost's marginal position as poet in a world of farming neighbors, and, even more, with his uneasiness about using their lives to further his poetic aims, "The Generations of Men" alludes to "the astonishing magnitude of . . . ambition" (*SL*, 20) that he had confided to Susan Hayes Ward

[30] My thanks to Richard Wakefield for first suggesting the importance of the cave image here and for noting "how the two cousins are like Frost, visitors to the rural world but more than visitors by virtue of their attenuated but real kinship with those long-gone cabin dwellers" (email of July 19, 2010).

in 1894 and had quietly sustained through the following nineteen years. The key to this connection lies in the name "Nausicaa," which Frost's young protagonist is told to call his cousin by the oracle he imagines in the brook. In Homer's *Odyssey*, Nausicaa is the Phaeacian princess who first lays eyes on Odysseus when he returns to human society after his release by the goddess Calypso, and, like so many of Frost's allusions, this playful reference provides only a narrow entry into a large intertextual space — in this case one that Frost himself found compelling.

Not only did Frost later list *The Odyssey* first among the books he liked (*CPPP*, 738); his singling out of two Homeric metaphors in "Education by Poetry" makes clear his fascination with a particular episode of that poem. One of these figures is that of an inverted shield by which Homer describes the outline of Scheria, land of the Phaeacians, which, in Book V, Odysseus discerns on the horizon. For Odysseus, clinging to the last bits of his raft destroyed by a vengeful Poseidon, the island is landfall, life, and all that it entails. The other Homeric image that Frost cites comes from the end of the same book, when the exhausted hero crawls under the fallen leaves of an ancient olive tree to survive the chill of the night, much as one covers with ash the "seeds of fire" to be fanned to flame the next day. "Seeds of fire," Frost repeats in his essay. "So Odysseus covered the seeds of fire in himself. You get the greatness of his nature" (*CPPP*, 724) — and also the extremity of his situation.

To understand what drew Frost to this particular part of Homer's epic, we must understand what reaching Scheria meant for Odysseus. Seven years earlier, he had been rescued by the goddess Calypso at a point near death, with all his companions lost. But, though Calypso adores him and grants him an eternity of youth, Odysseus weeps daily, looking out to sea. What he weeps for is not just his home and patrimony, his wife, son, and father, but a life of honor and renown among mortal peers and the struggle demanded by such a life. The classical scholar George Dimock connects Odysseus's repeated choices to the need to establish his name. As that name literally means "trouble" or "suffering," self-realization and recognition for Odysseus means embracing his full portion of trouble and trouble-making. On Ogygia, suffering the protection of Calypso, Odysseus was stripped of all his name stands for. Fittingly, the name Calypso literally means cover or concealment, so that hidden away on her island, his name obscured, he has exchanged his identity for nonentity, becoming the Noman he had called himself in the Cyclops's cave (Dimock, 411–12).

For Frost, the crucial connection to Odysseus is the momentous change represented by his return from nonentity and obscurity to the pursuit of renown in the human world. The change is signaled by the gaze of the maiden princess Nausicaa, who rather than frightened by the naked and salt-encrusted man who emerges from the leaf-litter, looks upon him first with equanimity, then compassion, and soon with desire, thinking "if only a man like *that* were called my husband" (6:270). For Odysseus, Nausicaa's admiration foreshadows things to come. Soon he will be welcomed by her father, the king. When, at the king's feast, Odysseus hears the Phaeacian bard celebrate his exploits at Troy, he finds that part of the renown he longs for has already been achieved. Unable to hide his tears, Odysseus reveals his name and tells of the wandering after Troy that brought him to this place — at this point a story known to no other living soul. In this way Odysseus becomes the poet as well as the doer of his deeds, prompting the king to say, "Keep telling us your adventures. They are wonderful. / I could hold out here till dawn's first light / if only you could bear, here in our halls, / to tell the tale of all the pains you suffered" (11:424–27). Winning the sympathy of the Phaeacians is crucial for Odysseus, who is without ship or companions and needs their help to return home. But revealing himself in this protectorate of Poseidon, Odysseus's sworn enemy, also involves considerable risk.

Much connects Odysseus in this crucial episode of Homer's poem with Frost in England in 1913, a year of intense work on *North of Boston.* Frost spent the year completing poems begun earlier and writing new ones, taking pains over the contents and design of the book, even educating literary friends in his sound-of-sense principles, creating knowledgeable reviewers for his forthcoming book. It was a year of determined effort to establish his name with an English audience that could, in turn, convey it back to America, as in fact it did. We know the risks he took in crossing an ocean in order to establish that name. In fact, the wish to "stand on [his] own legs as a poet and nothing else" (*SL*, 98) was a choice to keep risk at the center of life, and throughout his career Frost would repeatedly define poetry in heroic terms. No sooner did he return to America from England in 1915, than he would describe his years on the Derry farm as a temporary retreat "to save . . . and fix myself before I measured my strength against all creation" (*SL*, 158). Later he would speak of poetry as "prowess and feats of association" (Lathem, *Interviews*, 235); as "a figure of the will braving alien entanglements" (*CPPP*, 786); as "a way of taking life by the throat" (Pritchard, *Frost*, 58) or of pushing back against a nature that is always more or less cruel; and significantly as the task of "lodg[ing] a few poems where they will be hard to get rid of" (*CPPP*, 744). In "The Trial by Existence" from *A Boy's Will*, published the year before "The Generations of Men" was written, Frost affirms the lesson to which Homer's heroes wake in the "fields of asphodel": "that the utmost reward / Of daring [is] still to dare."

Such images of poetry as an effort at self-preservation and an assertion of identity against a hostile or indifferent world help to explain the appeal of Odysseus to Frost, whose driving force is also to create a name that will outlive him. Two decades after *North of Boston* appeared, Frost called *The Odyssey* "the first in time and rank of all romances" (*CPPP*, 738). Regarding its role in "The Generations of Men," we see expanding circles of relevance. The first circle is the poem's unfolding love story. The poem's young suitor — guided, he claims, by the brook's oracular voices and by his own faith in the power of words — renames his cousin Nausicaa not simply to flatter her but as an invocation, as if the name might inspire in her what Homer's lovely princess felt for the fugitive hero. In the wider context of *North of Boston*, the name of Nausicaa draws a larger circle that includes Odysseus's return to human society and to the mortal life whose unforgiving terms are explored by almost every poem in Frost's book and underlined by this poem's plot of loss and renewal, its courtship dance in the shadow of an abandoned house whose original inhabitants have faded to nonentity.

The widest circle of relevance, however, merges Frost's own story with that of his carpe diem protagonist. The moment when Odysseus arrives on the island of Scheria, leaving behind the nonentity and obscurity of his life with Calypso to seek renown among his mortal peers, had a deep resonance for Frost. In 1894, after confessing the "magnitude of [his] ambition" (*SL*, 20) to Susan Hayes Ward, Frost had declined his grandfather's offer of one year's support, asserting that he might need twenty to make his name as a poet. In 1913, as he composed "The Generations of Men," the twenty years were almost up, Frost was nearly forty, and *A Boy's Will* had not made his name, as Frost may well have expected it would not, for it provided only glimpses of the poetic craft he had worked toward during his Derry years and was now testing in poem after poem. Indeed, during this year devoted to *North of Boston*, the vernacular artistry Frost had achieved was seen by only a few British literary men, and Frost was probably alone in imagining himself one who could "do something to the present state of literature in America" (*SL*, 88). Though, at this point, Frost dared make this boast only to his friend and former student, John Bartlett, it reminds us, as Frost reminds himself, that the recognition he sought went beyond good reviews in England, beyond appreciation by "the critical few who are supposed to know," even beyond the sale of "books in their thousands" (*SL*, 98) through a major American publisher. And so, though unmentioned but alluded to, Odysseus, with twenty years of war and wandering behind him, is a source of meaning both for "The Generations of Men" and its poet. Just as the hope of the poem's young suitor is embodied in the unexpected figure who opens Nausicaa's eyes to love, so Frost's own ambition as a poet finds a model in the same Odysseus who, having arrived from nowhere, is about to take possession of his full identity and celebrated name.

Intimate Stranger: "The Fear"

"The Fear" was one of the last of the dramatic poems added to *North of Boston*,[31] and it provides yet another set of characters whose positions and concerns reflect those of the poet who saw the book as his last chance at public recognition and economic gain. The most obvious connection to the poet is seen in the stranger whose part in the story closely follows Frost's own experience, but the parallels go well beyond the biographical facts. By being briefly mistaken for a participant in the poem's primary drama, the stranger occupies a marginal position parallel to that of the poet's position both inside and outside the rural world portrayed in *North of Boston*. That the stranger gains entry into another's personal life quite by accident even parallels the way that Frost's initial retreat to Derry unexpectedly involved him in its rural culture, ultimately providing the materials for his "book of people." At the same time, the poem's female protagonist, who sees the stranger as an intruder, almost a voyeur, reflects another element of the poet himself, for her accusatory words resonate with Frost's own concern about trespass and violation, making "The Fear," like "A Hundred Collars" or "The Black Cottage," another of poems in which important aspects of the poet are mirrored by more than one of its characters.

The incident that became the starting point for "The Fear" occurred during the summer of 1907, when, seeking relief from hay fever, Frost took his family for a six-week stay at the John Lynch farm in Bethlehem, New Hampshire. During a late-evening walk with his son Carol, then five, he noticed that a local woman seemed alarmed as she passed them in her carriage and, soon after, when the two went by her farm, even accused Frost of prowling. Inquiring later with Mrs. Lynch, Frost learned that the woman had left New Hampshire for Boston, where she had trained as a nurse and married. Later falling in love with one of her patients, she returned with him to New Hampshire, where she lived in fear of discovery and reprisal by her abandoned husband. As Frost's final choice of title suggests, the poem he created from this story focuses on the woman's anxiety, leaving the background facts uncertain and the story itself closer to what he might have surmised without the juicy gossip provided by Mrs. Lynch. In any event, since nothing in the text suggests otherwise, we naturally take Joel and the unnamed woman in the poem to be husband and wife, making the feared intruder seem more like a spurned suitor or lover

[31] It may even have been the last of the dramatic narratives to be composed. In an August 7 letter to Bartlett listing twelve of the book's longer poems, Frost, calling it "The Lantern," reports that he had written the poem that very day. "Home Burial," the only dramatic poem absent from the list, was, however, probably written later. Had it been in existence at the time, it seems unlikely that Frost would have failed to mentioned it.

than an abandoned husband, and making "The Fear" the sixth and last of the book's poems to focus on marital relationships.[32]

"The Fear" opens with the woman and Joel arriving home, putting their horse and buggy in the barn, and debating whether the wife really saw a man's face in the bushes at the roadside, briefly lit by the carriage lamp as they passed. Joel, eager to calm his wife's fears and probably his own as well, exasperates her by suggesting that she has only imagined someone there. And when, a few moments later, she hears someone kick a loose stone, he reasons that, even so, it could hardly be the man she fears. But she is adamant. "It is," she insists, "— or someone else he's sent to watch." Like the husband in "Home Burial," obtusely hurtful where he means to soothe, Joel presses on, saying, "It's nonsense to think he'd care enough," prompting a sharper retort: "You mean you couldn't understand his caring." When she adds, as if to soften her rebuke, "Oh, but you see he hadn't had enough," we hear a lurking sympathy or regret, helping us to imagine some guilt or remorse underlying her fear of confrontation.

The man at the roadside turns out to be real but almost laughably innocent, making clear how fully the woman's emotion has affected what she saw. The lantern, which she takes from the carriage dashboard and holds onto through most of the dialogue, aptly parallels what her fear does to her perception, suggesting why Frost originally chose "The Lantern" as the poem's title. Besides being dangerously hot, the small circle of light it casts around the woman is more blinding than revealing, exposing her, as Joel seems to understand, more than it penetrates the surrounding dark. Unable to see beyond its glare, the woman calls out:

> "What do you want?" she cried to all the dark.
> She stretched up tall to overlook the light
> That hung in both hands hot against her skirt.

When at first no answer comes, seeming to confirm Joel's doubt, she tries again:

> "What do you want?" she cried, and then herself
> Was startled when an answer really came.
>
> "Nothing." It came from well along the road.
>
> She reached a hand to Joel for support:
> The smell of scorching woolen made her faint.

[32] If we include "The Generations of Men," with its courtship plot, it is the seventh. In order of appearance, the seven poems are: "The Death of the Hired Man," "Home Burial," "The Black Cottage," "A Servant to Servants," "The Generations of Men," "The Housekeeper," and "The Fear."

"What are you doing round this house at night?"
"Nothing." A pause: there seemed no more to say.

And then the voice again: "You seem afraid.
I saw the way you whipped up the horse.
I'll just come forward in the lantern light
And let you see."
. . . .
She stood her ground against the noisy steps
That came on, but her body rocked a little.

"You see," the voice said.

"Oh." She looked and looked.

"You don't see — I've a child here by the hand.
A robber wouldn't have his family with him."

"What's a child doing at this time of night —!"

"Out walking. Every child should have the memory
Of at least one long-after-bedtime walk.
What, son?"

"Then I should think you'd try to find
Somewhere to walk —"

"The highway, as it happens —
We're stopping for the fortnight down at Dean's."

The woman's bewildered and confused response brings about an abrupt ending to the narrative that tells nothing more about the intruder himself:

"But if that's all — Joel — you realize —
You won't think anything. You understand?
You understand that we have to be careful.
This is a very, very lonely place.
Joel!" She spoke as if she couldn't turn.
The swinging lantern lengthened to the ground,
It touched, it struck, it clattered and went out.

Has the woman simply dropped the lantern? Or has she, as suggested by her earlier response to the scorched woolen of her skirt, fallen in a faint? Either way, she experiences a sudden weakness perhaps brought on by relief, embarrassment, or disorientation. But she has undergone a loss of control at an even more basic level.

It began when the innocent stranger came forward into the circle of lantern light, suddenly challenging the reality created by her fear. No longer needing to convince Joel of another man's presence, she finds herself dismayed by what she has revealed in doing so. Judging by the repeated denials in her final speech, she seems to feel that, in validating her fear, she has said too much. In effect, this latter fear replaces the first, but she has felt both all along. Earlier, when she heard the man approach, she seemed more afraid of what Joel might hear than what the other man might do. Insisting on holding the lantern herself and preparing to face him, she had said:

> "You're not to come. . . . This is my business.
> If the time's come to face it, I'm the one
> To put it the right way. . . .
> . . . .
> Joel, *go* in — please.
> Hark! — I don't hear him now. But please go in."

She could, of course, have been concerned for the safety of one or both men, but by the end of the poem, with the immediate threat of confrontation gone, her greater concern lies with saving face, which includes controlling what Joel thinks: "You won't think anything. You understand?" Clearly, what's been left unresolved in her life has worked its way inward, leaving her compromised and vulnerable on two fronts. Unfreed from her past, she cannot live fully in the present.

Though "The Fear" has attracted little attention from literary critics and remains barely known to many Frost enthusiasts, Frost listed it in 1917 among his "stand-bys" for public readings (Barry, 75).[33] The danger, suspense, and sexual tension skillfully developed through the dialogue would explain its appeal to listening audiences. But beyond these "thriller" elements, and true to its title, "The Fear" rewards us not by answering our inevitable questions about the woman's past, but by dramatizing her feelings in the present, putting this poem among a handful of others in this and his next two volumes that focus on emotional pain in women: in this book, "Home Burial," "A Servant to Servants," and, to a lesser degree, "The Death of the Hired Man" and "The Housekeeper"; in *Mountain Interval* (1916), "The Hill Wife"; and in *New Hampshire* (1923), "Two Witches: The Witch of Coos" and "The Pauper Witch of Grafton." But in traversing this emotional ground, "The Fear" also joins the many *North of Boston* poems that reflect on the poet who, while set apart from his poetic subjects, appropriates for his own use the intimate substance of their lives.

---

[33] Frost makes this statement in a letter written July 11, 1917, to Lewis N. Chase. The letter resides at the Library of Congress and has been published only by Barry (173).

Like the botanist-auditor in "A Servant to Servants," like the exploring narrator in "The Mountain," like the playful young pair in "The Generations of Men," and like Frost himself in his Derry years, the stranger in "The Fear" is present by choice in a world that others inhabit by necessity, enjoying greater freedom and leisure than those who struggle to survive. In *North of Boston* Frost typically treats these inequities lightly, joking about theft in a way that alludes to the poet's work, but these ironies should not mislead us. Where the poet has qualms about such appropriation, he must, in fact, find ways to control them if he is to pursue the "actuality and intimacy" that Frost claimed as his right and called the artist's "greatest aim" (*SL*, 159). Ten years after *North of Boston*, Frost would say to Louis Untermeyer: "At bottom the world isn't a joke. We only joke about it . . . to let someone know that we know he's there with his questions" (*SL*, 300). In *North of Boston*, the questions of trespass or violation, whether voiced by the poems' narrators or characters, are Frost's own. His empathy for the people of his book drives the poems, but the poems he makes also serve his own ends, and his empathy makes his poetic use of their lives feel like a betrayal.

At first glance, however, "The Fear" does not make even the joking references to theft or betrayal that we have seen, for example, in "Blueberries" or "A Hundred Collars" and that we will see in "Mending Wall" and "The Wood-Pile." Yet the visiting stranger, who is modeled on the biographical Frost and exemplifies the poet's leisurely sort of exploration, is cast as a trespasser by the poem's protagonist. In fact, where the "The Mountain" and "Blueberries" cast aspersions on their narrators' poetic freedom only gently and obliquely, the woman in "The Fear" accuses the passing stranger quite directly. When he explains that he's just out for an evening walk, she says, "Then I should think you'd try to find / Somewhere to walk —," prompting his interruption — "The highway, as it happens." Though the stranger is quick to fend off her insinuation of trespass, the pleasant outing he has enjoyed with his child has become an ordeal for the woman and Joel, producing yet another analogue to the inequity between the poet and his rural subjects represented throughout the book. Such inequity was nothing Frost intended or desired, but given his artistic aims, his choice of subject, and his self-awareness, it was one he could neither avoid nor ignore.

In "The Fear," then, the stranger briefly mistaken for a participant in the poem's primary drama not only draws upon Frost's actual experience in the summer of 1907, but leads us back to the poet who in 1913 made a poem from the encounter. As the creator of his "book of people," Frost needed both access to the materials of his art and the poetic craft to bring them "to book" (*SL*, 159) — both an empathic involvement with his poetic subjects and an artistic distance from them. The man in "The Fear" who is seen at different moments as both intimate and stranger mirrors this joining of involvement and distance, paralleling the poet's ambiguous position both inside and outside the community from which he crafts his poems — a community to which he was deeply connected but not ultimately bound.

The stranger, moreover, is not the only character in "The Fear" to reflect Frost's concern with his role as poet. An important part of it is written into the woman. Twice she complains about the stranger's presence — "What are you doing round this house at night?" and "I should think you'd try to find / Somewhere to walk" — and these direct accusations remind us of the more ironic references to trespass and appropriation obliquely aimed at the poet in so many other poems. As in the real-life incident behind the poem, the stranger frightens the woman into an unintended exposure of her inner life, though not really to him. Only partly aware of what he has set in motion, he protests, in an effort to reassure, that "a *robber* wouldn't have his family with him" (emphasis added). Not that his innocence matters to the woman. However unaware, he has stolen into an intimate space, prompting an ordeal in which he does not share, and the woman's feeling that he does not belong there aptly complements the poet's concern about trespass.

As natural as the woman's objection may seem, it might seem surprising that the poet would share it. Admittedly, no poet such as Frost, with the professed aim of capturing intimacy and immediacy, can afford to give way to such qualms about intrusion, and in "The Fear" the woman's complaint is correspondingly cut short. But it is heard. Similarly, for the *North of Boston* poet, a concern about lives appropriated and boundaries breached, though buffered with jokes and other ironies, was not to be escaped. Along with corollary questions of violation and respect, this concern pursues Frost throughout the book, revealing itself frequently but obliquely, entering with its opening poem, "Mending Wall," in which a reticent New England farmer guards his privacy against his talkative neighbor, and staying through its last, "The Wood-Pile," where even in a frozen swamp a solitary walker feels accused of thieving intentions by a native of the place.

6: *North of Boston*'s Major Lyrics

When we consider the design and coherence of Frost's volume, we should almost be surprised if his uneasiness about the people of his book did not find expression in the first and last of its principal poems, as, in fact, it does. Both "Mending Wall" and "The Wood-Pile" — two of the three major lyrics that punctuate this volume — make overt though ostensibly joking references to theft. And though these accusations are buffered by elements of satire, hyperbole, and humor, they nonetheless convey a discomfort in the speakers of these poems that parallels the poet's own feelings of debt for the poetic materials he had made his own.

The Lyric Constellation

To appreciate the ways that such accusatory references reflect Frost's relation to his poetic subjects, we should recognize the role that the three major lyrics — "Mending Wall," "After Apple-Picking," and "The Wood-Pile" — play among the twelve dramatic narratives that portray Frost's vanishing New England. By focusing on a classic seasonal activity of rural New England life, even naming or alluding to it in its title, each of these lyric poems commemorates a signature task of this vanishing culture. Equally important, by placing these lyrics at the beginning, middle and end of the book's elegiac arc, Frost arranges them to measure, in their progression from spring to winter, the movement toward disappearance witnessed by the book as a whole.

To appreciate this feature of Frost's design, it is worth looking at the total arrangement of poems in the volume, including the distinction between the three major lyrics, all in blank verse or something very like it,[1] and the two short lyrics in tetrameter quatrains, "The Pasture" and "Good Hours," which serve as prologue and epilogue. These shorter lyrics were not listed in the book's table of contents and were further distinguished from the principal poems by being set in italics, as they are in the list below. I have also put the major lyrics in bold print to emphasize their strategic placement. All told, the poems of the volume were arranged as follows:

[1] I have briefly described the unusual verse-form of "After Apple-Picking" in note 2 of the introduction. One can see examples of it where I discuss the poem later in this chapter.

The Pasture
Mending Wall
The Death of the Hired Man
The Mountain
A Hundred Collars
The Black Cottage
Blueberries
A Servant to Servants
After Apple-Picking
The Code
The Generations of Men
The Housekeeper
The Fear
The Self-Seeker
The Wood-Pile
Good Hours

Among the first to comment on the lyrics as a group was Lawrance Thompson, who noted that as late as August 1913 Frost did not include them in his list of the book's prospective contents. Yet, "when the manuscript . . . was finally completed," Thompson writes, "the "five . . . lyrics were distributed symmetrically: two at the beginning ('The Pasture' and 'Mending Wall'), one in the middle of the volume ('After Apple-picking') [*sic*] and two at the end ('The Wood-Pile' and 'Good Hours')" (*Early Years*, 433). Matthew Parfitt says more about Frost's arrangement of these poems, distinguishing "The Pasture" and "Good Hours" from the longer lyrics, but does not include "After Apple-Picking" in the design:

> In the separate editions of *North of Boston*, "The Pasture" and "Good Hours" stood in italics outside the volume proper, one at either end. The table of contents does not include them, so they function as invitation and salutation, or perhaps front and back door, and give the whole volume a sense of an inside and an outside. "Mending Wall" and "The Woodpile" [*sic*] are thus the first and last poems in the book, and being like the exterior pair comparable in form and theme, they compose a second frame *inside* the volume proper. (58)

Parfitt ascribes an important thematic dimension to this structure, pointing out that when "The Pasture" and "Good Hours," are joined with "Mending Wall" and "The Wood-Pile" in "matching poem pairs," they not only frame a "volume of long dramatic poems" but "draw attention . . . to the importance of husbanding resources (both physical and psychological) against the wilderness," making them a "sketch of the [Virgilian] georgic theme in the volume as a whole" (58). Though Parfitt aptly places "After Apple-Picking" at the thematic "center of *North of*

Boston," citing its emphasis on the tenuousness of all human order, he does not connect it to the other lyrics in any schematic way.[2]

When seen in sequence with "Mending Wall" and "The Wood-Pile," however, "After Apple-Picking" forms a "constellation of intention"[3] that is felt throughout the book. Even as the first and last lyrics provide a containing envelope for the book, the triad of major lyrics creates an imbedded, internal framework that reflects the book's meta-narrative in a systematic and detailed way. Strategically placed among the twelve longer poems and celebrating three emblematic seasonal tasks, these three lyric meditations retrace the annual cycle, symbolically outlining the book's drama of disappearance — the story of traditional farming culture in retreat before both natural forces and a growing capital economy.

Set at "spring mending-time," "Mending Wall" opens the book upon a tradition of wall-building actively maintained even by the speaker who questions the wall, its on-going life underlined by his present-tense narration: "And on a day we meet to walk the line / And set the wall between us once again. / We keep the wall between us as we go." Autumnal in the middle of the collection, "After Apple-Picking" moves the season's work into the past tense, though barely so. Some fruit still hangs unpicked, the implements of harvest are still in place, the speaker's "instep arch" still feels the "pressure of a ladder-round," and the harvest, though formally ended, remains incomplete for this orchardist who will dream of apples, inwardly reaching for more even as he moves toward a sleep that hints at greater finalities. Finally, "The Wood-Pile" closes *North of Boston* with a barren winter landscape. Where the speaker of "Mending Wall" shares annual work with a neighbor and that of "After Apple-Picking" is still amidst the evidence of his labor, the narrator of "The Wood-Pile," alone and disoriented, struggles to connect with place or fellow creature. In the one sign of human presence that he finds, the abandoned cord of maple, the woodcutter's work is long enough past to be largely undone by time. "Cut and split / And piled — and measured," it speaks for the handiwork that once tamed a wilderness, but its distance from the speaker's present life is clear in its abandonment. Half sunken in the frozen swamp, left to rot "far from a . . . fireplace," it is no longer on anyone's road. Seen only by one willing to venture "far from home" and risk feeling lost, it is

---

[2] William Pritchard offers insightful comments about Frost's artful variation of genres and tonalities in the book, though he suggests nothing schematic about the arrangement (*Frost*, 91–92).

[3] I take this phrase from Sidney Cox's *Swinger of Birches* (78) by way of Reuben Brower's landmark study, *The Poetry of Robert Frost: Constellations of Intention* (1963). The idea originates in Frost's description in "The Prerequisites" of the way "poems hold each other apart in their places as the stars do" *CPPP*, 815.

beyond the loop of runner tracks in a world where runner tracks themselves recede into the past.

Placed as they are in the volume, these three poems outline the book's pervasive drama of disappearance, highlighting the human contest with nature made harder by economic decline. *North of Boston* continually reminds us of nature's power, from the "frozen ground-swell" that topples a boundary wall in its opening poem to the "smokeless burning of decay" that consumes an abandoned woodpile in its last. In the thirteen poems between, we see the run-off that erodes good cropland, the trees that invade unmown meadows, and the combined forces that blacken a derelict cottage and fill old an cellar hole. In all, *North of Boston* portrays a world in which all things "appear and disappear," "fall and break"; where all things "cut and split / And piled" return to the soil from which they came, and death is ready to claim first-born infants as well as old hired men. The grieving husband and father of "Home Burial" sounds the keynote of this world when he says, "Three foggy mornings and one rainy day / Will rot the best birch fence a man can build." Here, speaking of far more than fences, he builds on the loss of a child to mourn the transience of all we make with hands, heart, or loins. Like this young father's lament, each of the three major lyrics, by focusing on wall-building, apple-picking, and wood-cutting in turn, measures the power of entropy by a form of the human labor we mount against it. And in their first-person voices, each of these poems bears intimate witness to the struggle.

The Genesis of the Lyrics

When we consider the intricacy and power of the aesthetic and thematic design created by these major lyrics, it may seem surprising that all three were late additions to the book. Both Douglas Wilson and John Evangelist Walsh have established that "Mending Wall" was substantially if not wholly composed in September or October of 1913, soon after Frost and J. C. Smith had spent a day in late August walking and conversing among the unmortared stone walls outside Kingsbarns, Scotland. On November 24 of that year, responding to the packet of unpublished poems Frost had sent him, Smith wrote that he "recognized 'Mending Wall' at once as *the poem which had been suggested* by our walk at Kingsbarns" (Wilson, 73; emphasis added), suggesting in turn that, unlike the other *North of Boston* poems they had discussed that day, some of which Frost described in detail, this one was not then in existence. While Frost said that both "After Apple-Picking" and "The Wood-Pile" were "largely written . . . before he went to England" (Sergeant, 119) and that both poems were among those that he wrote "through without fumbling a sentence" (*Col-*

lected Prose, 161), both claims leave room for later revision.[4] An entry in one of Frost's English notebooks, for example — "As a bird that flies before you and thinks it is pursued" — clearly seems the kernel of an important passage in "The Wood-Pile" (*Notebooks*, 109; in Walsh, 221).[5] Despite Frost's claim of prior composition, Walsh also believes that "After Apple-Picking" was composed in fall of 1913 and that the lines, "I am overtired / Of the great harvest I myself desired," refer to the very work on *North of Boston* that he was just then bringing to a close (235). Whatever the facts about how much of these poems were written when, it seems clear that working them into *North of Boston* was a late as well as an inspired choice and that completing them and completing the book were parts of a single process.[6]

Including these three lyrics in the book clearly involved a change of heart in Frost himself. In a letter of August 7, 1913 to John Bartlett listing the book's prospective contents, Frost mentions eleven of its final twelve narratives but none of its three major lyrics, and two letters written three weeks earlier help to explain why. One was to Thomas Mosher, who had published "Reluctance" in one of his special-editions catalogues, and, preferring it to all other poems in *A Boy's Will*, had apparently asked

---

[4] Frost's claims of single-stroke composition for a number of poems have attracted considerable debate. In one of his longest notes to *The Early Years* (594–97), Thompson suggests that such claims are extravagant and reflect Frost's attraction to the romantic ideal of the inspired poet, citing evidence for revision of two of the most famous poems, "Birches" and "Stopping by Woods," that Frost had supposedly composed in a single sitting. In a note countering Thompson, Walsh defends Frost's claims, suggesting that "having occasionally written rapidly and with a sure touch . . . is all he intended by his 'one stroke'" (249). Walsh's comment comes close to something Frost wrote in 1950, when asked by Brooks and Warren to contribute to a new final chapter, titled "How Poems Come About," in their textbook, *Understanding Poetry*. In a letter to Charles A. Madison, the Holt editor who had conveyed the request, Frost names eight poems (including "After Apple-Picking" and "The Wood-Pile") as examples of those not "worried . . . into existence" and says, "With what pleasure I remember their tractability. They have been the experience I couldn't help returning for more of — I trust I may say without seeming to put on *inspired* airs" (*Collected Prose*, 161; emphasis added). Much though not all of Frost's statement was included in the third edition of Brooks and Warren, *Understanding Poetry* (523–24).

[5] Frost kept two notebooks of jottings in England, now collected as *Notebooks 8 and 9* in *The Notebooks of Robert Frost*. This entry comes from *Notebook 8*. The original is in the Frost Collection at the University of Virginia and is known as the Cohn Notebook because Frost gave it to Louis Cohn, a book dealer and friend, in 1948 (Walsh, 218).

[6] For a fuller discussion of the genesis of "Mending Wall," as well as its rhetorical and thematic complexities, see Sanders, "Earth, Time, and England."

Frost for others of that kind. In a letter of July 17, however, Frost puts him off: "I am made too self-conscious by the comment on my first book to think of showing another like it for some time." Frost goes on to mention the "volume of blank verse . . . already well in hand" (*SL*, 83). This comment strongly suggests that Frost, after the early reviews of *A Boy's Will*, felt stronger and less exposed on narrative and dramatic ground, where he reveals himself only indirectly through his characters.[7] Writing the same day to Wilbur Rowell, executor of his grandfather's estate, Frost says that the first book "has done rather well," reinforcing the point that this wild dreamer of a grandson was making good after all.[8] He demurs, however, about sending Rowell a copy, airing doubts about the book like those expressed to Mosher. "I am not too sure," Frost explains,"that you will care for my sort of stuff — so very personal in this first book [*A Boy's Will*] . . . practically all of it [written] five years ago on the farm in Derry." He adds, significantly, "The next book, if it comes off, should be more objective and so perhaps more generally interesting" (*SL*, 85).

Whether addressing Mosher, the committed aesthete who preferred poems like those in *A Boy's Will*, or Wilbur Rowell, man of law and business who may well have preferred no poems at all, Frost remains focused on his first book's lyric subjectivity and what it no longer says about him as poet. More than a year earlier, in March 1912, Frost had told Mosher, who had just sent Frost twenty-five dollars for "Reluctance," "that I . . . have others still under cover that more nearly represent what I am going to be" (*SL*, 47). The following year, in July 1913, Frost tells Rowell that *A Boy's Will* speaks for a former self that he's now outgrown and insists to Mosher that even this first book includes examples of his newer, more mature poetic voice. Of these Frost names "Mowing" and probably means "Storm Fear" as well,[9] for, in the language Frost uses with Rowell,

---

[7] My thanks for George Monteiro for suggesting this idea and calling my attention to Frost's express "self-consciousness" about "further lyrics" in his letter to Mosher — both in email correspondence of July 2007.

[8] Frost scrupulously qualifies the book's success by saying, "At any rate . . . it has introduced me to other people who write" (*SL*, 85). This was Frost's second mention of the book to Rowell. On June 6, when asking Rowell if he could send the annuity check a few days early, he had more pointedly suggested that his poetic ambitions were becoming actual achievements: "I have published a book here and expect to publish another before Christmas" (*SL*, 74). As we know, this timeline was extended, as much as anything by the redesign of the new book to incorporate the three major lyrics.

[9] Frost later described "Storm Fear" as "the youngest of the lot" that he included in *A Boy's Will*, "the last finished before publication" (Mertins, 106). But he might also have named "My November Guest," from which, in a letter to Bartlett, he cites three lines that demonstrate the "sentence sounds" — the spoken voice tones — he strives to capture. He even says that "one of the least successful of the poems in my book ["Asking for Roses"] is almost saved by a final striking sentence sound (*SL*, 112).

both poems "objectify" his feelings in more factual, pragmatic terms and display a tougher, more sinuous artistry than almost anything else in his first book. Their style is that of the new narratives affirmed by Frost's English friends in the weeks preceding these July letters to Mosher and Rowell — a style embodying Frost's "sound of sense" principles, infusing traditional poetic meters with the native notes of rural New England and using an "everyday . . . diction that," as Frost says to Mosher in boastful apology, "even Wordsworth kept above" (*SL*, 84). Hinting at the value he assigns to the new voice and style, Frost says, "In Mowing, for instance, I come so near what I long to get that *I almost despair* of coming nearer" (*SL*, 83; emphasis added).

Frost may have chosen this hyperbolic and somewhat histrionic phrase to appeal to Mosher, a valued and potentially valuable publisher-friend who preferred the more overt expressions of feeling that Frost had turned away from in his poems. Events in England make clear, however, that rather than "despair" at bettering his achievement in "Mowing," Frost was working to extend it — and not only in the blank-verse narratives he was showing to English friends. No sooner did Frost find affirmation for his more dramatic and vernacular style than he began to use it in longer lyric compositions, increasing their narrative and meditative dimensions in the manner of "Mowing," where emotion is not distilled and stated directly but embedded in observation, reflection, and even speculation that sometimes verges on analysis — and all of this in ordinary language, as if "Anything more than the truth would have seemed too weak." Or anything less. As he says in "Mowing" of his "long scythe whispering to the ground,"

> Perhaps it was something about the heat of the sun,
> Something, perhaps, about the lack of sound —
> And that was why it whispered and did not speak.

As we shall see, this way of presenting emotion is characteristic of the lyrics that Frost would use in *North of Boston*. As late as August 7, however, the list of prospective contents that Frost sent Bartlett still mentioned none of those that would appear in the book. But, it did include three dramatic narratives not mentioned to Frank Flint in July as well as a new, extended lyric called "Swinging Birches."

Like the three major lyrics that would soon structure the book, "Swinging Birches" is based on Frost's life in Derry and was probably started there. It also follows the "sound of sense" principles Frost developed there and was working to describe as well as to perfect in the summer of 1913. Still, when we see how the three chosen lyrics — "Mending Wall," "After Apple-Picking," and "The Wood-Pile" — encapsulate *North of Boston*'s drama of disappearance, and when we see how "Home Burial," the only dramatic poem added after August, deepens this elegiac plot, we can see why Frost would have saved "Swinging Birches" for another day.[10] What this final choice does not explain is why Frost even considered "Swinging Birches" for his new book on August 7 when, just three weeks earlier, he had told Mosher that "if I write more lyrics it must be with no thought of publication" (*SL*, 83). What would have changed Frost's mind?

It seems possible that in July, stung by the early reviews of *A Boy's Will*, as he himself explains, and perhaps worrying that "Mowing" was a lucky inspiration he could not equal, Frost was quite candid about putting lyrics aside, but that by August 7, bolstered by his new efforts and the comments of English friends, he felt a new confidence in the lyric voice that now incorporated his "sound of sense" principles. I would suggest, however, that even in mid-July Frost overstated his reservations about the lyric mode as a friendly way to put Mosher off and that, rather than forswearing lyrics altogether, he was simply ruling out the kind that Mosher wanted. He might also have felt that Mosher was not the right audience, and Mosher's limited-edition publications not the right place, for his new, more dramatic lyrics. Certainly one can see Frost's effort to differ with Mosher as agreeably as he could. Though he begins with reserved acquiescence to Mosher's praise — "I . . . am content to let you prefer Reluctance to any thing else I have written" — still he quarrels gently with that judgment, adding that *A Boy's Will* contains "a dozen poems that are at least good[11] in the same kind and for the same reason." He then cites "Mowing," a poem as unlike "Reluctance" as any in the book, as the example of what he most longs to achieve. In the next paragraph, as we have seen, Frost tells Mosher that what he *can* show him are those blank-verse dialogues written in "everyday . . . diction" (*SL*, 83–84) that, Frost jests, might just "frighten" Mosher. From the opening lines of his letter, then, we might read Frost as in effect announcing — as gently as he could to the man he valued as one of his first, few literary admirers — that "Any lyrics I do write for publication will have to be different from the ones you have most admired." And so they turned out to be.[12]

---

[10] It occupies a prominent place in *Mountain Interval* (1915), where it appears, revised and augmented, as "Birches."

[11] The phrase "at least good" is unusual enough to suggest that Frost meant "at least *as* good." I suspect however, that Frost has said exactly what he meant: in effect, that the other poems he has in mind have virtues similar to those of "Reluctance" and, if not quite that poem's equal, are "at least good."

[12] The combination of circumspection, gratitude, and concern for Mosher's feelings that I ascribe to Frost here are very clear in a letter to him the following summer (July 27, 1914), after *North of Boston*, published in May, had attracted highly favorable reviews. There Frost writes, "It has done so well here that I should almost venture to send you a copy in spite of your well-known predilection for the manner of the nineties. . . . Please tell me if on consideration you have reason to think you would care for the book and I shall be only too happy to see that you have one from my hand. You were one of the first to see me coming — you are nearly the only one thus far in America — and I should like to know that I had

In this regard, a September 15 letter from the very newest of Frost's admirers, J. C. Smith in Edinburgh, might seem prescient if we didn't know the extent of Smith's late-August conversation with Frost in Kingsbarns. On his return to Beaconsfield Frost had sent him *A Boy's Will*, which Smith had read aloud with his family and, clearly with little delay, had written back to Frost:

> I think on the whole "October" is my favorite; but other poems won other suffrages. My own taste is fairly simple, and I like you best when you are most objective. And I rather suspect that you are travelling in that direction yourself. I told them [Smith's family] that your forthcoming volume wd. . . . probably be more objective and austere. (in Walsh, 144)[13]

Having himself used the term "objective" in July to describe his forthcoming book to Wilbur Rowell, Frost would likely have used it in his August conversation with Smith. Almost surely, Frost meant to suggest a good dramatist's practice of providing the basis for assessment, especially of characters, rather than the judgments themselves. As he expressed the idea to Sidney Cox the following year, Frost said, "I make it a rule not to take a 'character's' side in anything I write" (*SL*, 138). As applied to his developing lyric style, however, "objectified" would be the more precise term and has less to do with taking sides than with how one conveys character and feeling. For, as we see in poems such as "Mowing" or the new lyrics for *North of Boston*, subjectivity remains the rule. But Frost shows who and what his lyric speakers are by how they perceive particular things. In his lyrics they convey their responses and assessments not in directly emotive or judgmental terms, but through description and reflection that carries a feeling or judgment with it.[14]

---

not lost favor with you at the same time that I was gaining it with really a good many important people over here" (*SL*, 129).

[13] This and the other letters Smith wrote to Frost in England are in the Rauner Collection at Dartmouth College Library.

[14] In his review of *North of Boston*, written for the August 1914 edition of *The English Review*, Edward Thomas confirms Frost's view of greater "objectivity," saying that "he has got free of the habit of personal lyric." Thomas at first implies that the change is a matter of genre, describing Frost's new book as "a collection of dramatic narratives, . . . some . . . almost entirely written in dialogue," and containing "only three" in which the poet is "chief character, telling a story . . . in his own words." He goes on, however, to describe the change as function of diction, locating its beginnings in *A Boy's Will*. There, he says, frankly echoing Wordsworth, Frost has "refused the 'glory of words' which is the modern poet's embarrassing heritage, yet succeeded in being plain though not mean, . . . reminding us of poetry without being 'poetical'" (Thornton, 29). It seems likely that Thomas's views reflect his conversations with Frost, whom he met in the fall of 1913.

In "The Wood-Pile," for example, what makes the speaker hesitate about going forward into the frozen swamp — whether uncertainty, uneasiness, disorientation, or all of these and more — is not named but implied by the "gray day," by "the hard snow" that "held" him "save where now and then / One foot went through," and by the "tall slim trees / Too much alike to mark or name a place by." Even his summation, "I was just far from home," leaves the feeling imbedded in the fact. With his lyric, as with his dramatic, personae, Frost nearly always provides the evidence for assessments and conclusions but leaves us to make or draw them ourselves. And by making us complete the loop of implication, he also leaves us free to reach alternative conclusions, creating important ironies. In "Mending Wall," for example, the speaker's final image of the neighbor as an "old-stone savage" who "moves in darkness" makes a summary judgment clearly grounded in what he's seen, heard, and told us. But not only does the speaker admit his own subjectivity: "as it seems to me," he says. By showing us what has led him to that judgment, Frost, as poet, provides the basis for our own, possibly different conclusions and even for a whole frame of reference beyond the speaker's own.[15]

In identifying the new direction for Frost's work as "more objective and austere," Smith was quite accurate, and to these two terms we might add "dramatic," especially with regard to "Mending Wall," on which Frost was almost surely at work when Smith's September letter arrived. As a remarkable poetic hybrid, creating a vivid interpersonal encounter that nonetheless maintains a single speaker's confidential address to his reader, "Mending Wall" becomes the starting point for both the lyric and dramatic strands of the volume, and it is intriguing to see just how Frost expands a meditative lyric to include two voices that never quite talk to each other, limiting yet intensifying the very drama he creates.

Lyric and Drama in "Mending Wall"

"Mending Wall" opens as a descriptive-meditative lyric familiar to English-language readers of verse since the eighteenth century, and at the start its main source of drama seems the difficulty of maintaining this human structure against natural forces, whose quiet, invisible operation outdoes the work of the wall's more furious adversaries:

> Something there is that doesn't love a wall,
> That sends the frozen ground-swell under it,
> And spills the upper boulders in the sun;
> And makes gaps even two can pass abreast.
> The work of hunters is another thing;

[15] For a fuller discussion of this particular example, again, see Sanders, "Earth, Time, and England."

> I have come after them and made repair
> Where they have left not one stone on a stone,
> But they would have the rabbit out of hiding,
> To please the yelping dogs.

The conflict with nature will gradually be pushed from the poem's spotlight by the entrance of a second figure who moves this solo meditation toward an encounter of two, though it's hard to say precisely where this change takes place. Still addressing the unseen agent of winter damage to the wall, the speaker says:

> The gaps *I* mean,
> No one has seen them made or heard them made,
> But at spring mending-time *we* find them there. (emphasis added)

In this, the poem's first "we," Frost deftly blurs the line where this lyric meditation becomes an encounter of two. On the one hand, with this plural pronoun, the speaker shares his knowledge of such gaps with us, just as he will soon share further confidences. At the same time, it refers ahead to the neighbor named in the very next line, with whom he will soon set to work:

> I let my neighbor know beyond the hill;
> And on a day we meet to walk the line
> And set the wall between us once again.
> We keep the wall between us as we go.
> To each the boulders that have fallen to each.
> And some are loaves and some so nearly balls
> We have to use a spell to make them balance:
> "Stay where you are until our backs are turned!"
> We wear our fingers rough with handling them.
> Oh, just another kind of outdoor game,
> One on a side. It comes to little more:
> There where it is we do not need the wall.

Even with the introduction of human interaction, the story at first remains focused on the shared task that unites the two men, and the only thing said — if it is even said aloud — is directed at the stones: "Stay where you are until our backs are turned!" At the same time, this mildly comic scene anticipates the coming clash of attitudes. The two men not only "set" but "keep the wall between [them]," the repeated phrase — "the wall between us" — creating an aural and visual analogue for the wall that puts them on opposite "sides" in their "outdoor game." The judgment that follows — that "we do not need the wall" — added as an afterthought, explains why all this work "comes to little more."

At this point, the speaker has said nothing about his neighbor's attitude, and when we see what Frost does next, we can appreciate the way he both developed and curtailed the poem's dramatic elements to create a hybrid form that, as it initiates the book's lyric triad, also anticipates the overt drama of the subsequent narratives. Having confided his own objection to the wall, the speaker becomes more expansive, yet elicits only the most sparing of replies:

> He is all pine and I am apple orchard.
> My apple trees will never get across
> And eat the cones under his pines, I tell him.
> He only says, "Good fences make good neighbors."
> Spring is the mischief in me, and I wonder
> If I could put a notion in his head:
> "*Why* do they make good neighbors? Isn't it
> Where there are cows? But here there are no cows.
> Before I built a wall I'd ask to know
> What I was walling in or walling out,
> And to whom I was like to give offense.
> Something there is that doesn't love a wall,
> That wants it down." I could say "Elves" to him,
> But it's not elves exactly, and I'd rather
> He said it for himself.

By this point, the shared problem of wall repair has become a problem of unshared feelings about the wall itself. Until now, the speaker has confided his view only to us. In fact, nowhere in the poem does he ever say to his neighbor anything so direct as "we do not need the wall." In joking that his apple trees pose no threat to his neighbor's pines, satirizing his neighbor's position, the speaker does nothing to narrow the distance between them. In addition, by keeping his discourse indirect, addressing us instead of his neighbor, he maintains a lyric enclosure around this drama of opposed attitudes, keeping it from becoming a direct debate. Rather than a conversation, Frost creates a failure of conversation in "Mending Wall" — and not only the failure of one person's words to reach another that we see in many of the book's dramatic poems. Here it is the failure of two characters to converse at all, the story of a monologue that verges on dialogue, only to collapse or retreat into itself.

Ironically, this turn takes place as the characters actually speak, and the ironies are multiple. Though the neighbor actually says, "Good fences make good neighbors," the words of this familiar proverb are not exactly his own, and rather than take up the invited discussion, they are meant to end it. Though the speaker's reply — "*Why* do they make good neighbors?" — seems to invite a response, he makes the question rhetorical by supplying all the answers, finally saying to his neighbor what he initially said to us — "Something there is that doesn't love a wall" — even sharpening his point by adding, "That wants it down." Yet even here, his circumspect phrasing stops short of standing behind it, and the "Elves" he considers naming as the enemy of walls only compounds his evasion.

Significantly, in this moment, where the speaker considers what he "could say" but says nothing, his approach to conversation becomes his withdrawal from it, and the poem's final eight lines form a private, reflective coda, shared only with the reader, in which the speaker observes his neighbor across what seems an evolutionary divide:

> I see him there
> Bringing a stone grasped firmly by the top
> In each hand, like an old-stone savage armed.
> He moves in darkness as it seems to me,
> Not of woods only and the shade of trees.
> He will not go behind his father's saying,
> And he likes having thought of it so well
> He says again, "Good fences make good neighbors."

We can see why the speaker would abandon his effort to converse with one who seems so unenlightened, even armed against self-examination. Where the speaker sees the fallen stones as making openings for new possibilities, including those of wordplay, the neighbor has used words like stones for closing such gaps. In the speaker's view, the neighbor makes the proverb into a mental wall to be kept in good repair — or even the very spell that keeps its stones in place.

There is, of course, much more to be said about the neighbor's position, about a speaker who says so much against the wall yet commits to its annual repair, and about a poem in which, as William Pritchard points out, "the few words spoken by another character . . . are conveyed . . . through the speaker's shifting terms (*Frost*, 91).[16] But for the moment let us notice the rhetorical dynamic of a lyric poem whose speaker, failing to draw his neighbor beyond his accustomed reticence, abandons argument, leaving "Mending Wall" in the form of a conversation proposed and declined, an opportunity for dialogue to be realized more fully in the volume's subsequent poems.

Lyric and Dramatic Personae

Despite the failure of genuine dialogue, "Mending Wall" nonetheless introduces the contrasting voices and divergent views that drive the dramatic

[16] Readers interested in the fuller complications of "Mending Wall" might begin by consulting Jonathan Barron's article on "Mending Wall" in *The Robert Frost Encyclopedia*.

narratives and emerge full-blown in the husband-wife dialogue of the book's next poem, "The Death of the Hired Man." At the same time, "Mending Wall" is also the first of the major lyrics that, in their subject matter, their narrative elements, and their progression from present to past tenses, spring to winter, symbolically outline the disappearance of a culture.

However much Frost made these three major lyrics more objective or dramatic than most of those in *A Boy's Will*, their meditative character remains nonetheless central to *North of Boston*. Not only do they reinforce the book's themes of survival through personal initiative and labor. Their intimate address to the reader affects the book's overall impact, fulfilling the prologue's invitation — "You come too" — in a way quite different from the longer, dramatic narratives. Three times in the course of the book, framing the longer poems yet placed among them, these lyric poems create islands of private reflection within the intensely peopled, interactive world of the narratives, where contesting characters take center stage. In the lyrics, by contrast, a single exploring consciousness brings various details of the New England landscape and culture — stones for a wall, a drinking trough after an overnight frost, the rungs of an orchard ladder, the apples themselves, a crust of old snow — to the foreground of attention, enlarging them in significance. Even in "Mending Wall," so focused on the question of relationship, the laconic neighbor and his defense of the wall is viewed through the lens of the speaker's subjectivity.

Frank Lentricchia, in *Modernist Quartet*,[17] suggests that, in "Mending Wall," the speaker's attempts at dialogue are a "pretext" and that, for Frost, the poem has more to do with later volumes than with *North of Boston*. He describes the poem as the book's "misleading tonesetter," departing from its main focus on the rural poor to unveil "a new kind of self-consciousness" by which Frost "creates an image of the writer he wanted to be . . . after *North of Boston*." Lentricchia sees the speaker's attempts at dialogue with his neighbor as just a way to show his verbal skill, suggesting that Frost's real concern is "the delightful peregrinations of his voice" and his real "subject . . . the bond that a writer would like to forge with his audience." The "jokes and puns, all shared with us . . . at the expense of the Johnny-one-note who is deaf to Frost's deft play" are, Lentricchia says, no more than the writer-speaker's attempt at "literary seduction [of] his possible public," who are naturally "honored by his confidence" (110–12). Though this ingenious reading overlooks the role of "Mending Wall" in *North of Boston*'s lyric triad (and a great deal more), it does raise the important question of how these lyric speakers relate to Frost as poet.

---

[17] This monograph studies four of the most influential American poets — Frost, Stevens, Pound, and Eliot — in the cultural and intellectual contexts of the early twentieth century.

Central to this study is the idea that the poems of *North of Boston* do reflect aspects of Frost himself, and I have already suggested ways that these feelings and concerns surface in both the characters and narrators of his dramatic compositions. We find equally important parts of Frost in his lyrics. We are encouraged to do so by a tradition of "sincere," personal lyrics, dating at least back to Wordsworth and other Romantics, whose speakers often evince feelings and convictions of the poet confirmed by letters, journals, or other expressions outside the poems. An even older tradition, dating at least from the Renaissance, reactivated by Blake, Tennyson, and Browning, and including many Frost contemporaries such as Ezra Pound, T. S. Eliot, and Edwin Arlington Robinson, embraces the dramatic lyric, whose speaker is a character other than the poet: an Achaean hero, a Renaissance monk, or a even a bored London socialite. But, such a distinction between types, even if clear in conception, inevitably blurs because poet and personae are never so neatly separated. Even in the most dramatic of lyrics, poets chose figures — whether mythic, historic, or invented — who rehearse their own concerns and conflicts. On the other hand, no matter how connected we might find poet and poetic persona to be, no equation between them is quite warranted or safe.

So it is with *North of Boston*'s lyric speakers. It is tempting to think, as Lentricchia does, that the speaker of "Mending Wall" is nothing more than the long-term persona Frost would create for himself. It is tempting because the speaker sounds more like a sophisticated poet than a New England farmer. Witty and nimble, he may also sound more like the lyric poet of Frost's later books than the restrained narrators of the longer poems in this one. As readers, however, we need not be so taken in by the speaker's charm and wit as Lentriccia imagines. We should also be careful about equating the speaker who argues against the wall with the Frost who later claimed to write the poem when he was "homesick for [his] old wall in New England" (Thompson, *Early Years*, 432–33). We should be even more careful about assuming too great a separation between the poem's laconic neighbor and the poet who himself makes such artful use of reticence. As we shall see, Frost leaves his speaker as much open to our judgment as the neighbor who defends his position by proverb. It would be hard, in fact, to identify the poet with either character even if Frost didn't lay claim to both their views, which he does. In 1938, Charles Foster quoted Frost as saying, "I am both wall-builder and wall-destroyer" (in Parini, 139).[18] In 1945 Frost said, "I played exactly fair in it. Twice

[18] Foster was a young poet who attended the Bread Loaf Writer's Conference in the 1930s and became a close friend to Frost around the time of Elinor's death in 1938. Parini (466) cites the "Notes of Charles Foster, DCL [Dartmouth College Library]."

I say 'Good fences' and twice 'Something there is'" (Cook, 355; in Cramer, 30).[19] The problem with Lentricchia's reading of "Mending Wall" is not the inspired connection he makes to Frost's later volumes, but the connections to this one that he ignores. Although the speaker's bond of confidentiality with his reader is a central element, it's not the only one, and the speaker himself is far more than a stand-in for Frost's later lyric persona, stowed away in *North of Boston* and waiting to emerge in subsequent publications. As we shall see, there are also connections between the poet and the poem's traditionalist neighbor that go beyond any doctrine of fairness or dramatic objectivity.

I have suggested that the intimacy of the lyrics complements the perspective of the longer poems, focused as they are on the conflicts between characters. The lyrics, by contrast, follow a single speaker's exploration which, anchored in immediate detail yet far-reaching in implication, invites a longer perspective on the very issues of time, change, and cultural decline taken up by the narratives. "Mending Wall," for example, describes a rough stone boundary wall whose very presence evokes a history of human culture under siege on various sides, from the "frozen-ground-swell" that "spills the upper boulders in the sun" to "the work of hunters" who, in flushing their quarry, "have left not one stone on a stone" — Frost's language here echoing Jesus's words on the end of days.[20] In "After Apple-Picking," the "pane of glass" that, on a cold morning, the speaker has "skimmed . . . from the drinking trough" to hold "against the world of hoary grass" not only registers the approach of winter and the passing of time but alludes to a host of biblical reflections on mortality — most prominently to Paul's description of earthly life as something seen "but through a glass darkly" (1 Cor. 13:12). No image more aptly captures *North of Boston*'s drama of disappearance better than the abandoned cord of maple seen by the speaker of "The Wood-Pile" on his walk into a frozen swamp. Reassured by this sign of human presence where he has found no other, he readily imagines the skilled acts of cutting, splitting, and piling that have put it there. But as he observes the artifact before him, the fact of human absence and the triumph of time slowly emerge.

---

[19] Cook's citation for this remark reads simply "At Middlebury College, Nov. 9, 1945" (355). Reginald Cook was professor of English at Middlebury and, from 1946–64, director of the Breadloaf School of English, with which Frost was closely involved. In his long friendship with Frost, 1925–63, Cook recorded much of what Frost said in conversation.

[20] In the synoptic gospel accounts, Jesus, speaking of the social upheaval that will come before the kingdom of God is established, looks at the Jerusalem temple and says "there will not be left here one stone upon another, that will not be thrown down (Matt. 24:2; see also Mark 13:2 and Luke 21:6).

> No runner tracks in this year's snow looped near it.
> And it was older sure than this year's cutting,
> Or even last year's or the year's before.
> The wood was gray and bark warping off it
> And the pile somewhat sunken. Clematis
> Had wound strings round and round it like a bundle.
> What held it though on one side was a tree
> Still growing, and on one a stake and prop,
> These latter about to fall.

The speaker's realization unfolds with his description, leading to an emblematic tableau of living tree against falling stake and prop, the human claim on this harvested wood literally lapsing as nature's claim literally grows.

Despite the scope of the drama here, which pits human effort against natural forces, the first-person voices of these lyrics create an intimate process of observation and discovery shared by speaker and reader. In a way that the longer poems and their narrators do not, the lyrics also invite us to imagine them as coming from a single source, much as, in theater, a dramatist's prologue invites the audience to imagine the single intelligence behind the characters about to take that single speaker's place on stage. I am reminded, too, of the theatrical first paragraph of Twain's *Huck Finn*, where Huck takes charge of his own first-person narrative by distinguishing himself from the "Mr. Mark Twain" who wrote that other book, *Tom Sawyer*. But even as Huck formally elbows Twain offstage in his own novel, he reminds us of the writer behind his story, whose name appears on the cover of the book Huck claims as his own.

Like Twain's Huck, Frost's lyric personae are poetic and somewhat dramatic creations that stand apart from him, their creator. If, on the other hand, these three lyric speakers who appear at intervals through the book remind us of the poet behind it, that is not an impression that Frost has exactly discouraged. In fact, his use of "The Pasture" and "Good Hours" as a prologue and epilogue conveying a writer's invitation and farewell further suggests Frost's wish not to be wholly forgotten when his characters come on stage. John Kemp, in *Robert Frost and New England*, assumes a single consciousness shared by all the lyric personae and narrators of the poems when he says that "In the 'larger design' of [the book], 'After Apple-Picking' reaffirms the persona's deep sensitivity to surroundings and thus strengthens the cogency of the entire collection as a record of his experience" (127). But we need not resolve the question whether the speakers of the three lyrics and the narrators of the longer poems merge into a single persona. We know that by the fall of 1913 Frost felt fully comfortable in having them stand together as his work. Even more, his late decision to build the three lyrics into *North of Boston*, especially considering the new writing they required, reflects Frost's confidence in his ability to write lyrics in the more "objective" manner of the dramatic poems, resulting in lyrics that speak more truly for the poet he had become by 1913 than most of those in *A Boy's Will* had done.

Arranged as they are in *North of Boston*, with "Mending Wall" and "The Wood-Pile" just inside the outer frame of prologue and epilogue, the three major lyrics offer a seamless transition from the poet's own persona to his various *dramatis personae* and back to the poet again. In "The Pasture," the book's short prologue, the poet-speaker's "You come too" explicitly invites us into the world of his book as he himself starts on a spring morning's work. Immediately following, "Mending Wall" gives us a lyric speaker with a strong narrative bent who tells of beginning a new season by repairing winter damage with his laconic neighbor. By introducing a second character vividly conveyed and directly quoted by this lyric speaker, "Mending Wall" anticipates the full dialogue of the dramatic poems, where the closest thing to the poet's own presence, the narrator's framing of scene and action, often disappears for long stretches, leaving the characters to speak for themselves. Once introduced, these dramatic voices populate Frost's "book of people" (*CPPP*, 790), creating a world of characters in dialogue suspended only briefly by "After Apple-Picking," with its elegy for the passing season in that earlier-established lyric voice, exacting and intimate. Following "The Self-Seeker," the book's final dramatic poem, "The Wood-Pile" offers a symbolic leave-taking from the poet's rural world, followed by an explicit farewell to both reader and book in "Good Hours," the poet's epilogue.

In giving this dramatic and thematic shape to *North of Boston* as a whole, the book's arrangement of poems takes on a biographical dimension. By presenting a succession of personae at varying distances from the poet himself, entering the world of rural New England in the prologue, exploring that world through fifteen poems of varied characters and voices, and departing from that world in the epilogue, the book offers a literary, almost narrative analogue for Frost's experience of the Derry world he had entered, lived in, and left, arriving with large poetic ambitions still unformed and taking from it a vision and voice shaped largely by the people he found there.

Pine Cones and Tailfeather: The Poet as Thief

Enter the Trespasser: "Mending Wall"

As they take their place in *North of Boston*'s rhetorical design, helping to make the book an abstract of Frost's relation to Derry's farming culture as well as an extended elegy for it, the three major lyrics inevitably reflect the poet's conflicted feelings about turning the decline of that culture to personal, artistic, and economic advantage. In "Mending Wall," the neighbor's defensive reticence fits his having so much more to lose than the clever modernist across the wall who narrates the poem and who seems to make light of what for the neighbor is no joke. For the neighbor, the wall is a patrimony that connects him to a personal and cultural past. He preserves that past by maintaining the wall and invokes that past by repeating his "father's saying," "Good fences make good neighbors."

It is this endangered past that, with *North of Boston*, Frost both celebrates and trades for his poetic future. It is true that the "Mending Wall" narrator does not directly oppose his neighbor's position, confiding his reservations most clearly and fully to the reader. And like the poet whose book preserves an endangered culture, he helps to maintain the wall. But like the poet who makes that vanishing past into a saleable commodity, this speaker lacks his neighbor's utter attachment to the wall and invokes its past only to sweep it aside. He is a questioner by temperament, yet when he interrogates the proverb — "*Why* do they [fences] make good neighbors?" — his follow-up to it — "Isn't it where there are cows? But here there are no cows" — is first merely rhetorical, and then reductive, as if all other values of a wall had gone the way of numerous, small-scale dairy operations.

Though we cannot simply equate the "Mending Wall" speaker with the poet himself, the parallels are hard to miss. Where the wall is irreplaceable for the neighbor, the speaker, despite his part in its annual repair, can imagine letting it go partly because, like the poet who turns his Derry years into one of the great books of American verse, he makes it into something else — or rather, into a number of things, all of them less tangible and less vulnerable to the attritions of time: an occasion for verbal performance, a symbol of resistance to change, even an impediment to thought. "He will not go behind his father's saying," he says of the neighbor, rendering him finally as "an old-stone savage" who "moves in darkness" and is "armed" — in short, as one outmoded, benighted, and potentially aggressive in defense of what he loves.

Despite this speaker's critique of his neighbor's position and refusal to debate, and as we might expect from a poet who claimed never "to take a 'character's' side" (*SL*, 138) in his poems, Frost is invested in both their perspectives, and even so dismissive an image of the neighbor has surprising dimensions. In a series of images from Frost's earliest writing to his latest volumes — in an essay on Petra for his high-school newspaper, in "To An Ancient" from *Steeple Bush*, and in many poems between — stone-age figures repeatedly represent our vulnerable humanity, which uses whatever is at hand to stave off the darkness of obliteration.[21] Notice too that Frost's only other use of the word "savage" in

[21] For a developed discussion of these related figures and references, see Sanders, "Earth, Time, and England."

North of Boston occurs in "The Self-Seeker," whose protagonist, The Broken One, attaches it to his friend Will's fierce effort to defend him against the insurance lawyer's tactics. In both these cases, in poems placed early and late in the book, the term is associated with stubborn defenders of the very cause to which the book itself is devoted.

Earlier in the poem an equally dismissive comment has more immediate resonance for the poet who may feel vulnerable to suspicion or worse. At first glance, the speaker's joke —

> My apple trees will never get across
> And eat the cones under his pines, I tell him —

is simply an attempt to make both the wall and its defender seem foolish. Clearly apple trees will not "get across" to eat pine cones, nor would the long-gone cows have wanted to. Yet, even as the speaker's satiric diversion misses or ignores the better reasons for a wall, including his neighbor's attachment to this one, his absurd pine-cone scenario hints at a concern with transgression that also suggests why he might read his laconic neighbor as resistant and defensive.

Let us, in fact, imagine the Frost in England who writes this poem to complete a book about a vanishing culture for which this tumbled-down wall is an emblem, keeping in mind that the book carries all of Frost's hopes for his economic future. Can we assume that the poet feels his appropriation of others' lives — his investment in their loss and the possible dividends from it — to be an inappropriate taking? Perhaps not. Yet there is an uncanny parallel between this image of thieving apple trees and the appropriations of a poet who would, remembering his English years, later cast himself as a poacher in this very time and place.[22] At the very least, the speaker's forceful denial of transgression in the book's first principal poem raises a question of trespass soon to be repeated throughout *North of Boston* and made conspicuous by its comic absurdity here.

The Elegiac Harvest: "After Apple-Picking"

"After Apple-Picking," the middle poem in the volume's lyric constellation, does not directly raise questions of debt and trespass but, while adding its voice to the book's drama of disappearance, also engages issues central to this transitional moment in Frost's poetic career. The poem

[22] See "A Romantic Chasm," written as a Preface to the British Edition of Frost's *A Masque of Reason* (1948). There, as mentioned earlier, Frost says that in 1913, as an American poet encountering English upper-class prejudice, he felt "hedged" out by "alien speech." But, he adds, "what was a hedge to the poacher in my blood . . ." (*CPPP*, 802). Though here Frost portrays himself as "taking" from the British aristocracy, not his Derry neighbors, he nonetheless makes clear that poetry, for him, required such acts of aggressive self-assertion.

exemplifies the way that, throughout *North of Boston*, Frost imparts symbolic dimensions to ordinary features of rural life — to a stone wall, a cellar hole, or a woodpile — all bearing witness to the ephemeral quality of earthly life and the work needed to maintain it. Most evocative here is the iced-over drinking trough that yields a melting "pane of glass" through which to view one's transitory world. In its focus on the end of the growing season marked by the first frost, the poem reflects the end not only of a cultural era which the book elegizes, but also of the twenty formative years that took Frost from his first published poem in 1894 to the end of his first year in England — an apprenticeship for which *North of Boston* would be his journeyman's piece.

Given such correspondences to Frost's own life, we can see more pointed parallels to the poet who had taken all he could from that Derry world before moving beyond it. John Walsh takes the poem to be "in some part symbolic of [Frost's] spent mood after his remarkable, nearly year-long spate of composition had abated in fall 1913" (234), focusing on the specific lines,

> I have had too much
> Of apple-picking: I am overtired
> Of the great harvest I myself desired.

This passage may well reflect a poet "weary of considerations"[23] after an arduous year of composition, revision, and literary politicking that for Frost made up most of 1913. Writing to Ernest Silver near the end of this process on December 8, Frost said, "I am clean shucked out by this last book — (North of Boston, I have decided to call it)" (*SL*, 103). Here, however, as throughout the volume, personal implications merge with universal ones. The lines above, for example, in which this orchard worker portrays himself as more exhausted than satisfied by his labor, build on the poem's opening images — the ladder "sticking through a tree / Toward heaven," the unfilled barrel, and the unpicked apples — to suggest the range of aspirations left unfulfilled by earthly life, while echoing the final sigh of the farm wife in the book's preceding poem, "A Servant to Servants": "I sha'nt catch up in this world, anyway."

The ladder image also leads us back to Frost's experience of Derry, which from the start he viewed as a world *through* which, but not *in* which, he could realize his aims as a poet. In this sense the whole Derry decade becomes the "pane of glass" skimmed from the "drinking trough" — the rural world that gave outline and substance to Frost's poetic vision but had to drop away before it could be realized in verse. Both the images of

---

[23] The phrase comes from "Birches" in *Mountain Interval* (1916) which, as "Swinging Birches" Frost considered for *North of Boston* as late as August 1913. See Frost's letter to John Bartlett dated August 7, 1913 (*SL*, 89).

incompletion that open the poem and the "trouble[d]" dreams to which the speaker looks ahead suggest the mixture of pride and doubt, the exhilaration and uncertainty of the poet who, with the addition of the three major lyrics, felt the book to be taking final form. Though he had his own convictions about its value, he also knew that, even after the months of composition and revision, of shaping and reshaping, and the years of work before that, the book must fall short of perfection and that public success would not be in hand until it was published and reviewed.[24] Nonetheless, with that success within reach, we might also hear the speaker's troubling dreams to reflect Frost's own feelings about the Derry neighbors from whose lives *North of Boston* was built. Though he would speak of this uneasiness only in the decades following the book's publication, it is one he would have felt most acutely as he brought that work to a close.

While alluding to many facets of Frost's poetic life in the fall of 1913, "After Apple-Picking" also deepens the book's elegiac thrust, ranging widely through our cultural resources to tie the passing of a traditional farming culture to the transitory nature of all earthly life. Most obvious of these is the Hebrew story of Eden that pervades this poem filled with images of fruit, reaching, and falling. Most striking is the frozen "pane of glass," which, as mentioned earlier, alludes to St. Paul's famous image of our mortal lives as something seen "through a glass darkly" (1 Cor. 13:12). The "world of hoary grass" seen through this farmyard lens draws, in addition, on a cluster of still older biblical texts that contrast human life to God's eternity. "All flesh is grass," says Isaiah, "while the word of God will stand forever" (40:6, 8). "I am withered like grass," sings the psalmist, "But thou, O Lord, shalt endure" (Ps. 102:10–11). In Psalm 103, our "days are like grass . . . / For the wind passes over . . . and the place . . . shall know it no more" (15–16). Apparently in contemplation, Frost's speaker holds his fragile lens "against" this world of change, but any suggestion of a buffer or shield or even a contrast is dispelled as he "let[s] it fall and break," signaling his own mortal descent. "But I was well / Upon my way to sleep before it fell," he adds, evoking mortal limits in yet another way shared by the Psalms, where "a thousand years" of human life is compared both to "a sleep" and to "grass which . . . in the evening is cut down and withereth" (90:4–6), while God "will neither slumber nor sleep" (121:4).

"After-Apple Picking" is also a Frostian ode to autumn, treasuring the ripeness and abundance of "ten thousand thousand fruit to touch, / Cherish in hand, lift down, and not let fall." But with Frost, as with

[24] Though Walsh says, "nothing at all is known about . . . the poem's composition," he concludes that it "was written in fall 1913, probably October" (234–35), and I concur. Since Frost had made no mention of the book's three major lyrics as late as August 1913, there is good reason to conclude that "After Apple-Picking," like "Mending Wall," was composed in September or October of that year.

Keats, to whom the poem owes so much, the value of that bounty is tied to its seasonal life — and death. Here, as the speaker details the beauty of those apples — "Stem end and blossom end, / And every fleck of russet showing clear" — they "appear and disappear," as if rehearsing the plot of mortality. Though the ladder pointing "Toward heaven still" gives an aspiring cast to the labor described here, it nonetheless sways to earthly movements and leaves the speaker in a world of tasks undone, partly because of his own fatigue. Indeed earth's tireless pull seems inescapable, for the speaker's "instep arch not only keeps the ache" but "the pressure of a ladder-round," a surprising distinction that reminds us of the effort required to turn earth's downward pull into a habit of ascent. Even the apples saved from a fall to earth end up "rumbling" in "the cellar bin," their below-ground storage becoming another kind of burial in the poem's array of downward movements, which include the fall and breaking of the "glass" and the speaker's own descent into sleep. In all of these details, Frost develops the figurative nature of his facts while subtly pointing to the facts underlying his figures, merging the literal pull of earth with all that conspires to return us to dust. And as the force of gravity in "After Apple-Picking" connects with the gravitas of the volume as a whole, it subtly anticipates "The Wood-Pile," the last of its lyric triad, where its questing speaker stays on top of the "hard snow . . . save where now and then / One foot went through," and where the abandoned "cord of maple," though still recognizable, is "sunken" into "the frozen swamp."

Almost Gone: "The Wood-Pile"

Where "After Apple-Picking" obliquely reflects issues that concerned Frost as the *North of Boston* poet, "The Wood-Pile," the last of the book's principal poems, directly revisits ideas of violation and trespass, made all the more noticeable when presented as the seemingly dismissible absurdity of "a small bird" who suspects the poem's speaker of thieving intentions. Described as guarding his integrity and tail-feather by being "careful / To put a tree between us when he lighted, / And to say no word to tell me who he was," the bird seems to share the suspicions of the "Mending Wall" neighbor — a feeling that with this clever intruder, no words of one's own are too few to be turned against one, no opening too small for his self-serving intentions. Don't let him get too close!

Like earlier characters, narrators, and auditors in *North of Boston*, the speaker of "The Wood-Pile" is on unfamiliar ground, and this last of the book's principal poems pushes his outsider-status to an extreme. The trees of this "frozen swamp" on this "gray day" are "too much alike to make or name a place by," leaving this uneasy venturer "just far from home" and quite ready to personalize the bird's instinctual behavior:

He thought I was after him for a feather —
The white one in his tail . . .

. . . .

One flight out sideways would have undeceived him.
And then there was the pile of wood for which
I forgot him and let his little fear
Carry him off the way I might have gone.

. . . .

He went behind it to make his last stand.

Frost's use of this creature, which might seem incidental in the poem, exemplifies his understated method as he makes the bird both what the speaker is and is not. On one hand, the bird mirrors the uneasy walker who feels nowhere and, a moment before, had almost turned back from the gray prospect before him. When he goes on but still feels lost, he gains distance from that uneasiness by belittling it, creating the story of the bird's "little fear" to explain its silence and its retreat to a mock-heroic "last stand" at the woodpile. By making the bird a victim of its own fear, he creates both a foil for his own venturing on into the swamp and a reminder of his own first impulse to turn tail and head home.

Like the decision to push beyond his fear, the speaker's inventive reading of the bird's behavior is also the "flight out sideways," a way of finding new perspectives, that the bird itself cannot take. In this sense the bird returns us to other *North of Boston* figures — old Silas in "Death of the Hired Man" or the neighbor of "Mending Wall" — who cannot or will not adopt new ways. Like many members of a depleted traditional culture threatened by the next modernity, this bird and the "Mending Wall" neighbor might both be viewed as closing ranks against the outsider by shutting their mouths. Like the neighbor who takes comfort in his father's proverb, and like most of the local people of Frost's book, the bird takes a "stand" behind another emblem of this once-vigorous culture, and he makes it in even fewer words than the wall-mending neighbor. Ironically enough, their defensive refusal to define themselves in speech gives the poet even greater freedom to make of them what he will, and what he must.

When the suspicion and accusation are attributed to a bird rather than to a human neighbor, as they are in "Mending Wall," these attitudes are even more clearly the speaker's own projection, more strongly suggesting the concern with intrusion and trespass to be his own. He even describes the bird, the first of his alter egos in the poem, in self-mirroring terms as "one who takes / Everything said as personal to himself." Like the narrator of "Mending Wall" and like Frost in Derry, the speaker of "The Wood-Pile" is a relative outsider who does not live or die on the same terms as those native to the place. Like the poet who saw this second book of verse as a "last stand" in his effort to launch a poetic career, this speaker comes to "see" rather than to settle in this landscape and culture. For him survival means plucking its mystery, if not its tailfeather, and moving on.

Similarly, Derry had given Frost both the material and means of his vocation: a natural world that would sustain a lifetime of poetic reflection and provide the central drama of his work; a vigorous local vernacular that gave his poetic voice its defining character and music; and, inseparable from these, a rural people that enabled him to celebrate — as he later described it — the "originality and initiative . . . I ask for my country" (*CPPP*, 778). Frost's own pain of breaking with this life can be heard in the poem's final reflection on the absent woodcutter who, in moving forward, "Could so forget" the "handiwork on which / He spent himself." The poignancy of this forgotten handiwork for this speaker reminds me of Frost's own urging, nearly a plea, to John Bartlett in November 1913, as *North of Boston* neared final form, asking that Bartlett not "grow cold in letter writing" and explaining, "You are about all that I saved from the years I spent in Derry, you and Margaret, and the three children born to us on the farm, and the first book that was mostly written on the farm" (*SL*, 97).

It is Frost himself who has left behind farming, wall-building, woodcutting for a cultivation of publishers, patrons, and public audiences; and the abandoned cord of maple, like the earlier apples left unpicked "upon some bough," speaks for that world of small-scale farms and local economies relegated to history and poetry by social and economic changes. That Frost remains on both sides of that divide is what makes him the poet of this disappearing culture, recording in verse and saving in imagination what must be lost in fact. Throughout this volume — in such poems as "Mending Wall," "Death of the Hired Man," "A Hundred Collars," "The Mountain," and "The Self-Seeker," to name just a few — we have seen a wide range of figures who take on various roles in the personal drama of Frost's effort to realize himself as a poet.

In a way both striking and ironic, "The Wood-Pile" includes a character notable for his absence — the woodcutter thought to have "forgotten" the "labor of his ax." Like the bird seen to act out of fear and suspicion rather than instinct, this woodcutter is another of the speaker's inventions, though one that speaks for a different part of Frost himself. For, in "turning to fresh tasks" this imagined woodsman makes the saving "flight out sideways" that the bird could not make and parallels the poet who had ventured to England on the proceeds of the Derry farm, at once relieved and grieved to leave behind the rural world to which he owed his maturity as a poet.

The poet's grief infuses the six-and-a-half-line coda that ends the poem, subtly undercutting the optimistic surmise by which the speaker explains the woodpile's abandonment. But this grief begins to take form earlier, almost at the discovery of the woodpile, for no sooner does the narrator see it than he sees evidence of its abandonment, complicating what he has found. At first, this "cord of maple, cut and split / And piled — and measured, four by four by eight," affirms his decision to go forward into the swamp. "And not another like it could I see," he adds in an emphatic, iambic, one-sentence line. As the only human thing he finds in this barren place, the woodpile transforms the featureless landscape. Unlike the silent bird, it speaks to him. He knows the work that goes into a cord of wood and the dimensions that once defined a unit of currency in this northern culture. In his imagination he identifies with its maker, rehearsing the very acts that had put once-living trees into ordered ranks so like the lines of a poem. Yet the description that follows is an unfolding realization that this artifact has passed out of human hands. Left for years, "the wood . . . gray" and "the pile somewhat sunken," it doubly recedes into the gray landscape. In the absence of "runner tracks looped near it," clematis has "wound strings round and round it" in an act of repossession.

As the human claim on the woodpile literally lapses with the "stake and prop . . . about to fall," so the culture it represents, created by human labor, also recedes into the past, much like the poet's Derry world. Understandably, the speaker so excited at finding the woodpile is disturbed to recognize its abandonment, though at first he does not sound so:

> I thought that only
> Someone who lives in turning to fresh tasks
> Could so forget his handiwork on which
> He spent himself, the labor of his ax,
> And leave it there far from a useful fireplace
> To warm the frozen swamp as best it could
> With the slow smokeless burning of decay.

Explaining the abandonment as a mere forgetting, he exchanges its failure to reach "a useful fireplace" for "fresh tasks," making the unreturning woodcutter much like himself, who on sighting the woodpile had forgotten the bird.

The poem, however, contains not one unreturning woodcutter, but two. Alongside this expression of the speakers's optimism — this imagined figure too busy to retrieve "the labor of his ax" — is the companion of his grief, an unmentioned figure unable to return and beyond either remembering or forgetting — a shadowy alter ego for whom the half-sunken woodpile is not expendable excess, but essence. Though unnamed, this unmentioned woodcutter is implicit in the cost and waste of "the handiwork on which / He spent *himself*" and in the futile "warming" of a "frozen swamp." In the passages from Hawthorne's *American Notebooks* and *The Blithedale Romance* that became Frost's literary sources for this episode,[25] the abandoned woodpile is far more decayed and overgrown, old enough that its maker must be dead and the pile his symbolic burial mound. In the novel, Hawthorne's narrator, Miles Coverdale, describes

> a heap of logs and sticks that had been cut for firewood, a great while ago, by some former possessor of the soil, and piled up square, in order to be carted or sledded away to the farm-house. But being forgotten, they had lain there, perhaps fifty years, and possibly much longer, until, by the accumulation of moss, and the leaves falling over them and decaying there, from autumn to autumn, a green mound was formed, in which the softened outline was still perceptible. In the fitful mood that then swayed my mind. . . . I found the long-dead woodman, and his long-dead wife and children, coming out of the chill graves, and essaying to make a fire with this heap of mossy fuel. (211–12.)

Clearly, Hawthorne's "heap of logs . . . cut . . . and piled up square, in order to be . . . sledded away" provided a model for Frost's "cord of maple, cut, and split / And piled" and left to await returning "runner tracks" in the snow. And just as Hawthorne's woodpile prompts his narrator to imagine the current state of its maker, so does Frost's. In fact, Hawthorne's ghostly image of the "long-dead woodman" returning to "make a fire" may even have suggested the ironic "burning of decay," insufficient to warm the living, that sounds the final note of Frost poem.

By making his woodpile's abandonment more recent, however, Frost leaves its maker's fate uncertain, with life and death in precarious balance. This sense of standing at the crossroad of life and death, and the assertion of life within the shadow cast by death, is the classic stance of the elegist, and is reinforced by an allusion to the most famous elegy in English, John Milton's "Lycidas," which ends with the elegist's turn away from death toward future possibilities:

> At last he rose and twitched his mantle blue:
> Tomorrow to fresh woods and pastures new.

Frost, who knew both Milton's poem and its Classical models, signals his awareness of this long tradition by his use of the word "fresh." Though

[25] Two studies in *Frost: Centennial Essays* explore these passages. J. Donald Crowley (288–309) considers the one in *The American Notebooks*; Edward Stone (282–83) looks at the one in *The Blithedale Romance*, strikingly similar but slightly shorter and adapted to the character and situation of Hawthorne's narrator, Miles Coverdale. In *Robert Frost and the New England Renaissance* (66–69), George Monteiro discusses the passage from the novel, citing Stone and Crowley, and pointing out that Alexander C. Kern had earlier connected Frost's poem to Hawthorne in *The Explicator* 28 (February 1970), item 49.

Frost's phrase, "in turning to fresh tasks," might suggest no further reference to many modern readers, those who know Milton's famous close will find the echo unmistakable. In making the same turn back to life made by Milton's "Tomorrow to fresh woods," Frost's "in turning to fresh tasks" precisely duplicates Milton's cadence while placing the key word "fresh" in the corresponding, emphatic position, as part of a spondee. For a prosodist such as Frost, this echo is no accident, and it hints at the widening circles of context — personal and cultural, American and English, ancient and archetypal — in which Frost places this intersection of past and future.

For the speaker of "The Wood-Pile," this turn toward the future asserts the same optimism that earlier prompted him, even in this gray, bleak place, to "go on farther — and . . . see." In both spatial and narrative terms, death, always a possibility, remains an understory in his poem. He is not yet Lycidas, "Sunk . . . beneath the watery floor" (line 167). For him, what lay beneath the "hard snow . . . where now and then / One foot went through" also remains submerged in his story of "turning to fresh tasks." In detaching the woodcutter from the burial and decay of his woodpile, the speaker distances himself from these elements although, as we see, they remain powerfully present in his language. But this "go[ing] on farther" and "turning to fresh tasks" speaks for the poet as well. For Frost the death of the rural farming culture he came to know in Derry, if inevitable, was not yet accomplished, as we see in the wall-repair underway in the book's opening poem. And, like the speaker of this closing poem, Frost had kept his means of "extrication."[26] Selling the Derry farm and going to England was an ambitious poet's decision not to go under with a sinking culture, but rather to leave behind both the limitations of that world and the fears of risk and failure that might have kept him in New Hampshire.

Leaving that world behind was nonetheless an end, another kind of death involving loss and grief — emotions that infuse the poem's closing lines, almost the last of the entire book. Looking again at the speaker's reflection on the abandoned wood left

> To warm the frozen swamp as best it could
> With the slow smokeless burning of decay,

we see a perfect example of Frost's artistic tact, combining prosody and fact to objectify feeling in a bold yet understated way. Even as

---

[26] The term occurs in "From Plane to Plane" (*CPPP*, 368), a dramatic dialogue begun in England, though not published till 1948. The dialogue involves two farm hands, one a young man "fresh and full of college," the other seasoned by fifty years of toil, whose conversation ranges broadly and allusively to consider labor and leisure as well as different kinds of work and knowledge.

the "*slow smoke*less burning" suggests the invisible work of natural and historical change, this spondee of two long "o" syllables ruffles the iambic cadence and slows the line, adding a mournful note to its statement of loss. Just as this speaker is held by the decaying artifact even as he frees its maker — and vicariously himself — for "fresh tasks," so the poet conveys the pull of the world it represents and the costs of having left it. In reflecting this enduring attachment to a vanishing culture, *North of Boston* expresses the poet who mourns this loss even as he seeks to profit from it.

7: Welcome and Farewell: Prologue and Epilogue

Both "Mending Wall" and "The Wood-Pile," the first and last of the book's principal poems, present speakers who are "inside outsiders" in their rural world and whose mix of connection and detachment provide clear parallels to the poet who needed both involvement in and distance from the rural culture that inspired his verse. This dynamic of division, written into so much of the book, reaches even to "The Pasture" and "Good Hours," the shorter lyrics used as prologue and epilogue to the New York edition — though "Good Hours," in closing the volume, expresses this division more fully and openly than does "The Pasture" in its introductory role.

I have mentioned that *North of Boston*'s arrangement of lyric and dramatic poems, in which the poet dissolves into his *dramatis personae*, then reemerges from them, provides an analogue for Frost's own decade in Derry — for the people and culture with which he involved himself yet also kept apart and finally broke away from. Within this analogous arc, "The Pasture" and "Good Hours," taken together, reflect the changes in Frost wrought by these ten years. At his entrance to the book, as if to the decade, the relative brevity and simplicity of "The Pasture" fits the aspiring poet who approached Derry mainly as a refuge "from the world that seemed . . . to 'disallow'" him (*SL*, 159). At the end of the book and decade, "Good Hours," with its uneasy turnings, reflects the poet who looks back on a world from which he has kept his means of "extrication" (*CPPP*, 368) only to find that he has not left it wholly behind and cannot ignore the claims it has made upon him.

Like the poet who completed *North of Boston* far from its New England setting, these two poems stand just outside the volume proper. This degree of separation is partly a matter of visible form. Unlike the major lyrics, each of which runs from forty to forty-five lines of blank verse (or, in the case of "After Apple-Picking," something very like blank verse), these framing poems are in rhymed tetrameter quatrains — two and four of them respectively. Unlike the principal poems, these two lyrics were originally printed in italics and did not appear in the book's table of contents. In narrative, dramatic, and psychological terms, their two lyric speakers are also placed just outside the *North of Boston* world. However much the speakers of the major lyrics may feel different from the local people or be viewed as outsiders by them, they are also immersed in that world, actively repairing a wall, picking apples, cutting and stacking cord wood or recalling just how this work is done. "The Pasture" and "Good Hours" take this separation a step further, viewing such engagement in prospect or retrospect.

"The Pasture": You Come Too

In "Good Hours," which closes the volume, the speaker looks back on his separation from a community of which he only "thought" he'd been part. In a complementary way, the speaker of "The Pasture" looks *toward* the Derry world that the poet will take us into. All is intention and expectation — what he is literally "going" to do:

> I'm *going* out *to* clean the pasture spring;
> I'll only stop to rake the leaves away;
> (And wait to watch the water clear, I may):
> I sha'n't be gone long. — You come too.
>
> I'm *going* out *to* fetch the little calf
> That's standing by the mother. It's so young,
> It totters when she licks it with her tongue.
> I sha'n't be gone long. — You come too. (emphasis added)

In addition to the language of anticipation, the refrain of both stanzas — "I sha'n't be gone long — You come too" — also foregrounds the poet-reader relationship, so that, even though the speaker seems to consider the farm home, the rural world remains an excursion from the literary one in which he addresses us and to which he promises a return.

This narrator, in short, is as much the poet inviting us into his book as he is the farmer inviting us on his seasonal or daily rounds. To be our guide, of course, the poet must know that world, and the images of pasture and spring come from Frost's Derry farm. But the terms of his invitation have him reentering with us from outside, much like the part-time farmer Frost was in Derry, or like the poet who had moved from the farm to Derry village in 1910, when he wrote the poem, or even like the poet removed to England, where he published it. From such a vantage point, "I sha'n't be gone long" might refer not only to this short circuit of pasture and spring, but to the whole Derry decade, 1900–1911, as the temporary sojourn Frost always meant it to be — the place he went, as he would write upon his return from England, "to . . . fix myself before I measured my strength against all creation" (*SL*, 158).

In sensibility, "The Pasture" tilts more toward nostalgia than *North of Boston* as a whole. While its central use of the spring clearly alludes to the Derry world as a poetic source, its images of bucolic innocence seem more to offset than to introduce the painful human material Frost found there. Not that "The Pasture" lacks complication. In his essay "Frost and Invitation," Guy Rotella reviews the tonal complexities many readers have found in the poem, from the "teasing" qualities heard by Reuben Brower (11) to the interweaving of contraries noted by Robert Hass (64–66), but concludes that such "precariousness . . . doesn't obviate the simplicity and warmth so many readers feel and respond to in [the poem]" (36–38). It may be its predominantly cheerful tone that explains why, in 1930, Frost removed "The Pasture" from *North of Boston*, making it the prologue to all editions of his *Collected Poems*, with their broader range of material.

Nonetheless, the idea of looking into the clouded spring suggests the psychological and emotional depths that the volume will explore in a way that simply clearing the dead leaves and fetching the calf do not. Offered as an afterthought — "(And wait to watch the water clear, I may)" — this more probing impulse is the book's first, almost subliminal hint of the needs and concerns that made Frost's rural world a human one from the start. Looking back in 1940, Frost spoke of his pleasure in watching "the uncloudiness displace the cloudiness" of a cleaned-out spring, adding, "It might be taken as a figure of speech. It is my place to see clarity come out of talk and confusion" (Smythe, 56–57; in Cramer, 10).[1] Just as Frost invoked Wordsworth as a model for the "level of diction" he "dropped into" (*SL*, 83–84) for *North of Boston*, so this formulation about emerging clarity owes something to Wordsworth's idea that poetry "takes its origin from emotion recollected in tranquility."[2] The idea that emotion is ordered by reflection certainly applies to *North of Boston*'s dramatic poems, which give the clarity of a poet's insight and form to the disorderly passions of its characters. Bringing clarity specifically to "talk" also suggests the orderly, metrical use Frost was able to make of "a language absolutely unliterary," his "mak[ing] music out of . . . the sound of sense" (*SL*, 102, 79) — the principles of prosody that he first formulated in the summer of 1913 and for which *North of Boston* was the proving ground.

The sediment stirred up by dredging this source — what must resettle or be carried off in order for the water to clear — is another figure borrowed from Wordsworth's idea that poetry orders what arises from below consciousness. Frost's unsettled feelings about using the lives of his Derry neighbors, feelings inevitably stirred by his work on the book

[1] Smythe recorded these words from a conversation with Frost in March 1940 at the home of John Holmes, a friend of the poet and a member of the Tufts University faculty.

[2] This phrase comes from Wordsworth's Preface to *Lyrical Ballads, with Pastoral and Other Poems* (1802). In Wordsworth's *Literary Criticism*, 57.

through 1913, may provide an analogue for the clouding and troubling of this rural source that has made its way even into the book's overtly cheerful prologue. Whether this water ever fully cleared in the long years of Frost's economic success and public recognition remains a question. The joking references to his own prosperity in "New Hampshire" and "Poetry and Poverty," written roughly ten and twenty years after *North of Boston* appeared, suggest that Frost came to accept the gain reaped from others' failures and losses as inevitable to his vocation. But, for one who would describe irony as "a kind of guardedness" and humor as the "most engaging cowardice" (*SL*, 299, 300), this later joking suggests that, however accustomed to these inequities and conflicts he may have grown, some uneasiness remained.

John Kemp has noticed "some faintly discordant notes of uncertainty and self-consciousness" in the speaker of "The Pasture," which he reads as the sign of a conflict "explor[ed] more thoroughly in the rest of the collection." He points to various "tentative, apologetic phrases" — "I'll only stop," "I may," "I sha'n't be gone long," and the hesitation in "— You come too," suggesting that all of them convey the speaker's discomfort with the pastoral mantle he assumes (107). He quotes earlier critics Leo Marx and John Lynen, who, missing such discordant notes, see the classic invitation into an "ideal pasture" where the speaker will share "glimpses of delicate beauty" (Lynen, 22) and "clear a channel to a hidden source of renewal and creativity" (Marx, 258). But "unlike the conventional swain," Kemp suggests, "Frost's persona is unsure of his approach to the experience he contemplates" because, while he proposes a simple rural task, his "motives are devoid of practical, agricultural purpose." The pasture spring, Kemp points out, is used only by animals who don't care about the dead leaves or the water's clarity. Nor does the cow need help with her newborn calf. For the speaker who wants only to "watch" and look, these actions are nothing more than an "indulgence in contemplative recreation" (107).

In separating its speaker from classic pastoral conventions, Kemp illuminates the prologue's connection to *North of Boston* as a whole. Nothing in the book is idyllic. Its most beautiful moments and images are austere or poignant and underlined with gravitas. In setting aside an overly simple reading of the poem's pastoral elements, Kemp anticipates Robert Hass, who suggests that, by giving us a speaker who "clear[s] away rotten leaves from the spring . . . like the classical poets who cleansed Helicon," Frost links renewal and decay and "rides the pastoral tradition into the twentieth century." In its avoidance of both "romantic and naturalistic excesses," its joining of "tough-minded and tender-minded perceptions," writes Hass, "The Pasture" epitomizes Frost's view of "lived experience," making it a fitting prologue to his *Collected Poems*, which it became in 1930.

This complexity of attitude has specific relevance to *North of Boston* as well. For, as Hass points out, "The Pasture" goes beyond "an invitation to communion and leisure" to touch on "the . . . sometimes unpleasant annual rituals" that a farmer must perform to "ensure his future survival" (66). Contrary to Kemp's assertion, the "motives" of this speaker are not "devoid of practical . . . purpose" (107). One might argue that clearing sediment from the spring satisfies an aesthetic or symbolic impulse more than a practical need, but "fetch[ing] the little calf" does not. Farmers separate calves from their mothers to meet human needs,[3] not to help either mother or calf. Still, despite his plan to take the "little calf," the speaker is touched by its newborn vulnerability and by the maternal bond he is about to break. "It's so young," he says, "It totters when she licks it with her tongue." By placing this tender response alongside his pragmatic intent, "The Pasture" opens *North of Boston* with an act of appropriation accompanied by feelings that oppose it, subtly introducing a conflict developed in the poems that follow. For what is difficult for this farmer has also been difficult for Frost as poet of this New England farming culture. Just as "The Pasture" shows feelings that complicate its speaker's practical errand, so the following sixteen poems reveal the qualms of a poet committed to making *dramatis personae* out of the friends and neighbors of his Derry years.

While leisurely contemplation is not the prologue's only theme, it too remains central both here and throughout the volume. By engaging in such contemplation and imagining more of it, the speaker in "The Pasture" anticipates figures in "Mending Wall," "The Wood-Pile," "The Mountain," "A Servant to Servants," and "Blueberries," among still other poems, who do things mainly in order to see, talk, and reflect, and whose indulgence in this pleasure sets them apart from their dramatic counterparts in much the way that Frost himself felt separated from his real farming neighbors. But if Frost's persona in "The Pasture" — who "may" wait long enough "to watch the water clear" — leaves his planned excursion somewhat undetermined, it is not, as Kemp suggests, because he "is unsure of his approach to the experience he contemplates"(107), but rather that he insists on his openness to possibilities of the moment, his liberty to explore and respond. It is a declaration of freedom from necessity. If his feeling about living a life of reflection in a laboring world reaches the point of self-consciousness, it anticipates the many poems of the volume that set labor and subsistence against leisurely contemplation.

[3] One reason for the separation might be that the calf "has not met the farmer's staunch criteria for successful husbandry" (Hass, 66). Another is that calves alone will not stimulate cows to their fullest milk production, and sharing the milk with a suckling calf can be difficult because the mothers often become very protective of calves left with them more than a day or two.

And it surely falls short of apology. Rather, in his oblique and understated way, Frost serves early, subtle notice of the departures from traditional pastoral that the surface of his prologue might seem to promise. This is hardly surprising for the poet whose "Pan with Us," in *A Boy's Will*, had portrayed the sylvan faun without a song to play for a world that had "found new terms of worth," including new ways of seeing nature itself.

In exercising a poet's license to alter inherited conventions, "The Pasture" also anticipates the repeated allusions, in the poems that follow, to the poet's special work, which includes describing and even celebrating the sorts of husbandry and cultivation that Frost preferred to do rather little of himself, much like the narrator of his later poem, who finds it "restful" to consider the economic austerities of New Hampshire from his relative prosperity in Vermont. But in playing with pastoral expectations at the entry to *North of Boston*, Frost also anticipates, in an almost prescient way, an unsettled relation to an audience that would, in fact, come to gratify and disappoint him at once — an audience that he needed, courted, and appreciated, but also knew would fail to meet him where he was. On New Year's Day of 1917, about three years after sending *North of Boston* to press, Frost wrote Louis Untermeyer, saying:

> You get more credit for thinking if you restate formulae or cite cases that fall in easily under formulae, but all the fun is outside[,] saying things that suggest formulae that won't formulate — that almost but don't quite formulate. I should like to be so subtle at this game as to seem to the casual person altogether obvious. The casual person would assume that I meant nothing or else I came near enough meaning something he was familiar with to mean it for all practical purposes. Well well well. (*CPPP*, 692)

In that final "Well well well" we hear the self-consoling mischief of a poet disappointed by the "casual" readers unable or unwilling to engage the tougher ironies that resist resolution. To the end of his life Frost remained aware, like the narrator of "Directive," that many would be lost before they reached the "height of the adventure." In "On Extravagance: A Talk," delivered at Dartmouth College on November 27, 1962 — close to his last public appearance — Frost uses the children's game, Snap the Whip, played on ice skates, to suggest the readers left behind by the poet's insinuating line. In poetry, Frost says, there is always the element of extravagance that may stretch meanings beyond the reader's understanding. "It's like snapping the whip, you know. . . . Are you still on? . . . Are you with it? Or has it snapped you off?" (*CPPP*, 907).

"On Extravagance" may be Frost's last, somewhat extravagant expression of the "lover's quarrel" (*CPPP*, 322) he had with an audience that often adored him for less than he was and was not entirely to be depended on. His choice to use "The Pasture," inviting yet tentative about our response, as the doorway to *North of Boston* might be seen as one of the first such expressions.[4] It announces a poet who urges us, with a touch of uncertainty, to follow his exploratory path into his Derry world. Such uncertainty is not too surprising at the beginning of 1914, when Frost completed the book, and through much of the preceding year. For, once the reviews of *A Boy's Will* began, in the summer of 1913, to make clear that the book had not revealed the poet Frost believed himself to be, it also became clear that his arrival as a poet rested with the book in preparation. Considering the urgency of this task for Frost, it is not surprising that questions of reception and receptivity hinted at in "The Pasture" are again, and more directly, raised by the speaker's unresponsive neighbor in "Mending Wall," the book's next poem.[5]

Just as "The Pasture," at the threshold of the book's poetic world, looks ahead to its reception in the literary marketplace, so the epilogue, "Good Hours," at its close reflects a similar awareness of the poet's audience. Admittedly, the poem's more obvious concern is with the people of Frost's book. These are represented by the "village" from which the speaker walks away, then returns to, remaining ambiguously connected and disconnected throughout the four stanzas of the poem. At the same time, by calling attention to this unseen observer of village life, "Good Hours" reminds us of the poet's backstage presence in the book's unfolding drama, and in doing so, it addresses us, his audience. Or it almost does, asking our "leave" at the end of poem. The speaker's "by your leave" is a curious bit of courtesy having, as we shall see, more than one reference. Among them, however, is the poet's request for permission to depart from the book, leaving it in our hands. In one sense, the request is needless and ironic, for simply by publishing the book, he has already chosen to do just that. But when we consider that the poem dramatizes the moment of that choice, and when we understand all that the poet now entrusts to us, his readers, an element of deference is understandable. As we shall see, for a closing poem, "Good Hours" remains unusually fraught and unsettled, reminding us one last time of the costs encountered by the poet who, in making *North of Boston*, exchanged a community of rural neighbors to which he was never fully joined for an audience of readers of which he was far from assured.

---

4 "Into My Own," first published in 1909, later to become the first poem in *A Boy's Will*, may be considered an earlier expression of these unresolved tensions. Robert Newdick traces its origin to the spring of 1894 when Frost taught school in Salem, Massachusetts (43–44; in Cramer, 13) and shortly after "My Butterfly" was accepted by *The Independent*.

5 For a fuller discussion of this idea see Sanders, "Earth, Time, and England."

"Good Hours": "By Your Leave"

While "Good Hours" touches on questions about the poet and his audience, the poem takes a more direct look at the relationship between Frost and those who became his poetic subjects. Extending the pattern of excursion-and-return introduced in "The Pasture," "Good Hours" concludes *North of Boston* by revisiting the questions of connection and separation, possession and appropriation, trespass and violation, that persisted for the poet whose path always pointed beyond his rural village and who worried that he had taken more from its people than he had given of himself. In this regard, Frost's surmise, in his September 1913 letter to Cox, about the reciprocity between Robert Burns and the rural people of his poems betrays a certain longing. As an eighteenth-century Scot in a time of English oppression, Burns's affirmation of his native dialect and culture made him his people's champion in a way that Frost, as a New Englander and farmer by adoption, could never feel equally sure about.

In exploring the tension between Frost's connection to his "people" and his need to remain apart, "Good Hours" dramatizes a number of painful feelings — regret, apology, atonement, and exclusion, among still others — that attached to his chosen degree of separation. Here, too, Frost treats these feelings with some irony. What is striking is how strong they are and, overall, how much goes on in this short, blandly titled lyric that, in closing the book, might seem a mere formality. The poem describes the narrator's evening walk beyond a village and his late return, where he is the sole unquiet thing:

> I had for my winter evening's walk —
> No one at all with whom to talk,
> But I had the cottages in a row
> Up to their shining eyes in snow.
>
> And I thought I had the folk within:
> I had the sound of a violin;
> I had a glimpse through curtain laces
> Of youthful forms and youthful faces.
>
> I had such company outward bound.
> I went till there were no cottages found.
> I turned and repented, but coming back
> I saw no window but that was black.
>
> Over the snow my creaking feet
> Disturbed the slumbering village street
> Like profanation, by your leave,
> At ten o'clock of a winter eve.

As in "The Pasture," and more than in any of the book's major lyrics, the speaker in "Good Hours" is again the *North of Boston* poet. And now, replacing his *dramatis personae* on stage, he completes a number of the book's organizing designs. Where "The Pasture" opens the volume with a morning excursion in springtime, "Good Hours" closes it on a winter return near midnight, the diurnal progression complementing the seasonal one traced by the three major lyrics. And just as these major lyrics move from the fellowship and conflict of "Mending Wall" to the solitude of "The Wood-Pile," so the invitation of "The Pasture," "You come too," both offers and asks companionship, while "Good Hours" asks us mainly to witness the speaker's chosen isolation. The figure who had addressed us directly in the prologue, only to dissolve into his dramatic characters through most of the book, now reappears in the epilogue sounding very like the poet both connected to and separate from his *dramatis personae.* In fact, as he considers "the folk within" the cottages that he now views from outside, we are reminded of all the houses full of lives and characters that the poet has taken us into through his poems, all of which he now consigns to us, his readers, with a "by your leave," as if, having done his work, he asks our permission to depart. The apparently simple dredging of the rural source promised in "The Pasture" has in fact discovered not only a world of complex characters and relations, but a set of conflicted feelings in the poet which, in the dark place he conjures up here, stay with him to the book's final line.

While addressing the poet's relationship to Derry more directly than anything else in the volume, "Good Hours" is also a last opportunity to underline its central concerns, and Frost makes good use of it. By dramatizing the speaker's marginal position in the village, Frost maintains the book's concern with human relationships but widens it to include the poet. As the narrator struggles throughout the four stanzas to affirm a connection to his fellow villagers, who are snug in their houses while he walks into the night, it seems clear that what sets him apart is his own need to move beyond village life. Despite his express concern with belonging and possession, he is largely dispossessed: his "walk" — his passing through — is the only thing he unequivocally calls his own.

By contrast, the speaker's claims of "I had" — five in the first eight lines — are all qualified, some to the point of denial. The direct object of the first "I had" — "*No one at all* with whom to talk" (emphasis added) — is prominent and emphatic, taking up the whole second line, and quickly establishes the speaker's apartness within "his" community. The next line — "But I had the cottages" — promises to buffer this exclusion but falls far short, for these village faces "Up to their shining eyes in snow" remain largely masked to the speaker, yielding only an unblinking communal assessment that, ironically, he will feel even more on his return, when the lights are out.

The speaker's marginal position in the village grows clearer, and his connection-by-way-of-possession thinner, as he tries to get behind those shining windowpanes. The qualification that opens stanza two — "And I *thought* I had the folk within" (emphasis added) — an idea no sooner uttered than corrected, embodies disappointment, bringing us close to the poet who, in writing this poem, recognized that he had to be apart from the people who would become his poetic subjects.[6] Richard Wakefield comments that the narrator's "thinking he 'had the folk within' is a lot like what [Frost] does with the neighbor in 'Mending Wall' and the bird in 'The Wood-Pile'": because neither will say much, each speaker "can make what he will of them."[7] Here, in the retrospect of an epilogue, the speaker reveals the price of such freedom and poetic license. What he could "have" of the folk in one way is denied him in another. What he could he has captured in the book's fifteen principal poems. What he could not is made clear by this narrative of solitude.

By conveying an earlier sense of belonging now revised downward — what he "thought" but no longer thinks — the poet-speaker readies us for further evidence of separation, which soon comes. His only uncorrected "had" attaches to "the sound of a violin." Poignant and disembodied, it alone leaves the lighted houses to follow him into the dark, while the "forms . . . and . . . faces" of the villagers remain behind curtained windows and closed doors. Here we have almost a paradigm of the poet who made "music out of . . . the sound of sense" (*SL*, 79) — who captured the music of a community's speech while never really entering into it. Almost prophetically, in a letter to John Bartlett on July 4, 1913, written in the midst of his involvement with the book, Frost described the "sound of sense" as the dramatic tones of meaning one might hear "from voices behind a door that cuts off the words" (*SL*, 80) — in effect, as the sound of a conversation from which one is excluded. Later, when recounting his Derry years to William Braithwaite, recalling the interest he took in his neighbors' gossip and attributing to it the "actuality and intimacy" that an artist must aim for, Frost again casts himself more in the role of eavesdropper rather than participant (*SL*, 159).

Mark Richardson reads "Good Hours" "as one of many parables of his experience in American villages that Frost told in the 1910s" (72) and rightly connects it with the January 1913 note to Frank Flint in which Frost contrasts his newfound fellowship among poets in London to his experience in American villages where he felt his poetic vocation as a kind of pariah-hood. Tyler Hoffman suggests the poem reflects

---

[6] Thompson (*Early Years*, 433) reports that the poem was written in Plymouth, New Hampshire in the winter of 1911–1912, when Frost had decided he would leave teaching to write full-time in a place outside New England.

[7] Wakefield made this observation in comments on an earlier draft of this chapter (July 23, 2006).

Frost's "marginalized status" not only "as a poet in a utilitarian world" but more specifically as ethnographer-poet in rural New England, whose role as participant-observer helps to explain "his oblique and ambivalent position to the back-country he is seeking to record" ("Poet as Anthropologist," 6). To both of these views I would add the complicating factors of conscience, ethics, and economics that we have seen throughout *North of Boston.*

Frost's repeated use of "I had" in "Good Hours" makes explicit the question of possession that the book's principal poems raise through their many references to appropriation and violation, trespass and theft. It is hardly surprising that this poem raises the issue more directly, for here the speaker is more clearly the poet who, as we know, was determined to pursue his vocation and, thus, to make others' lives into the saleable commodity that Frost needed his verse to be. But a corollary "truth" divulged by *North of Boston* and confirmed by "Good Hours" is that Frost also felt the claims of community and a real connection to the people of his poems, creating an irreducible conflict for one who needed to make his vocation a livelihood. He cared deeply about the people to whom his book was both dedicated and devoted. He cared about the language and human materials from which he had forged a poetic vision. He cared, intellectually, about the culture of Derry, which he had left behind to complete and publish the book that would preserve it.

And so, in "Good Hours," even as the speaker leaves the lighted cottages behind him, he carries with him an acute sense of "the folk within." Like the music, it follows him. In this regard, the line "I had such company outward bound" equivocates deftly. When spoken by this lone walker, the claim of "such company" might at first seem hollow, only a brave face put on loneliness, the best he can make of a separation that will feel even greater on reentering the sleeping village. But when we see this speaker as Frost himself, the claim suggests something more mysterious and imaginative, the presence-in-absence of something longed for and internalized. "The folk within" the cottages remain within this poet-speaker even as he walks beyond the village, reminding us of the way in which Frost's rural neighbors remained alive in his imagination even as he left Derry and New England. The term "such company" even alludes to the "company" of *dramatis personae* that they would become in *North of Boston* — a transformation made possible only by the creative separation, the "good hours," that the poem's speaker both suffers and celebrates here.

In important ways, "Good Hours" anticipates "Acquainted with the Night," written about ten years after *North of Boston*, describing another excursion into the dark and offering a more pointed parable of the poet who follows his own impulses but is followed in turn by the values and judgments of the wider community he both needs and needs to escape. In this later, more vivid dramatization of the poet's place apart, the speaker tells how, when passing "the watchman on his beat," he has "dropped [his] eyes, unwilling to explain." Just as the violin music follows him in "Good Hours," he is pursued in the later poem by "an interrupted cry / . . . from another street, / But not to call me back or say good-by." In "Acquainted with the Night," however, the narrator has also "looked down the saddest city lane." Aided by an allusion to Dante's *Inferno* in the poem's *terza rima*, and also, as Lawrance Thompson has suggested, to the "man of sorrows . . . acquainted with grief" in Isaiah 53:3 (*Early Years*, 627; in Cramer, 94), "Acquainted with the Night," even more than "Good Hours," portrays the poet as drawn by his nature to the forms of darkness we normally avoid: to death, grief, disappointment, loneliness, confusion, the indifference of the social and natural worlds — all forms of suffering that *North of Boston* explores in depth.

We cannot simply inject "Acquainted with the Night" back into "Good Hours." But we should recognize that the earlier poem suggests what the later poem fully implies and that, for one ready to explore the darker regions of experience, as *North of Boston* has shown Frost to be, the same dichotomy and paradox apply.[8] The villagers in their lighted cottages exhibit the good sense of ordinary folk on a winter night, staying warm and close, affirming communal bonds. The poet, moving beyond such comforts, not only probes the darkness they shun, but sees both the comforts and the confinements of community in a way that those in its fold cannot. To each these evening "hours" are "good" in different ways. The villagers, freed from workday demands, share comradeship and recreation in their dwellings, allowing the poet to wander unobserved, freed from immediate social demands, though carrying with him the sense of otherness recorded here. Quiet as his footsteps may be on snow, they are enough to mar the consensus of his fellow citizens, to "profane" the silent unanimity that the sleeping village has reached by ten o'clock! What makes the poet's wandering hours "good" is also what makes them painful. He claims the freedom both to transgress such communal observances and to suffer for doing so.

The most striking and telling moments of the poem, as Mark Richardson has noted, are created by the two words, "repented" and "profanation," that resonate with Frost's own uneasiness about his distance from the Derry "folk." If Thompson and other biographers are right in placing the poem's composition at Plymouth, New Hampshire, in the winter of 1911–12 (Cramer, 43), it coincides with Frost's choice to leave Derry. And when we consider that he would commit to only one year of teaching at

[8] In discussing Frost's use of parataxis, Tyler Hoffman associates these two poems as expressions of the poet's struggle with "alienation" and "estrangement" from his society at large (*Politics of Poetry*, 78–80).

the Plymouth Normal School, that he sold the Derry farm that November, and that his 1911 Christmas letter to Susan Hayes Ward promises "the long deferred forward movement . . . to begin next year" (*SL*, 43), when he went to England, it seems clear that the poem documents the moment when Frost has decided to exchange a promising teaching career for an uncertain future as a poet, and his life in Derry village for that of its poetic champion, in which his former neighbors would provide "such company" as his memory, his imagination, and his poems could sustain. Having gone "till there were no cottages found," he says in "Good Hours," "I turned and repented, but coming back / I saw no window but that was black." In going far enough to satisfy his need for separation, he has sacrificed social connection, and the formerly lighted windows, now black, make an apt if ironic rejoinder to his own foray into darkness.

Among Frost's most influential literary forebears, Thoreau championed the artist's separation from the American village, while Hawthorne explored its more troubling recesses and complicities. Frost's brilliance lies in testing its balance point, or what Tyler Hoffman has aptly characterized as "the play between . . . the [poet's] twin impulses to cede to and outstrip social constraints" (*Politics of Poetry*, 80). We have seen abundant evidence that Frost recognized the cost of his artistic choices and the violation of communal values they entailed, which he partly confirms here by calling his speaker's return a "repentance" and saying that his footsteps in the late-night village silence are "like profanation."

In ways we have seen throughout the book, however, Frost qualifies that confirmation with three words — "by your leave" — added to this "profanation," subtly recollecting the drama of the poem and the book as a whole. By asking our "leave," bringing forward our presence as audience against the more separated "folk" of "the slumbering village," this three-word insertion points to Frost's exchange of one community for another entailed in the making of these poems. By making his Derry neighbors into poetic subjects, he has, in effect, transformed a relationship with them into one with his readers, a transformation paralleled by the wordplay that makes his "creaking feet" on the village snow into the metrical yet varied "feet" of his poem. At the same time, there is something elusive in his "by *your* leave," especially when we compare this oblique leave-taking with the direct invitation of "The Pasture," "*You* come too" (emphasis added). Here in this lone farewell near midnight, the poet asks his readers' permission to depart but also, it seems, our indulgence. But for what?

Whatever it is surely includes his own hyperbole, which has described his return to the dark village as "repentance" and now amplifies the sound of his footsteps on snow into a "profanation" of its quiet hours. Mark Richardson notes the irony in Frost's use of "repentance" and the "sardonic politeness" of the poem's final stanza but suggests that the poem "is as much concerned with a symbolic return to the village — and . . . accommodation within its cultural boundaries — as with extravagance from it" (69). Such a "symbolic return" was a major concern for Frost, and one might view his entire public persona from 1915 onward as a continued effort in that direction. But I would stress the reservations attached to that return here, as the poem's ironies suggest.

In the first of these ironies — in what Richardson aptly calls a "mocking acknowledgement" (69) of the villagers' judgment — "Good Hours" affirms the poet's excursion beyond village boundaries. While "I turned and *repented*" (emphasis added) ostensibly marks the moment where the poet capitulates to village culture, the excess of this *mea culpa* does seem mocking, undercutting any real sense of atonement. Nor does his reentry to the village in the rest of the sentence read like a return to its fold. "[B]ut coming back," he says, "I saw no window but that was black." Alone in the dark and silent streets, he remains the outsider. In much the same way as "repented," the poem's penultimate line — "Like profanation, by your leave" — resists the very judgment of transgression that it seems to admit. Even as a simile — not quite the thing itself — "*Like* profanation" (emphasis added) seems overstated. While we can imagine the otherwise perfect silence of the village to be "disturbed" or even marred by the poet's "creaking feet," "profanation" becomes ironic through its excess, and seems aimed more at the social conformity that makes a sacred precinct of these late hours than at the wayward poet who violates this implicit article of village faith.

We have seen a similar use of hyperbole in "Blueberries" when the narrator playfully assumes the label of "thief" for picking the same wild berries that his poorer neighbor Loren harvests for needed sustenance or income. That narrator of course understands and partly shares the social logic that gives Loren and his hungry children the prior or greater claim. But by exaggerating that judgment, reducing his lesser claim, based on mere desire, to the status of theft, the speaker subtly challenges that logic, using his poetic license to defend his personal freedom, and by extension, his poetic vocation. In "Good Hours," by specifically asking our "leave" for his claim of "profanation," the speaker subtly acknowledges it as overstated and questionable. It's a verbal wink at the reader, an "if you will" in which the speaker, having aired the accusation, also implies its absurdity and shares with us his disavowal of it. The poem's title, counting the speaker's "evening walk" as "good hours," subtly adds its judgment of the religious conformity of village life that prompts the speaker's apology, implying that a poet's hours, and perhaps his best ones, may need to violate social norms. Yet, resist them how he may, the poet who cares about these people, wander though he will, cannot move beyond range of their values. As this speaker's verbal posturing reminds us, he feels a need to defend the social marginality entailed by his vocation.

These compounded ironies return us to others throughout *North of Boston* that both question and defend the poet's right to defy the social and practical demands that make poetry an extravagance. As mentioned above, there is the narrator of "Blueberries," who, because he competes for the same berries that his neighbor Loren picks for survival, playfully adopts the name of "thief," yet undercuts the charge by choosing a term that overstates it. We have the narrator of "Mending Wall," whose joke about his apple trees poaching his neighbor's pine cones, while satirizing the neighbor's defense of the wall, also alludes to transgressive aspects of his own joke, and more, of making light of what the neighbor holds sacred — all of which are part of the poet's making a poem of this neighborly encounter. The speaker of "The Wood-Pile" feels accused by the bird of wanting to steal a white tailfeather, when all he wants — and he wants no less — is to turn what he sees (including the bird) to his own uses, just as the poet behind him does in his poem. There is Lafe in "A Hundred Collars" whose own pursuit of happiness and survival feels to him, and may well be, a betrayal of those he calls his neighbors and fellow Democrats. And there is Frost himself, who confessed to feeling "reproach" when he learned that one of the women he "wrote into" "A Servant to Servants" had suffered a complete breakdown.

In each of these cases, as in "Good Hours," the speakers both feel and resist an accusation or suspicion whose source lies partly within and partly without — a feeling that, through complex rhetorical postures, they partly acknowledge and partly deny. And, as we have seen, all of these figures wrestling with their degrees of marginality have counterparts in still other *North of Boston* poems ("The Mountain," "The Code," "A Servant to Servants"), all of whom are outsiders, less constrained than the local inhabitants by local mores or the pressures of survival, and thus more open to suspicion, resentment, or envy. "Listen to that!" says the trapped wife in "A Servant to Servants" to the visitor who, like Frost himself, had come to Lake Willoughby on a botanizing trip: "You let things more like feathers regulate / Your going and coming." All of these encounters, whether actual or imagined in the poems, whether subtle or overt, internal, external, or both, lead us back to Frost himself, for all of these outsiders in the poems are figures for the poet who, in recording the rural culture of his Derry years, cared about the people he made into poetic subjects but who, in living among them, could never be one of them and never meant to stay. As *North of Boston* tells their stories, it sheds indirect light on the poet who turned these people into his own public success, preserving that transformative decade of his life in the very book that provided his extrication from it.

Works Cited

Barron, Jonathan. "Mending Wall." In *The Robert Frost Encyclopedia*, edited by Nancy Lewis Tuten and John Zubizarreta, 203–5. Westport, CT: Greenwood Press, 2001.

Barry, Elaine. *Robert Frost on Writing*. New Brunswick, NJ: Rutgers UP, 1973.

Brooks, Cleanth, and Robert Penn Warren. *Understanding Poetry*. 3rd edition. New York: Holt, Rinehart and Winston, 1960.

Brower, Reuben. *The Poetry of Robert Frost: Constellations of Intention*. New York: Oxford UP, 1963.

Brown, Dona. *Inventing New England: Regional Tourism in the Nineteenth Century*. Washington, DC and London: Smithsonian Institution, 1995.

Buell, Lawrence. "Frost as a New England Poet." In *The Cambridge Companion to Robert Frost*, edited by Robert Faggen, 101–22. Cambridge, UK: Cambridge UP, 2001.

Bulletin of Yale University: Obituary Record of Yale Undergraduates, 1914–1915. Eleventh series, no. 19. New Haven: Yale UP, July 1915.

Burnshaw, Stanley. *Robert Frost Himself*. New York: George Braziller, 1986.

Cook, Reginald L. "Robert Frost's Asides on his Poetry." *American Literature* (January 1948): 351–59.

Cox, Sidney. *A Swinger of Birches*. New York: Collier Books, 1961.

Cramer, Jeffrey. *Robert Frost among His Poems: A Literary Companion to the Poet's Own Biographical Contexts and Associations*. Jefferson, NC and London: McFarland, 1996.

Crowley, J. Donald. "Hawthorne and Frost: the Making of a Poem." In *Frost: Centennial Essays*, edited by Jack Tharpe, 288–301. Jackson: UP of Mississippi, 1974.

Derry Historic Research Committee. *From Turnpike to Interstate, 1827–1977: The 150 Years of Derry, New Hampshire*. Canaan, NH: Phoenix, 1977.

Dimock, G. E., Jr. "The Name of Odysseus." *Hudson Review* 9, no. 1 (1956): 52–70. Reprinted in Homer, *The Odyssey*, translated and edited by Albert Cook, 406–24. Norton Critical Edition. New York: Norton, 1974.

From Turnpike to Interstate: 1827–1977. See Derry Historic Research Committee.

Frost, Robert. *Collected Poems, Prose, and Plays*. Edited by Richard Poirier and Mark Richardson. New York: Library of America, 1995.

———. *The Collected Prose of Robert Frost*. Edited by Mark Richardson. Cambridge, MA: Harvard UP, 2007.

———. *Farm Poultryman*. See under Lathem and Thompson.

———. *The Notebooks of Robert Frost.* Edited by Robert Faggen. Cambridge, MA: Harvard UP, 2006.

———. *Selected Letters.* Edited by Lawrance Thompson. New York: Holt, 1964.

Frost, Robert, and Elinor Frost. *Family Letters of Robert and Elinor Frost.* Edited by Arnold Grade. Albany: State U of New York P, 1972.

Hass, Robert Bernard. *Going by Contraries: Robert Frost's Conflict with Science.* Charlottesville: UP of Virginia, 2002.

Hawthorne, Nathaniel. *The Blithedale Romance.* New York: Oxford UP, 1991.

Heine, Heinrich. *Songs of Love and Grief: A Bilingual Anthology in the Verse Forms of the Originals.* Translated by Walter W. Arndt. Evanston, IL: Northwestern UP, 1995.

Hoffman, Tyler. *Robert Frost and the Politics of Poetry.* Hanover: UP of New England, 2001.

———. "Robert Frost: The Poet as Anthropologist." Paper presented at a meeting of the American Literature Association, Long Beach, California, May 25, 2002.

Holmes, Richard, and William Dugan. *Derry Revisited.* Portsmouth, NH: Arcadia, 2005.

Homer. *The Odyssey.* Translated by Robert Fagles. New York: Penguin, 1996.

Jarman, Mark, and Robert McDowell. "The Elephant Man of Poetry." *The Reaper* 4 (1981): 45–60.

Kemp, John C. *Robert Frost and New England: The Poet as Regionalist.* Princeton, NJ: Princeton UP, 1979.

Lathem, Edward Connery, ed. *Interviews with Robert Frost.* Guilford, CT: Jeffrey Norton, 1997.

Lathem, Edward Connery, and Lawrance Thompson. *Robert Frost: Farm Poultryman.* Hanover, NH: Dartmouth, 1963.

Lentricchia, Frank. *Modernist Quartet.* Cambridge, UK and New York: Cambridge UP, 1994.

Lynen, John. *The Pastoral Art of Robert Frost.* New Haven: Yale UP, 1960.

MacArthur, Marit. *The American Landscape in the Poetry of Frost, Bishop, and Ashbery.* New York: Palgrave/Macmillan, 2008.

Marx, Leo. "Pastoral Ideal and City Troubles." *Journal of General Education* 20 (1969): 258–59.

Mertins, Louis. *Robert Frost: Life and Talks Walking.* Norman: U of Oklahoma P, 1965.

Milton, John. *Complete Poems and Major Prose.* Edited by Merritt Y. Hughes. New York: Odyssey Press, 1957.

Monteiro, George. *Robert Frost and the New England Renaissance.* Lexington: UP of Kentucky, 1988.

Newdick, Robert. *Newdick's Season of Frost: An Interrupted Biography of Robert Frost*, edited by William A. Sutton. Albany: State U of New York P, 1976.

Parfitt, Matthew. "Robert Frost's 'Modern Georgics.'" *Robert Frost Review* (Fall 1996): 54–70.

Parini, Jay. *Robert Frost: A Life*. New York: Holt, 1999.

Pritchard, William H. *Frost: A Literary Life Reconsidered*. New York and Oxford: Oxford UP, 1984.

———. "*North of Boston*: Frost's Poetry of Dialogue." In *In Defense of Reading: A Reader's Approach to Literary Criticism*, edited by Reuben A. Brower and Richard Poirier, 38–56. New York: Dutton, 1963.

Quinn, Gerard. "Frost's Synechdochic Allusions." *Resources for American Literary Study* 25, no. 2 (1999): 254–64.

Richardson, Mark. *The Ordeal of Robert Frost*. Urbana: U of Illinois P, 1997.

Robbins, J. Albert. *An Interlude with Robert Frost: Being a Brief Correspondence with the Poet and Recollections*. Bloomington, IN: The Private Press of Frederic Brewer, 1982.

Robert Frost (VHS), No. 5 in the series, *Voices and Visions: The Poet in America*. South Carolina Educational Television Network, New York Center for Visual History, and Annenberg/CPB Project. Santa Barbara, CA: Intellimation, 1988.

The Robert Frost Encyclopedia. See under Tuten, ed.

Rotella, Guy. "Frost and Invitation." *Robert Frost Review* (Fall 2005): 36–49.

———. "'Synonomous with Kept': Frost and Economics." In *The Cambridge Companion to Robert Frost*, edited by Robert Faggen, 241–60. Cambridge, UK: Cambridge UP, 2001.

Sanders, David. "Earth, Time, and England: New Light on Frost's 'Old-Stone Savage' and 'Mending Wall'." *Robert Frost Review* (Fall 2007): 43–59.

———. "Revelation as Child's Play in Frost's 'Directive'." In *Frost: Centennial Essays II*, edited by Jack Tharpe, 267–77. Jackson: UP of Mississippi, 1976.

Sergeant, Elizabeth Shepley. *The Trial by Existence*. New York: Holt, Rinehart and Winston, 1960.

Sheehy, Donald. "Pastoral Degenerate: Frost and Rural Sociology." *Robert Frost Review* (Fall 2006): 18–30.

Smythe, Daniel. *Robert Frost Speaks*. New York: Twayne, 1964.

Stone, Edward. "Other 'Desert Places': Frost and Hawthorne." In *Frost: Centennial Essays*, edited by Jack Tharpe, 275–87. Jackson: UP of Mississippi, 1974.

Tharpe, Jack, ed. *Frost: Centennial Essays*, complied by the Committee on the Frost Centennial for the University of Southern Mississippi. Jackson: UP of Mississippi, 1974.

Thompson, Lawrance. *Robert Frost: The Early Years, 1874–1915*. New York: Holt, Rinehart and Winston, 1966.

———. *The Years of Triumph*. New York: Holt, Rinehart and Winston, 1970.

Thornton, Richard, ed. *Recognition of Robert Frost: Twenty-Fifth Anniversary*. New York: Holt, 1937.

Tuten, Nancy Lewis, and John Zubizarreta, eds., *The Robert Frost Encyclopedia*. Westport, CT and London: Greenwood Press, 2001.

Walsh, John Evangelist. *Into My Own: The English Years of Robert Frost*. New York: Grove, 1988.

Wikipedia, The Free Encyclopedia. http://en.wikipedia.org/wiki/John_Burroughs.

Wilson, Douglas. "The Other Side of the Wall." *Iowa Review* 10, no. 1 (1979): 65–75.

Wordsworth, William. *The Literary Criticism of William Wordsworth*. Edited by Paul M. Zall. Lincoln: U of Nebraska P, 1966.

Index